Modern Privacy

Modern Privacy

Shifting Boundaries, New Forms

Edited by

Harry Blatterer
Macquarie University, Australia

Pauline Johnson
Macquarie University, Australia

and

Maria R. Markus
University of New South Wales, Australia

palgrave
macmillan

First published 2010 by
PALGRAVE MACMILLAN

Palgrave Macmillan in the UK is an imprint of Macmillan Publishers Limited, registered in England, company number 785998, of Houndmills, Basingstoke, Hampshire RG21 6XS.

Palgrave Macmillan in the US is a division of St Martin's Press LLC, 175 Fifth Avenue, New York, NY 10010.

Palgrave Macmillan is the global academic imprint of the above companies and has companies and representatives throughout the world.

Palgrave® and Macmillan® are registered trademarks in the United States, the United Kingdom, Europe and other countries.

ISBN 978–0–230–24611–9 hardback

This book is printed on paper suitable for recycling and made from fully managed and sustained forest sources. Logging, pulping and manufacturing processes are expected to conform to the environmental regulations of the country of origin.

A catalogue record for this book is available from the British Library.

Library of Congress Cataloging-in-Publication Data

Modern privacy: shifting boundaries, new forms/edited by Harry Blatterer, Pauline Johnson, Maria R. Markus.
p. cm.
Includes bibliographical references.
ISBN 978–0–230–24611–9
1. Social psychology. 2. Privacy. I. Blatterer, Harry. II. Johnson, Pauline, 1953– III. Markus, Maria R., 1936–
HM1033.M63 2010
302—dc22

2010027493

10 9 8 7 6 5 4 3 2 1
19 18 17 16 15 14 13 12 11 10

Printed and bound in Great Britain by

CPI Antony Rowe, Chippenham and Eastbourne

Contents

Acknowledgments

Our thanks go to the contributing authors whose generosity of spirit was equaled only by their scholarship. Bernard Leckning not only provided invaluable assistance during the editing stages. Equally important was his critical, constructive engagement with the intellectual premises of the text. We are grateful to Senior Commissioning Editor Philippa Grand at Palgrave Macmillan for her interest in and support of the project from the outset.

Harry Blatterer
Pauline Johnson
Maria R. Markus

List of Contributors

Zygmunt Bauman is Emeritus Professor of Sociology at the Universities of Leeds and Warsaw and among the leading critical thinkers of our time. In 1992 he was awarded the European Amalfi Prize for Sociology and Social Sciences. In 1998 he received the Theodor W. Adorno award of the city of Frankfurt. He is the author of over 50 books including *The Art of Life* (Cambridge: Polity, 2008), *The Individualized Society* (Cambridge: Polity, 2001), and *Liquid Modernity* (Cambridge: Polity, 2000).

Harry Blatterer is Lecturer in the Department of Sociology at Macquarie University. He is author of *Coming of Age in Times of Uncertainty* (New York and Oxford: Berghahn Books, 2007, 2009).

Günter Burkart is Professor of Sociology at the Leuphana Universität, Lüneburg. He is author of numerous publications on family and intimate relationships, gender, the life course, social theory, the sociology of the body, and new media. His most recent books include *Familiensoziologie* (Köln: UTB, 2008) and *Handymania: Wie das Mobiltelefon unser Leben verändert hat* [*Cell Phone Mania: How the Cell Phone has Changed our Lives*] (Frankfurt: Campus, 2007).

Norbert Ebert is Lecturer in the Department of Sociology, Macquarie University. His research centers on theories of individualization and the experience of work. He is author of *Identität aus dem Nichts: Überlegungen zu Schopenhauer, Nietzsche und Scheler,* [*Identity from Nothingness: Reflections on Schopenhauer, Nietzsche and Scheler*] (Norderstedt: BoD, 2003).

Arthur Glass is Associate Professor in Law, University of New South Wales. His research focuses on the philosophy of law, constitutional law and migration law. He is author of numerous articles and co-author of *Australian Constitutional Law* (Sydney: Butterworths, 1994, 1998) and *Australian Federal Constitutional Law: Commentary and Materials* (Sydney: LBC, 1999).

Pauline Johnson is Associate Professor of Sociology at Macquarie University. She has published widely in feminist theory and on the work of Jürgen Habermas. Her major publications include *Feminism as Radical Humanism* (Sydney: Allen and Unwin, 1994) and *Jürgen Habermas: Rescuing the Public Sphere* (Routledge, 2006). She is co-editor of *Culture and Enlightenment: Essays for Gyorgy Markus* (Ashgate, 2002).

Maria R. Markus, a member of the Budapest School of critical theorists, taught sociology at the University of New South Wales, where she is now a visiting scholar in the School of Social Sciences and International Studies. She is the author and co-author of several books and has published over 60 papers in various volumes and scholarly journals. Among these those most directly connected to the present volume are "Decent Society and/or Civil Society," *Social Research*, vol. 68, no. 4, 2001, "In Search of a Home," *Contemporary Perspectives in Critical and Social Philosophy* (Leiden: Brill, 2004), and "Lovers and Friends: Radical Utopias of Intimacy," *Thesis Eleven*, no. 101, 2010.

John Rundell is Associate Professor in the School of Philosophy, Anthropology and Social Enquiry, Melbourne University. He is a past editor of *Thesis Eleven*, and current editor of *Critical Horizons* and *The Social and Critical Theory Book Series* (Leiden: Brill). He is co-editor of *Critical Theory After Habermas: Encounters and Departures* (Leiden: Brill, 2004), *Contemporary Perspectives in Social and Critical Philosophy* (Leiden: Brill, 2004), and *Recognition, Work, Politics New Directions in French Critical Theory* (Leiden: Brill, 2007).

Eli Zaretsky is Professor of History at the New School for Social Research. His interests are in twentieth-century cultural history, social and cultural theory, the history of capitalism, and the history of the family. His most recent book is: *Secrets of the Soul: A Social and Cultural History of Psychoanalysis* (New York: Random House, 2005). He is the editor of *The Polish Peasant in Europe and America* (Chicago: University of Illinois Press, 1984), and the author of *Capitalism, the Family and Personal Life* (New York: Harper and Row, 1976).

Introduction

Harry Blatterer, Pauline Johnson, Maria R. Markus

The distinction of *polis* and *oikos* in Greek antiquity, and the assignment of men to the one and women and children (and slaves) to the other, is etched in the Western imagination as constitutive to the development of our shared history, and so has over time become the quasi-natural template for the differentiation of the private and the public spheres along lines of power. However, with the emergence of what Agnes Heller (1999) has called "the modern social arrangement" with its double-edged freedoms—freedoms that both allow and compel us to carve our individual destinies from highly contingent institutional and normative contexts—the lived contents of these spheres of action become contestable and contested. From then on, the contestability of privacy as an entitlement and desired good depended on the formation of public institutions which listened, gave voice to and advocated for individuals whose autonomy became the conceptual bedrock for liberal-democratic privacy (Habermas, 2002; Rössler, 2005). The development of modern privacy, then, is best understood in terms of its articulation with the public realm. In the more literal sense, that articulation has long included a defense against undue interference by the state, as well as pressures to open the private realm to scrutiny in order to expose and then curtail the violence of gendered power.

Privacy can thus be characterized as a dynamic process. Its definitions, the expectations that surround it and the experiences from which these originate, are bound to cultural, political, economic and technological changes. And because social change is the central marker of modernity (however conceived), the meaning of privacy too is never settled. This is no trivial matter. For the importance of changes to the way privacy is defined and made sense of becomes central as soon as we make the connection between privacy and autonomy. The contributors to this volume all recognize this connection, and in their various ways elaborate its forms and consequences; they recognize that what is at stake is not simply a clarification of the manifold uses of "privacy," but that to value privacy is to value important aspects of the conditions for our individual and thus collective flourishing. Hence, the authors are concerned to critically discuss and interpret various points at which the public and the private meet, to give their original accounts of the shifting boundaries between these spheres, and to reflect on the social consequences of the changes they analyze.

The chapters collected here address new and emergent transformations of privacy in Western societies from a multidisciplinary and international perspective. Of course, not all problems that lie at the intersection of the public and the private can be addressed in a volume such as this. For one, the issue of government surveillance—increasingly important in the post 9/11 context—is not directly explored, partly because the literature on the topic is vast and growing, and partly because the topic is not cognate with the authors' areas of expertise. For similar reasons we have decided to exclude mainstays in discussions of the private sphere such as "the family." What the collection does address, however, are salient contemporary issues of privacy in relation to large-scale social transformations. The range of empirical instances that the authors take up includes uses of "new media" and their impact on social interactions and cultural trends, feminism and the public/private divide, privacy and the law, the blurring of privacy and work, the transformation of erotic love, therapy culture and narcissism. By raising these issues we hope that the collection not only makes for interesting reading, but also invites further discussion.

We want to stress that while the collection provides a multidimensional analysis of the transformation of privacy with the understanding that history is irreversible, the authors do not suggest that people are passive sufferers of historical transformations. People not only create these transformations, but can also control their impact on their own lives. Therefore, the implication of the analyses is not a nostalgic reconstruction of the past, but a question which is, by way of reflection on the volume, taken up in the concluding chapter: in what society do we wish to live, and what problems have to be addressed under new conditions in order to approach this goal?

The contributions

Chapter 1 constitutes one of the darker, more pessimistic works of *Zygmunt Bauman*. While the general message of this chapter is not dissimilar to Bauman's other writing, it is cut off at the point when hope could (and to a degree does) enter. The chapter thus not only expresses despair, but a warning to us all. In the first section, Bauman investigates the nature of the borders between the public and the private, emphasizing the continuous struggle between the two spheres. In "liquid modernity" public institutions constantly relinquish their functions and transfer the responsibility for their fulfilment to individuals. Simultaneously, they transport ever bigger volumes of private information from the private sphere. On the other hand, the very idea of "secrecy" as marking private territory is disappearing. What now frightens people more than possible violations of privacy is, according to Bauman, not being able to put their secrets on display for all to see, transforming the public sphere into a "light-entertainment variety theatre" (p. 16). This points to the degradation of both spheres, and as a consequence we are now more than ever vulnerable to humiliation and the denial of dignity. This is the background against which Bauman investigates the possibility of utopia. And he concludes, pessimistically, that in an individualized consumer society in which the hope to make the world a better place is in jeopardy we can merely "fight against losing" (p. 29). It is not surprising that such a utopia does not in any way provide meaning to life. When—for whatever reason—a time for reflection comes, it is usually "too late to oppose its present shape and effectively dispute and challenge its propriety" (p. 33). This is Bauman's warning.

In Chapter 2, *Günter Burkart* discusses what he sees as a culture of reflexive individualism that emphasizes self-reflection and self-thematization. A "culture of confession" emerges as norms which were once embedded in religious and later in therapeutic contexts enter the public terrain. Today, the new media especially offer a forum for the public presentation of privacy; they aid a trend whereby, for Burkart, "privacy goes public." While this trend may not be new, it has accelerated considerably with the rise of the new media. But rather than offering a straight diagnosis of the confessional turn, Burkart asks whether it isn't already in decline as it morphs into a public culture of staging. In the intimate sphere, however, the culture of self-disclosure, of reflection and intimate communication, does not disappear altogether. The author's prognosis errs on the side of caution. What Burkart sees as the blurring between the public and the private spheres will make it increasingly difficult for intimates to recognize one another's authentic selves.

Pauline Johnson (Chapter 3) explores feminism's attempt to come up with an alternative to liberal faith in "ready made" private freedoms. Specifically, she identifies and then challenges two troubled approaches to the task: one that unsuccessfully tries to refill descriptions of private freedoms with normative contents drawn from commitments of a democratic public, and another that affirms normative discontinuities between the private and public spheres but can't avoid the grip of naturalizing ideologies. Discussing the way in which these two approaches have been used to reflect on the normative contents of contemporary intimate life, she finds that Giddens looks at the value of intimacy in terms borrowed from a democratic polity, while Honneth is persuaded that the intimate sphere constructs its own little world of feelings and affections. However, for Johnson, neither account adequately describes the complexity of our investments in intimate life, nor are they able to respond adequately to a feminist interest in the reconstruction of private freedoms. In the final section of the chapter she develops an alternative account of the values of the intimate sphere, one that provides a more useful framework for reflecting on its dynamic and self-critical tendencies that have fed feminist motivations.

Legal scholar *Arthur Glass* (Chapter 4) stresses the embeddedness of modern privacy laws in different normative, social contexts and raises some of the practical legal difficulties that arise from this circumstance. Glass discusses how the liberal state has, against the background of social, political and technological transformations, responded to the need for the legal protection of privacy under conditions where privacy is best conceived as a complex, differentiated concept and need. Turning to the normative link between privacy and subjects' autonomy, he shows that while neither can be reduced to the other, various protections of the right to privacy prevent state violations that would adversely affect our capacities to exercise personal autonomy. In the liberal democratic polity personal autonomy also, and vitally, translates into political autonomy. Privacy law, then, both ensures and transcends individual rights.

In Chapter 5, *Harry Blatterer* investigates the motivations for disclosing behavior on social networking sites such as *Facebook* and *MySpace*. Taking issue with all-too-easy explanations that point to a rampant individualism as the main driver of trends, Blatterer contextualizes people's willingness to trade some of their privacy for publicity in a need for visibility. That need is, in turn, anchored in our human, social constitution. Technology, rather than determining collective behavior, in this view no more than facilitates the pursuit of that need. There is, then, a tension between the need for privacy and the need for visibility. That tension deserves particular vigilance because, so Blatterer argues, it more than promises significant consequences for the collective autonomy of liberal subjects.

Maria R. Markus (Chapter 6) deals with one particular aspect of personal life in late modernity: the devaluation of "solitude." Searching for an explanation for people's willing exposure of some of the most intimate aspects of their lives, she investigates two recent cultural trends: the striving for visibility and connectedness. Markus argues that these trends transform personal relationships and reduce the meaning of "public." While the former becomes redefined as "connectivity," the latter is divested of political content and is diminished to "publicity." By extension, the space for solitude—for reflection on our relation to the world—narrows. This, in turn, has consequences for our capacities to enter into meaningful relations of intimacy, because, as Markus explains, intimacy is also "shared solitude" (p. 153). And so her exposition of privacy provides us with yet another crucial aspect of its role: it is a shelter from external noise in which reflection and self-reflection become truly possible, autonomy gains its meaning and relationships can flourish. Solitude, she argues, empowers people to face the world on their own terms.

Philosopher *John Rundell* (Chapter 7) explores a tension at the heart of modern erotic love. All about passionate, unwilled attachments driven by an erotic force, love promised freedom to newly self-conscious modern individuals. However, the cultural entwinement between love and freedom is out of step with the experience of contemporary individuals who are caught by the caprice of love in a whirl of disappointments and frustrated longings. To grasp the complexity of modern love it will be necessary to track five distinct, sometimes competing, at times complementary, constructions. Love is an active, always particular, synthesizing and erotic reaching out to the other. It draws up a difficult negotiation between sexuality, bestowal, sensuousness, passion and care. From the standpoint of modern cultural life, this dynamic and uneasy fusion promises the creative disruption of heightened subjectivity. For the individual though it spells trouble; as Beck and Beck-Gernsheim (1995) suggest, we are caught in "the normal chaos of love."

Pauline Johnson (Chapter 8) critically responds to what she sees as sociologists' trouble in spelling out their objections to the triumph of therapy culture. Shaped by the "helping professions," therapy culture offers itself as a bundle of techniques and "life skills" that only wants to support us to achieve our own existential goals. Johnson argues that therapy culture is able to sidestep critiques that suggest that it one-sidedly advocates particular ways of valuing individual freedoms. Having no fixed agendas of its own, therapy culture is able to move easily between them. However, its interest in fixing existential problems means that it necessarily describes the values it appropriates in particular, limited terms; in terms that can be converted into sets of competencies to be taken up by the troubled individual. This means that therapy culture is unable to appreciate the cultural potentials of the ideals it champions (like rational autonomy and authentic subjectivity) in their rich complexity. In particular, it means that therapy culture blocks our insights into the way in which the pursuit of these individual ideals can lead us to an appreciation of our web of interconnecting dependencies on others.

Norbert Ebert (Chapter 9) reflects on the relationship between work and privacy in late modern societies. Work holds an obscure position when it comes to distinguishing between the private and the public spheres. On the one hand, with the rise of modernity, work has become a defining feature of who we are and how we live our lives. Questions of income, qualifications and lifestyle have become indispensable reference points for identities based on work. On the other hand, while work readily lends itself to establishing personal identity markers in the private sphere, it plays an equally important economic and political role in the definition and maintenance of the public sphere. For Ebert, "work is messy and seeps through each and every facet of our lives" (p. 208). This results in a narrowing of privacy: it becomes a resource in the pursuit of managerial objectives.

In Chapter 10, *Eli Zaretsky* situates the debate over narcissism in the context of postindustrial society. What he calls "the redemption of narcissism" (p. 235) has, in his view, a strong performative dimension closely related to the changing boundaries between the public and the private which, in turn, is rooted in the emergence of a postindustrial, even post-economic consciousness. Drawing his trajectory from Freud, via post-Fordist capitalism to the psychoanalytic movement in their Lacanian and American relational modes, Zaretsky's survey concludes that our critical attitude toward narcissism, and so toward the global/intellectual nuclear family with its origins in the 1960s, remains unachieved.

It is our hope that all the contributions included in this collection provide sufficient material for readers' reflections. We offer our own in the concluding chapter, and in so doing extend an invitation to collective debate and an exchange of ideas.

References

Beck U. and E. Beck-Gernsheim (1995), *The Normal Chaos of Love* (Oxford: Polity Press).

Habermas, J. (2002), *The Structural Transformation of the Public Sphere* (Cambridge: Polity).

Heller, A. (1999), *A Theory of Modernity* (Oxford: Blackwell).

Rössler, B. (2005), *The Value of Privacy* (Cambridge: Polity).

1

Privacy, Secrecy, Intimacy, Human Bonds, Utopia—and Other Collateral Casualties of Liquid Modernity

Zygmunt Bauman

1.1.

Alain Ehrenberg (1995), a uniquely insightful analyst of the convoluted trajectory of the modern individual's short yet dramatic history, attempted to pinpoint the birthdate of the late-modern cultural revolution (at least of its French branch) that ushered in the liquid-modern world which we continue to inhabit, design as well as overhaul and refurbish day in, day out; a sort of Western cultural revolution's equivalent of the salvo of the battleship Aurora that gave signal to the assault and capture of the Winter Palace and triggered the seventy years of the Bolsheviks' rule. His choice was an autumnal Wednesday evening in the 1980s, on which a certain Viviane, an "ordinary French woman," declared during a TV talk show and so in front of several million spectators, that her husband Michel suffers premature ejaculation and for that reason she'd never experienced an orgasm in the course of her marital life.

What was so revolutionary about Viviane's pronouncement? Two inextricably interrelated things. First: a confession of things quintessentially, even eponymically *private*, was made *in public*. And second: the *public* arena had been used to vent and thrash out a matter of a thoroughly *private* concern. Between themselves, the two upheavals legitimized public use of the language of the private. More precisely, they initiated the designing and authorizing of a new language meant to be used for narrating private experience (in the sense of *Erleben* rather than *Erfahrung*) in public, and for the consumption and use of public audience.

To cut the long story short, we may say that Viviane's appearance in front of millions of French men and women glued to their TV screens also ushered the watchers, and their near and dear, into the *confessional society*; a kind of society in which microphones have been installed in confessionals, heretofore receptories of the most private and secret of secrets, the sort of secrets which could be divulged only to God or his earthly plenipotentiaries; and where loudspeakers have been installed on public squares previously reserved solely for brandishing and thrashing out the issues of common, shared interest and public urgency. The entry into confessional society was the moment of the ultimate triumph of privacy, that foremost modern invention, and the beginning of its vertiginous descent from the peak of its glory.

1.2.

What is "private"? Anything that belongs to the realm of "privacy." To find out what in our days is understood by "privacy," let's consult Wikipedia, the website known to promptly and diligently seek and record whatever is currently believed/accepted by popular wisdom to be the truth of the matter, and to update its findings day in and out, following thereby closely its target notorious for running faster than even the most dedicated of its pursuers: "Privacy," we could read in the English-language version of Wikipedia (2009):

> is the ability of an individual or group to seclude themselves or information about themselves and thereby reveal themselves selectively ... Privacy is sometimes related to anonymity, the wish to remain unnoticed or unidentified in the public realm. When something is private to a *person*, it usually means there is something within them that is considered inherently special or personally sensitive ... Privacy can be seen as an aspect of security—one in which tradeoffs between the interests of one group and another can become particularly clear.

And what is a "public arena"? A space with an open access for everyone who may wish to enter. Everything that may be heard and seen in a "public arena" may be, in principle, heard and seen by anybody. Considering that (to quote Wikipedia once more) "the degree to which private information is exposed depends on how the public will receive this information, which differs between places and over time" (Wikipedia, 2009), keeping a thing, an event or an action private and making any of them public are obviously as much at cross-purposes as they are interdependent. "Private" and "public" are at loggerheads. For each of the two notions, self-defining and self-assertion mean opposition to the other.

As a rule, the semantic fields of the two notions are not separated from each other by borders inviting/allowing a two-way traffic, but by frontlines—preferably tightly sealed and heavily fortified on both sides against trespassers (the habitual turncoats accustomed to sitting across the barricade, but most particularly the deserters). Yet even if a war hasn't been declared and warlike actions have not been undertaken (or if hostilities have been suspended), borders as a rule tolerate a *selective* cross-traffic only: a free-for-all traffic would defy the very notion of a boundary and render the boundary redundant. Control, and the right to decide who or what is allowed to pass the borderline and who or what is bound to stay put on one side only, and so also the right to decide what items of information have the prerogative to remain private, and which ones are allowed or decreed to be made public, are as a rule hotly contested. If you wish to know which side is presently on the offensive and which is (pugnaciously or half-heartedly) trying to defend its inherited or acquired rights against invaders, you could do worse than ponder on Peter Ustinov's (1956, p. 19) prophetic foreboding: "This is a free country, madam. *We* have a right to share *your* privacy in a public space" (my emphases).

1.3.

For most of the modern era, the assault on the current private-public frontier, and yet more importantly a univocal revocation and arbitrary change in the extant rules of the border traffic were almost exclusively expected/feared to come from the side of the "public": public institutions were widely suspected of the intention to invade and conquer the sphere of the private and take it under their administration, and thereby to severely curtail the realm of individual or group free will, depriving human individuals or groups of individuals of shelter and, in consequence, of personal or group security. The most sinister and harrowing demons haunting the times of "solid modernity" were vividly portrayed in George Orwell's (1977, p. 267) trope of a "boot stamping on a human face."

Somewhat inconsistently yet not groundlessly all the same, public institutions were suspected of the practice or intention of erecting barricades blocking many a private concern access to the agora or other sites of free mutual communication in which the recasting of private troubles into public issues could be negotiated. Obviously, the gruesome experience of the two similarly rapacious and cruel twentieth-century varieties of totalitarianism (which between themselves, as if to top despair with hopelessness, seemed to have exhausted the spectrum of visible choices—one claiming the legacy of Enlightenment and its modern project, the second decrying that foundational act of modernity as a crime, and rejecting the modern project as a recipe for disaster) lent veracity to the suspicions and justification to resulting anxiety.

Though by now past their peak, such suspicions linger, and anxiety refuses to abate—galvanized time and again, resuscitated and reinvigorated by the news of one or another public institution arbitrarily transferring ever larger swathes of their own functions and obligations from the "public" to the "private" realm, in blatant violation of usages firmly settled in democratic mentality even if uncodified—while transporting in the opposite direction, openly or surreptitiously, ever bigger volumes of indisputedly private information. And yet whatever was the case of the assumed greed/rapacity of the "public" and its imputed or anticipated aggressiveness, and however the perception of each might have been changing over time, alarms of the impending invasion and conquest of the public sphere by private interests and concerns were at best few and far between. Defending the private domain from undue meddling by the powers that be was the sole task inspiring most of our ancestors and older generations to take to arms.

Until recently, that is. Today, triumphant reports of the "liberation" of successive areas of public territory by advancing troops of the private, greeted as a rule with applause and jubilation by avidly watching crowds, are mixed with (thus far faint) somber premonitions and (thus far sparse and tentative) warnings that the ostensible "liberation" bears all the marks of imperialist conquest, ruthless occupation and rapacious colonialism.

1.4.

On secrecy (and so obliquely on privacy, individuality, autonomy, self-definition and self-assertion—as far as secrecy is an indispensable, and crucial, ingredient of them all), Georg Simmel, arguably the most insightful and far-sighted among the founders of sociology, observed that to stand a realistic chance of surviving intact it needs to be acknowledged by others. A rule needs to be observed that "what is intentionally or unintentionally hidden is intentionally or unintentionally respected" (Simmel, 1950, p. 330). The relation between these two conditions (of privacy and individual entitlement to self-assertion) tends to be however unstable and tense—and "the intention of hiding" "takes on a much greater intensity when it clashes with the intention of revealing" (Simmel, 1950, p. 330). If that "greater intensity" fails to emerge, if the urge to defend secrecy tooth and nail against the interlopers, meddlers and busybodies disrespectful of one's secrets is absent, privacy is in danger. And this is now the case—as Peter Ustinov, updating Georg Simmel's pronouncement, reflected on the mood of our times, only by a few decades younger than Simmel's study.

Occasional warnings of the terminal dangers to privacy and individual autonomy emanating from the apparent "liberation" of the public arena for private concerns, and from the gradual yet relentless transformation of the public arena into a light-entertainment variety theater, find little if any repercussion in the public agenda, media programming and first and foremost in the popular attention. The paradox of "deregulation" (the state's retreat from a great number of its past jealously guarded prerogatives) and "individualization" (abandoning of a great number of the state's past functions to the individually managed and operated realm of "life politics"), leading to the sapping of the foundations of individual autonomy while stripping that autonomy of its past attractions and devaluing it in the effect, is all but covered up in the process, passes by almost unnoticed, attracting little, if any attention and triggering little, if any action.

Secret, by definition, is that part of knowledge the sharing of which is refused and/or prohibited or closely controlled. Secrecy, as it were, draws and marks the boundary of privacy; and one's privacy is the realm that is meant to be one's kingdom, the territory of one's undivided sovereignty, inside which one has the power to decide "what and who I am," and from which one may launch and relaunch the campaigns to have and keep her/his decision recognized and respected. In a startling U-turn from the habits of our ancestors, we've lost somehow the guts, the stamina, and above all the will to persist in the defense of such rights, the building blocks of our autonomy. In our days, it is not so much the possibility of betrayal or violation of privacy that frightens us, but the opposite: shutting down the exits, the area of privacy turning into the site of incarceration, the owner of private space being condemned and doomed to stew in his/her own juice. In other words, the absence of avid listeners eager to wring out and tear out our secrets from the ramparts of privacy, put them on public display, make them everybody's property and make everybody wish to share them. We seem to experience no joy in having secrets, unless these are the secrets meant to enhance our egos through being displayed on the Internet, on TV, on the first pages of tabloids and inside glossy magazines.

As the result of all that, it is now the public sphere that finds itself flooded and overwhelmed, having been invaded by the troops of privacy.

But are those troops flowing out of their enclosures prompted by the urge/desire to conquer new outposts and spawn new garrisons, or are they rather running away, in despair and panic, from the barracks of the past, now found to be no longer inhabitable? Is their zeal a symptom of a newly acquired spirit of exploration and conquest—or rather an outcome of and a testimony to expropriation and victimhood? Is the task they have been ordered to perform in our liquid-modern times—the task of finding out and/or deciding "what and who I am"—too daunting to be seriously undertaken inside the skimpy plot of privacy? Bound to reveal that, when trying many tentative approaches and/or putting on and taking off many different dresses, the harder one tries the less likely looks the prospect of reaching the self-confidence one hoped to acquire?

This is but one of the questions with no obvious answer. There is another question, thus far waiting for an answer similarly in vain. Secrecy, after all, is not only the tool of privacy, of cutting out a space entirely of one's own, of setting oneself apart from intruders and unwelcome companions; it is also a most powerful building-and-servicing tool of togetherness, of the tying up and protecting of arguably the strongest among the known and conceivable interhuman bonds. By confiding one's secrets to some selected, "very special" people while barring them from all the others, the webs of friendship are woven, one's "best friends" appointed and retained, infinite commitments entered into and maintained (indeed, blank checks are signed, in as far as the commitments are indeterminate and the withdrawal clause absent), loose aggregates of individuals recast into tightly knit and firmly integrated, probably long lasting, groups. In short, the enclaves are cut out of the world inside which the troublesome and vexing clash between belonging and autonomy is for once laid to rest; in which the choice between private interest and the well-being of others, between altruism and selfishness, self-love and care for another, stops tormenting and no longer foments and fans repetitive pangs of conscience.

But, as Thomas Szasz (1973, p. 11) observed already in 1973,

> traditionally, sex has been a very private, secretive activity. Herein perhaps lies its powerful force for uniting people in a strong bond. As we make sex less secretive, we may rob it of its power to hold men and women together.

Sexual pursuits served until recently as a genuine epitome of intimate secrets meant to be shared with utmost discretion and with only the most carefully and laboriously selected others: in other words, as the prime example of the strongest binding, most difficult to break, most reliable interhuman bonds. But what applies to the most prominent guardian of privacy, applies even more to its lesser companions, inferior substitutes and paler copies. *The present day crisis of privacy seems to be, in other words, inextricably connected with the weakening and decay of interhuman bonds.* In this intertwining between collapse of privacy and falling apart of bonds, one factor is an egg and the other the chicken, and it is a waste of time to quarrel which is the first and which comes second.

1.5.

The other face of the decay of social bonds is the rapid promotion of the fear of inadequacy and of humiliation to the rank of the most ubiquitous, obtrusive and harrowing demons of our liquid-modern world of affluent (or expecting to become affluent) consumers. Those demons haunt the catacombs of privacy making them, for many a practical intent and purpose, uninhabitable.

Humiliation, the denial of dignity, is the alternative to social recognition. In a recent Dennis Smith (2006, p. 38) definition, "the act is humiliating if it forcefully overrides or contradicts the claim that particular individuals ... are making about who they are and where and how they fit in." In other words, if the individual is, explicitly or implicitly, denied the recognition which s/he expected for the person s/he is and/or the kind of life s/he lives; and if s/he is refused the entitlements that would have been made available or continued to be available following such recognition. "A person feels humiliated when s/he is brutally shown, by words, actions or events, that they cannot be what they think they are. ... Humiliation is the experience of being unfairly, unreasonably and unwillingly pushed down, held down, held back or pushed out" (Smith, 2006, p. 38).

In the society of individuals like ours, the pain, envy, vengefulness, and the peeve bred by the sentiment of having been humiliated is arguably the most venomous and implacable variety of Nietzsche/Scheler's *ressentiment* (wrath, rancor, bitterness, ill blood) which a person may feel, and these days arguably the most common and prolific cause of conflict, dissent, animosity, rebellion and thirst for revenge. *Denial of recognition, refusal of respect and the threat of exclusion have replaced (or are rapidly replacing) exploitation and discrimination* as the formulae most commonly used to explain and justify the grudge individuals might bear toward society, or to the sections or aspects of society to which they are directly exposed (personally or through the media) and which they thereby experience (whether first or second hand).

The shame of humiliation breeds self-contempt and self-hatred, which tends do overwhelm us once we realize how weak, indeed impotent, we are when we attempt to hold fast to the identity of our choice, to our place in the community we respect and cherish, and to the kind of life we would dearly wish to be ours and remain ours for a long time to come; once we find out how frail our identity is, how vulnerable and unsteady are our past achievements, and how uncertain must be our future in view of the magnitude of challenges we face daily. That shame, and so also the self-hatred, rise as the proofs of our impotence accumulate—and as the sense of humiliation deepens in the result.

Self-contempt and self-hatred are, however, unbearably tormenting, unendurable states to be and stay in: they need, and desperately seek, a safety valve, an outlet—they must be let out and channeled away from our inner self, which they may otherwise seriously damage or even destroy. The chain leading from uncertainty, through feelings of impotence, of shame and humiliation, to self-disgust, self-loathing and self-hatred, ends up therefore in the search for the culprit "out there, in the world"; of that someone, as yet unknown and unnamed, invisible or disguised, who conspires against my (our) dignity and well-being, and makes me (us) suffer that excruciating pain of humiliation. Discovery and unmasking of that someone is badly needed, as we need a target on which the pent up anger might be unloaded. Pains must be avenged, though it is far from clear on whom. Exploding, self-hatred hits targets at random—mostly those closest to hand, though not necessarily those most responsible for one's fall, humiliation and misery.

We need someone to hate because we need someone to blame for our abominable and unendurable condition and the defeats we suffer when trying to improve it and make it more secure—and this need is one more powerful stimulus for the exploratory public ventures of the private self. We need someone to hold in contempt in order to unload (and so hopefully mitigate) the devastating sense of our own unworthiness. Both "someones" can be easiest to locate on city squares; or better still—much better—in their contemporary high-tech replacement, the Internet, that renders drawing and redrawing of frontlines facile and instant, and unloading toxic bile risk-free, since unopposed and unpunishable.

For that unloading to be successful, the whole operation needs, however, to thoroughly cover up all hints of a *personal* vendetta (here as well, the shield of detachment and anonymity offered by the electronic web comes in handy: the grudge and the adversary are de-personalized and "objectivized," while the blow is personally delivered and bears all the coveted marks of subjective achievement). The intimate link between the perception of the loathsomeness and hatefulness of the chosen target on one hand, and our frustration seeking an outlet on the other, must be kept secret. In whatever way hatred was conceived, we would rather tend to explain its presence, to the others around us but also to ourselves, by our will to defend good and noble things which they, those malicious and despicable people, denigrate and conspire against; we would struggle to prove that the reason to hate them, and our determination to get rid of them, have been caused (and justified) by our wish to make sure that an orderly, civilized society survives. *We would insist that the reason to hate is our urge to wipe the world clean of hatred.*

It does not agree perhaps with the logic of things, but it does chime well with the logic of emotions, that the "underclass"—homeless refugees, the uprooted, the "not belonging," the asylum-seekers-but-not-finders, the *sans papiers*—tend to attract our resentment and aversion and become a most favored outlet for self-therapy. *Si non è vero è ben trovato.* All those people have been as if made to the measure of our fears. They are walking illustrations to which our nightmares wrote the captions. They incarnate the idea of inadequacy and being cast at the receiving end of refusal of dignity and, therefore, of humiliation. They are living tokens and reminders (signs, sediments, embodiments) of all those mysterious forces, commonly called "globalization," we hold responsible for the threat of being forcefully torn away from the place we love (in the country or in society) and pushed onto a road with few if any signposts and no known destination. They represent admittedly formidable forces, but they themselves are weak and can be defeated with the modest weapons we possess and know how to handle. *Summa summarum,* they are ideally suited for the role of an effigy in which those forces, indomitable and beyond our reach, may be burned, even if only by proxy.

1.6.

Each kind of utopia is pregnant with its own dystopias—genetically determined, like all offspring are. When they move into the *Lebenswelt,* the embryos turn into life's inner demons. And if you wish to learn what pulls and pushes your contemporaries, look at those demons. You need to know what sort of *alternative* your contemporaries dream of—but also, and probably first and foremost, what kind of *prospect* frightens them most.

In Michel Houellebecq's (2006) *The Possibility of an Island,* the first great dystopia of the liquid-modern era of forceful and relentless individualization and the crumbling of interhuman bonds, the final sentences jotted down by Daniel 25, the last (by his own choice) in the long (infinite by design) series of cloned Daniels, are:

> I had perhaps sixty years left to live; more than twenty thousand days that would be identical. I would avoid thought in the same way I would avoid suffering. The pitfalls of life were far behind me; I have now entered a peaceful space from which only the lethal process would separate me ... I bathed for a long time under the sun and the starlight, and I felt nothing other than as slightly obscure and nutritive sensation ... I was, I was no longer. Life was real.
>
> (2006, p. 336)

Somewhere in between these meditations, Daniel 25 concludes, "Happiness was not a possible horizon. The world had betrayed" (Houellebecq, 2006, p. 337). In Houellebecq's rendering, this was to be, inescapably, the end of a long story. But what was the beginning? How it all started?

Twenty-five clonings earlier, and before the "First" and the "Second Decrease" of the human population of the planet (code names for the credit collapse? Or ecological collapse? Or another war of all against all?)—those catastrophes that transformed the meager remnants of the erstwhile human species into scattered gangs of cannibalistic savages, leaving the memory of the human past to the sole possession, guardianship and care of "neohumans" in order to, as Daniel 25 would *retrospectively* surmise and impute, "shelter from destruction and pillage the whole sum of human knowledge"—Daniel 1 (the last of the Daniels born of a mother) noted in his diary:

> I no longer feel any hate in me, nothing to cling to any more, no more landmarks or clues ... There is no longer any real world, no world, no human world, I am outside time, I no longer have any past or future, I have no more sadness, plans, nostalgia, loss or hope
>
> (2006, p. 296)

In a remarkable recent article on the persistence of utopia, Miguel Abensour quotes William Morris insisting in 1886 that

> men fight and lose the battle, and the thing that they fought for comes about in spite of their defeat, and when it comes it turns out not to be what they meant, and other men have to fight for what they meant under another name.
>
> (2008: 407)

Let us note right away, though, that however much they might have varied in other respects, all utopias written by Morris's predecessors and contemporaries (including Morris himself), a hundred years before the vision of serial Daniels could possibly germinate in Houellebecq's visionary mind, were all sketches/projects of a world in which battles for "things that are not" will no longer be on the cards: such battles will be neither required nor wished for, as the last stone in the search for final perfection will have been already turned and turning any more stones could only be done at the cost of diminishing the perfection already reached. So, if we agree with Morris, the "big thing" missed and thus *fought for* by people who had it in their nature to fight for things missing and missed (whatever names they gave to the things they currently fought for—provisional and on the whole contentious names), was, paradoxically, the *end to fighting*; the end to a need, the must, the desire and desirability, to fight. And the *big* thing that kept "coming about" in the aftermath of lost battle (only to turn out "not to be what they meant" and to prompt other people to fight again for the same thing under another name), was the condition of having no axe to grind and thus no fight to be fought. Restlessness of the compulsive/addicted draftsmen/chasers of utopias was propelled and sustained by the intractable *desire of a rest*. People ran into battle chasing the dream of laying down arms—forever.

To be born, utopian dreams needed two conditions. First, the overwhelming (even if diffuse and inarticulate) feeling that the world was not functioning properly and had to be attended to and overhauled to set it right. Second, the confidence in human potency to rise to the task, belief that "we, humans, can do it"—being armed as we are with reason, able to spy out what is wrong with the world and find out how and with what to replace its diseased parts—and with the flair and proficiency needed to graft such designs on human reality: in short, trust in human potency to force the world into a shape—better fit for the satisfaction of human needs whatever those needs already are or yet may become.

One can say that if the premodern ideal-typical posture toward the world was akin to that of a gamekeeper, it was the gardener's attitude that could best serve as a metaphor for the modern world-view and practice. The main task of a gamekeeper is to defend the land assigned to his wardenship from all and any human interference, in order to defend and preserve, so to speak, its "natural balance"; the gamekeeper's task is to promptly discover and disable the snares set by poachers and to keep alien, illegitimate hunters from trespassing. His services rest on the belief that things are at their best when not interfered and tinkered with; that the world is and is meant to remain a divinely conceived and executed chain of being in which every creature has its rightful and useful place, even if human mental abilities are too limited to comprehend the wisdom, harmony and orderliness of God's design.

Not so the gardener; he acts on the assumption that there would be no order in the world at all, were it not for his constant attention and effort. Gardeners know best what kind of plants should and what sort of plants should not grow on the plot entrusted to their care. They first work out the desirable arrangement in their heads, and then see to it that these images are engraved on the plot. They force their preconceived design upon the plots by encouraging the growth of the right type of plants and uprooting and destroying all the others (now renamed "weeds"), whose uninvited and unwanted presence disagrees with the overall harmony of the design.

It is the gardeners who tend to be the most ardent and dexterous producers of utopias. It is on the gardeners' image of ideal (perfect) harmony, first blueprinted in their heads, that the gardens "always land," archetyping Oscar Wilde's image of humanity always landing in the country called "utopia." If one hears today phrases like "the demise of utopia," or "the end of utopia," or "the fading of utopian imagination," repeated often enough to take root and settle in common sense so firmly as to be taken for self-evident—it is because the gardener's worldview, posture, and the ways to procede are nowadays giving way to that of the *hunter's.*

Unlike the two types that happened to prevail until his tenure started, the hunter could not care less for the overall "balance of things"—whether "natural," or designed and contrived. The sole task hunters pursue is another "kill," big enough to fill their game-bags to capacity. Most certainly, they would not consider it to be their duty to make sure that the supply of game roaming in the forest will be replenished after the hunt. If the woods have been emptied of game due to a particularly successful hunt, hunters may move to another relatively unspoiled wilderness, still teeming with potential hunting trophies. True, it may occur to them that sometime, in a distant and still undefined future, the planet could run out of non-depleted forests; this is not, however, an immediate worry and certainly not *their* worry—as it won't jeopardize the results of the present hunt. And so, surely, this is not a prospect which a single hunter or a single hunting association would feel obliged to ponder, let alone to do something about.

We are all hunters now, or told to be hunters and called/compelled to act like hunters, on the penalty of eviction from hunting, if not of relegation to the ranks of the game. No wonder then, whenever we look around, we are likely to see mostly other lonely hunters like us, or hunters hunting in packs which we also occasionally try to do. What we do and see is called "individualization." And we would need to try really hard to spot a gardener who contemplates a pre-designed harmony beyond the fence of his private garden and then goes out to bring it about. We certainly won't find many gamekeepers with similarly vast interests and sincerely entertained ambitions (that being the prime reason for the people with "ecological conscience" to be alarmed and to try their best to alert the rest of us). That increasingly salient absence is called "deregulation."

It stands to reason that in a world populated mostly by hunters there is hardly any room left for utopian musings; and that not many people would treat utopian blueprints seriously, were they offered them for consideration. And even if we knew how to make the world better and took making it better to heart, the truly puzzling question will be who might have sufficient resources and strong enough will to do it. Those and suchlike expectations as to a suitable agent used to be vested with the resourceful authorities of nation states—but as Jacques Attali (2004, pp. 9–10) observed a few years ago, "nations lost influence on the course of affairs and have abandoned to the forces of globalization all means of orientation in the world's destination and of the defence against all varieties of fear." And the "forces of globalization" are anything but notorious for their "gamekeeping" or "gardening" instincts or strategies; they favor hunting and hunters instead. Roget's Thesaurus, justly acclaimed for its faithful (and authoritative) recording of the successive changes in verbal usages, has every right to list now the concept of the "utopian" in close proximity to "fanciful," "fantastic," "fictional," "chimerical," "air-built," "impractical," "unrealistic," "unreasonable," or "irrational." And so perhaps we are indeed witnessing the end of utopia?

1.7.

Increasingly, *escape* (private by definition) becomes now the name of the most popular game in town. Semantically, escape is the very opposite of utopia, but psychologically it is its sole available substitute: one would say—its new rendition, refashioned to the measure of our deregulated, individualized society of consumers. You can no longer seriously hope to make *the world* a better place to live, you can't even make really secure that better *place in the world* which you might have managed to cut out for yourself.

What is left to your private, personal, individual concerns and efforts, is the fight against *losing*: try at least to stay among the hunters, since the only alternative is to find yourself among the hunted. And the fight against losing is a task which to be properly performed will require your full, undivided attention, twenty-four hours a day and seven days a week vigilance, and above all keeping on the move—as fast as you can.

The dream of making uncertainty less daunting and happiness more permanent by changing one's ego, and of changing one's ego by changing its dresses, is the "utopia" of hunters: the "deregulated," "privatized," and "individualized" version of the old-style visions of good society, society hospitable to the humanity of its members. In that privatized utopia, the world outside the private realm enters life's pursuits solely in the role of a container full of items, useful, useless or harmful for the task of pandering to *amour de soi*.

Hunting is a fulltime task, it consumes a lot of attention and energy, it leaves time for little else; and so it averts attention from the infinity of the task and postpones *ad calendas graecas* the moment of reflection in which the impossibility of the task ever to be fullfilled would need be faced point blank. As Blaise Pascal (1966, pp. 67–8) centuries ago prophetically noted, what people want is "being diverted from thinking of what they are ... by some novel and agreeable passion which keeps them busy, like gambling, hunting, some absorbing show." People want to escape the need to think of "our unhappy condition," and so "we prefer the hunt to the capture." "The hare itself would not save us from thinking" about the formidable but intractable faults in our shared condition, "but hunting it does so."

The snag is, though, that once tasted, hunting turns into addiction, compulsion and obsession. Catching a hare is an anticlimax; its only positive impact is to render yet more seductive the prospect of another hunt, as the hopes that accompanied the hunt are found in retrospect to have been the most delightful (the only fully and truly delightful?) experience of the whole affair. Catching the hare signals an end to those hopes—unless another hunt is immediately planned.

Is that the end of utopia? In one respect it is—in as far as the early-modern utopias envisaged a point in which time will come to a stop;

indeed, the end of time as *history*. There is no such point though in the hunter's life, no moment where one could say that the job has been done, the case open and shut, the mission accomplished—so that one could look forward to the restful remainder of time, enjoying the trophies from now to eternity. In a society of hunters, a prospect of the end to hunting is not tempting, but frightening—since it may arrive only as a personal defeat. The horns will go on announcing the start of another adventure, the greyhounds' bark will go on resurrecting the sweet memory of past chases, the others around will go on hunting, there will be no end to universal excitement ... It's only me who will be stood aside, excluded and no longer wanted, barred from other people's joys, just a passive spectator on the other side of the fence, watching the party but forbidden or unable to join the revelers, enjoying the sights and sounds at best from a distance and by proxy. If a life of continuing and continuous hunting is another utopia, it is—contrary to the utopias of the past—a utopia of *no end*. A bizarre utopia indeed, if measured by orthodox standards; the original utopias promised temptingly the end to the toil—but the hunters' utopia encapsulates the dream of toil never ending.

Strange, unorthodox utopia it is—but utopia all the same, as it promises the same unattainable prize all utopias brandished, namely the ultimate and radical solution to human problems past, present and future, and the ultimate and radical cure for the sorrows and pains of the human condition. It is unorthodox mainly for having moved the land of solutions and cures from the "far away" into the "here and now." Instead of living *toward* the utopia, hunters are offered a living *inside* the utopia. "Private" is no longer something to be fought for and achieved at a far away finishing line of protracted efforts. "Private" is to be lived now and in every one of the moments into which the pointillist time of liquid modernity is sliced. Or, rather, life is to be lived, and tends to be lived indeed, as if the world was already the self's *Lebensraum,* the territory of expansion and conquest by the private, the private self's playground and grazing ground.

For the gardeners, utopia was the end of the road—whereas for hunters it is the road itself. Gardeners visualized the end of the road as the vindication and the ultimate triumph of utopia. For the hunters, the end of the road would be the lived utopia's final, ignominious *defeat*. Adding insult to injury, it would also be a thoroughly *personal* defeat and proof of personal failure. Other hunters won't stop hunting, and non-participation in the hunt can only feel like the ignominy of personal exclusion, and so (presumably) of personal inadequacy.

Utopia brought from the misty "far away" into the tangible "here and now," utopia *lived* rather than being *lived toward*, is immune to tests; for all practical intents and purposes, it is immortal. But its immortality has been achieved at the price of frailty and vulnerabity of all and each one of those enchanted and seduced to live it.

Unlike the utopias of yore, the hunters' utopia does not offer a meaning to life—whether genuine or fraudulent. It only helps to chase the question of life's meaning away from the mind of living. Having reshaped the course of life into an unending series of self-focused pursuits and with each episode lived through as an overture to the next, it offers no occasion for reflection about the direction and the sense of it all. When (if) such an occasion finally comes, at the moment of falling out of or being evicted and banned from rejoining the hunting life, it is usually too late for the reflection to bear on the way in which life, one's own life as much as the life of others, is shaped; and so it is also too late to oppose its present shape and effectively dispute and challenge its propriety.

References

Abensour, M. (2008), "Persistent Utopia," *Constellations*, vol. 15, no. 3, 406–21.
Attali, J. (2004), *La voie humaine* (Paris: Fayard).
Ehrenberg, A. (1995), *L'individu incertain* (Paris: Calman-Lévy).
Houellebecq, M. (2006), *The Possibility of an Island*, G. Bowd (trans.) (London: Phoenix).
Orwell, G. (1977), *1984* (London: Penguin).
Pascal, B. (1966), *Pensées*, A. J. Kreilsheimer (trans.) (London: Penguin).
Simmel, G. (1950), *The Sociology of Georg Simmel*, K. H. Wolff (ed. and trans.) (Glencoe: Free Press).
Smith, D. (2006), *Globalization: The Hidden Agenda* (Cambridge: Polity Press).
Szasz, T. (1973), *The Second Sin* (New York: Anchor Press).
Ustinov, P. (1956), *Romanoff and Juliet: A Comedy in Three Acts* (London: Harper Brothers).
Wikipedia (2009), "Privacy," http://en.wikipedia.org/wiki/Privacy, date accessed 8 March 2009.

2

When Privacy Goes Public: New Media and the Transformation of the Culture of Confession

Günter Burkart

Media researchers are accustomed to the view that in the mass media there is a growing number of acts of self-disclosure and self-exposure, of publicizing private matters. This seems to be true especially for the new media: the Internet, new forms of television, but also mobile phone usage in public places. More and more people, it is said, are eager to reveal intimate details of their private lives in public, to expose themselves in an indecent, shameless manner. As a consequence, there seems to be a dissolution of the boundaries between the private and the public spheres, enabled by the new media.

When we talk about self-disclosure and self-exposure, we assume that once there was a time when the personal self of the subject was separated from the public, hidden and protected in a sphere of intimacy from observation by a sensation seeking crowd. And, vice versa, we tend to think that the public sphere was protected from obtrusive privacy. Indeed, historical evidence shows that a sphere of privacy—which did not exist before in the same way—emerged in the eighteenth century, in the context of bourgeois society. This development was accompanied by the rise of a more reflexive form of individualism, a culture of self-thematization (*Selbstthematisierung*),[1] a refinement of techniques of confession, which gradually became released from religious and juridical contexts. This culture of self-thematization reached its peak in the twentieth century with the invention of psychoanalysis, the rise of therapy culture, and the transfer of the therapeutic mode into everyday life. Authenticity became a central value of self-presentation in public situations.

Today, in media culture, there is a tendency toward a dissolution of the boundary between the private and the public; toward intensified penetration of the public into the realm of privacy, and of privacy into the public sphere. When the private self goes public, however, the character of authentic self-disclosure begins to shift to a dramatized, strategic self-presentation and theatrical self-expression. With this, the culture of reflexive self-disclosure begins to dissolve or may even begin to disappear.

2.1. The rise of privacy

We may believe that privacy has existed for all times. However, before the eighteenth century a sphere of privacy as we know it today did not exist. In the vast literature on the private/public distinction we can find two basic meanings of *privacy/private* (Sennett, 1977; Weintraub, 1997). First, private is the secret, the hidden, the non-visible; an inner sphere separated by a boundary from the publicly visible world. Second, private is the very personal, the individual, something not shared with any other person. In this sense, private is both one's credit card number as well as one's sexual behavior.[2]

There are further, more complex definitions and distinctions, some emphasizing the right of access to private things, others stressing the sphere of intimacy or some other characteristics. Whatever the definition, two basic complementary aspects are: on the one hand, the *protection of privacy* (of private ownership, information and space), that is, protection from unwanted intrusions by the state, commercial institutions or the media. On the other hand, the *autonomy and freedom* of the individual to be on her own and to go public of her own accord (decisional privacy without limits or restrictions from the public). So, there is an asymmetric structure in so far as the individual wants to have protection of her privacy, and control over attempts at outside intrusion, but also the freedom to go public. Harry Blatterer (this volume, Chapter 5) identifies a growing tension between the desire of being invisible (private) and the pursuit of visibility (see also Markus, this volume, Chapter 6).

Historical origins of the distinction between public and private reach back to antiquity, specifically to the Greek distinction between *oikos* and *polis*. The house (*oikos*) did not represent privacy in a modern sense, just as the Roman word *familia* did not mean family in a modern sense of an emotionally based community, but an economic community and a system of domination (domestic power). And this is also true for the *house community* of premodern Europe. The beginning of the separation between the private and the public spheres is marked by the separation between household and economy in the early bourgeois family. With the separation between production and reproduction a new sphere of intimacy within the house emerged. The house became a shelter of family safety, a place offering security (*Geborgenheit*), and later a "haven in a heartless world" (Lasch, 1979). The realm of work was outsourced, so to speak. The public was excluded from certain parts of the house, although there was, however, a place within the house to which the public had access. Therefore, the separation between private and public is not equivalent to the separation between family and society. "Family" is not analogous with "the private sphere." Rather, it is the place where the private and the public meet and, in part, merge—where the two spheres are balanced. As Jürgen Habermas (2002, p. 45) commented regarding early bourgeois society, "The line between private and public sphere extended right through the home. The privatized individuals stepped out of the intimacy of their living rooms into the public sphere of the *salon*, but the one was strictly complementary to the other." Still today, the line runs between bedroom and living room.

The boundary between private and public is not fixed once and for all. It can be pushed or pulled to either side, and therefore the realm of the two spheres can increase or diminish. From this perspective we may distinguish between four levels of privacy. From level to level, the boundary between the private and the public sphere is shifting from the inside to the outside (if we accept, for the time being, a spatial metaphor). On the first level, "private" is the inner world of a subject, separated from the outer side of the person as well as from the whole world outside the subject (high personal or inner privacy). On the second level is the personal sphere of individuality, autonomy and free will separated from social relationships (individual privacy). Third, there is the sphere of intimate relationships (sexual privacy and love; shared secrets or reciprocal self-disclosure between two lovers or intimate friends). Finally, on the fourth level we may envisage the domestic sphere of family community (household privacy), separated from the whole world outside the family. So, we have, from level to level, an extension of the private sphere at the cost of (a diminishing) public sphere.

2.2. Individualism and self-reflection

The culture of self-recognition and confession is part of a long-term process of individualization, of a growing significance of individualism. To a certain degree, this process has its roots in antiquity, but began to develop substantially only from the twelfth century and intensified in later eras: the Renaissance, the Enlightenment, the Age of Sentiment, German "Klassik," "Sturm und Drang," the Romantic period.

"Individualization" in general means a growing importance of individualism as a central western value. However, what is individualism, and which of its elements gain growing significance? In German sociology, during the last three decades, there was a widespread debate about a new thrust of individualization after World War II, or, after "1968." Unfortunately, however, there was no great effort to clarify the terms "individualization" or "individualism." So, it remained unclear which dimension of individualization was supposed to be on the rise. I propose to distinguish three dimensions of individualism which are also historical stages in the long-term process of individualization.[3]

The first dimension is *autonomy*, related to social processes of *liberation* (*Freisetzung*), that is a dissolution of traditional forms of bonding, releasing the individual from collectivities and strong structures, family ties and religious ligatures, and today even from gender roles. This leads to more individual autonomy and self-determination, more options and room for decision-making, but on the other hand compels the individual to show self-reliance, to be active and self-oriented.

The second dimension is *uniqueness* related to social processes of *distinction*. When individualization in the sense of liberation is widespread, chances for further differentiation increase, class structures become more permeable, and so refined distinctions are necessary. Ranking-systems emerge, and efforts for even stronger distinction between peculiar individuals are encouraged (Bourdieu, 1984). Historically, the Romantic era emphasizes uniqueness; an understanding of the individual as a very special person, not comparable to anyone else. The highest form of individuality is the genius.

The third dimension is *self-reflection*. It is related to social processes of the institutionalization of self-reflection, and to social discourses which evaluate the processes of liberation and distinction. Self-awareness of the individual becomes more important, self and identity becomes an issue, the whole of life is becoming the subject of biographical narratives. In order to enable self-reflection there must exist *institutions* of self-reflection, of self-thematization. Without such institutions it would be much more difficult to reflect upon one's self, since we can assume that there is no natural need for such reflection (Hahn, 1987). Those institutions offer patterns for the construction of identities and selves, for the generation of biographical narratives and for controlled self-disclosure and confession. Modern cultures developed techniques, media and institutions for self-reflection, from simple routines of thinking ("Who am I?") to narrative patterns and special forms of self-expression such as letters, diaries, autobiographies, and other *ego-documents*, which testify to the individual's searching for a real self, for authentic needs, for the true personality, and so on. Today, there seems to have developed new forms of ego-expression, like weblogs, chat rooms and social networks on the Internet.

The three dimensions of individualism can also be interpreted as forming a historical sequence. The first dimension (liberation) was on the rise up to and during the eighteenth century, with the Enlightenment, economic and political revolutions (autonomy of markets, freedom for citizens). The second dimension (uniqueness) can be connected historically to the Romantic era, where the cult of the genius was prevalent, while the third dimension emerges with psychoanalysis in the twentieth century.

There is, of course, a close connection between individualism and privacy.[4] On the one hand, the separation of a private sphere reinforces individualism, and on the other hand the growing significance of individualism is raising the chance for more autonomy, but also for privacy to penetrate into the public sphere. The necessity to express one's individuality is a permanent incentive for trying to be "private" or "natural" also in the public sphere—to break rules, to ignore roles, standards and etiquette (something Sennett (1977) was afraid of). For modern individuals there is a permanent pressure to fulfill contradictory expectations: to be authentic and self-related, but at the same time, to carry out roles.[5] In this sense, growing individualism has perhaps contributed to the blurring of the boundaries between the private and the public, because it compels privacy to go public.

2.3. Self-reflection as a culture of confession

Making intensified efforts for self-recognition, self-evaluation and self-realization also puts the onus to reveal personal insights onto others. Self-reflection can develop into a *culture of confession*. What does "confession" mean? We have, at least, four basic meanings of the term or similar terms: (a) confession of sin (of guilt in religious terms); (b) confession of a bad deed or crime (of guilt in terms of the law and of norm systems); (c) confession of a faith, of a value; standing up for one's convictions, for belonging to a community of shared values; (d) confession of a desire, including sexuality. Historically, the meaning of confession gradually shifted from the religious, moral and juridical confession of sin and guilt to the disclosure of intimate desires (as in confessions of love, and later in psycho-therapy). In therapeutic contexts it is not a question of good or bad, but of honestly revealing dark, inscrutable fantasies and declaring one's own suffering, pains and passions. There is also a shift from confession as a marker of belonging to a value-based community, toward individualistic disclosures of secrets and further hidden aspects of intimate inner life.

According to Michel Foucault (1977; 1990), we can consider modernity as an era that gave rise to a culture of confession. Thinking about oneself, problematizing one's own self, and communicating these insights to certain professionals becomes the precondition for being ascribed subject status, for the recognition of subjectivity and normality. Persons being labeled deviant should be led to normality by self-reflection and confession, if necessary with expert help. Foucault (2007), referring to the figure of the Christian Shepherd, identifies "pastoral power" as an early form of this professional assistance/power. Being obliged to confess becomes a new technique of domination.

One of Foucault's (1990) famous historical examples is sexuality. In Christian Europe, he claims, in opposition to conventional wisdom, sexuality was not suppressed, but, on the contrary, people have been forced to reflect their desires, to become aware of and talk about their sexuality. So, according to Foucault, social control has shifted from the institutions of bodily punishment to the institutions and professions of bringing us to think and talk about ourselves.

Foucault developed a model of historical stages. At the first stage, the individual is typically punished by bodily torture. At the second stage, disciplines (at school, in military institutions, at work) are developed, and soon—with the entrance to the third stage—individuals begin to keep themselves under surveillance, to monitor themselves. Further steps are refinements of this self-control by techniques of confession, which at the beginning are related to notions of good and evil, later to problems of the self, to one's imperfection and suffering, finally to the desires of the flesh. Thus, psychiatrists, therapists, sexual researchers and coaches for intimate matters have taken the place of priests and judges. They all are working on the discourse of normality and are engaged in upholding social order (control and discipline) including the sphere of sexuality and intimacy. There is a fourth stage in Foucault's oeuvre, however, a more utopian one. It is the utopia of self-governed individuals who take care of themselves, worry about themselves (*souci de soi*) and are thus able to self-govern. More recently the discourse of *gouvernementalité* has focused on self-management and the entrepreneurial self.

The peak (for the time being) of this culture of self-reflection and confession was reached in the last third of the twentieth century, in the proliferation of psychotherapies and the permeating into everyday life of the therapeutic ethic and of therapeutically informed talk. We now have a "therapy culture" (Furedi, 2004; see also Johnson, this volume, Chapter 8). A new norm emerged claiming that within personal relationships you are obliged to confess whatever you have in mind, your desires and fears, your hopes and fantasies. Authenticity is an important value, and so, for example, infidelity may be tolerated as long as it is confessed and sincerely talked about. Another indicator for a culture of confession is the prominence and popularity of the interview both in the social sciences and in the media, for example in talk shows. With the success of the narrative interview in qualitative social research, which encourages biographical self-reflection, more and more life histories are produced. And in the self-help literature, instructions for autobiographical writing are available, indicating that more and more "normal" people are writing their autobiography (Kraus, 2006).

Finally, some forms of self-reflection and psychological self-thematization have become crucial even in the context of *work*. Scholars like Eva Illouz (2007) and Arlie Hochschild (2003) emphasize the growing importance of psychology for capitalism. Illouz shows how psychological theories have infiltrated management techniques. Hochschild (2003) refers to certain fields of work where emotional competences are needed, such as air hostesses who are advised to treat their customers as if they were their personal guests at home: their smile ought to be sincere. Boltanski and Chiapello (2006), in a study of management advice manuals, found that a growing importance is placed on creativity, autonomy, self-reliance and flexibility—all including some degree of self-reflection—for the "new spirit" of capitalism (Foucault's self-governance fits into this picture).

Of course, psychologically trained self-reflection and self-expression in the world of work is not identical with authentic confession. When going into the field of work, reflexive individualism is changing its form and institutional setting: from therapy to coaching; from self-reflection to self-presentation; from confession to controlled and strategically oriented self-expression; from authenticity to dramatized self-presentation. Self-management becomes a strategic endeavor, which includes some basic skills in self-reflection and self-control, but does not necessarily include confession—certainly not in the sense understood in psychotherapy.

In general, we can state a closer connection between emotional and rational aspects (which may be related to the blurring of private and public) in the economy as well as in politics. But also in the field of living arrangements, we can observe a blurring of the private/public divide: the rise of the concept of *partnership* in couple relationships indicates a growing importance of normative concepts developed in the public sphere, like egality, negotiation, rational communication, etc.—instead of "confluent" love (Giddens, 1992), non-verbal communication and very private intimacy. Another form of this blurring of the lines between private and public forms of living is the shared, communal living arrangements between non-kin, where the line between personal privacy and public space has to be continuously negotiated. And in the context of therapy culture new forms of group therapy have been developed which change fundamentally the culture of confession: there is no longer a "shepherd," a "father confessor" or a therapist; rather, the confession is now made in an egalitarian context, within a peer-group of people on the same level of competence and affliction.

What happens when the media take a hold of the private sphere and the culture of confession? Can we interpret the new trends in the media as a further step in the development of the culture of confession, reflexive individualism and the relative dominance of the private sphere? Does the presentation of privacy in the media support the notion of "authenticity" and thus "privatize" the public sphere? Or, on the contrary, is privacy severely threatened by new media technologies? I will turn to these questions in what follows.

2.4. Media culture as a culture of confession and self-disclosure

When privately owned television was introduced and came into competition with public television in the 1980s, in Germany and in other western countries, a debate was initiated about a new culture of shamelessness and vulgarity. Trends toward increasing self-disclosure and exposure were being observed; trends toward deliberate, perhaps even lustful revelations of people's intimate lives which hitherto were considered shameful and were therefore concealed from the public. The new media, it is said, offer a forum for the public presentation of privacy. The threshold of shame is moving; the self leaves the protected sphere of privacy, the boundary between public and private begins to dissolve (Weiß and Groebel, 2002).

Media scholars argued that naive lay actors are exposed—mostly in an indecent way—to the public in so-called real-life soaps; that they are exposed to mockery or make laughing stocks of themselves and so become the object of public amusement. Television was labeled a "zoo of people" with shows such as *Big Brother, Girls Camp, Germany's Next Top Model* being at the center of critique. Complaints were rampant about a new vulgarity, the decline of quality, loss of discretion, the tyranny of intimacy, about the advance of the obscene, the noisy and loud. In the USA, critics of TV talk shows (related to its "classical" form through the 1990s) have characterized it as sordid, raunchy, immoral, sleazy, bizarre, trashy, degrading, repulsive and so on (Orrego et al., 2000, p. 251). Much of the talk shows' popularity was "due to their increase in the controversial and sensational nature of guests' disclosures ... Talk shows are 'public confessionals' that encourage private revelations of intimate personal information" (Orrego et al., 2000, p. 249).

The complaints about the intrusion of the private into the public is influenced by critics such as Richard Sennett (1977) who believes that the public sphere is going to be destroyed by the invading forces of privacy, turning personal feelings, authenticity and intimacy into norms of public life. These critiques reflect a social debate about normality, about rules of appropriate behavior in public—after all, it is a debate about de-civilization. Therefore, we may also characterize the derogatory stance of some media scholars as a bourgeois critique of the conquest of the public space by an underclass or by members of popular culture. On the other hand, positive judgments, emphasizing the triumph of popular culture, are rarely made.[6]

This trend is not quite new, of course. In general, with the introduction of technical media of communication into households and families (with its *domestication*), the television, computer and telephone became interfaces between the two spheres. Via media the public enters the private sphere, and begins to change personal relations, modes of perception of reality, one's "sense of place" (Meyrowitz, 1985), and the relation between absence and presence (Gergen, 2002). On the other hand, mediated publication of privacy is not quite new either, even in the print media. Journalists discovered, in the early stages of newspaper production, that the reading public was rather interested in private matters (especially sex and crime). But, the trend seems to be considerably amplified by commercialized television and the Internet.[7] Especially the Internet with its "odd mix of personal and public information" is "boundary-shattering" (Meyrowitz 2002: 171).

The great success of the cell phone is another element of the culture of confession and the making public of private matters. Observers have stated that with the growing occurrence of cell phones in public places the public/private barrier was weakened, the threshold minimized and so allowed people to talk publicly about private, even intimate, matters (Haddon, 1998; Katz and Aakhus, 2002; Ling, 2004; Burkart, 2007; Katz, 2008). What is disturbing is not only the intruding noise of ring tones (increasingly loud music) but more being forced to listen to private conversations. Emanuel A. Schegloff (2002, p. 286) tells a story which is instructive for the confusion caused by the missing boundary between private and public, by the "intersection of worlds." A young woman is sitting in a train with a cell phone. Evidently, she has some troubles with her boyfriend, and she is even shouting. Most people do not seem to take notice—Goffman's *civil inattention*—pretending not to listen (though it is not possible not to hear). Only one passenger reacts, if timidly. He looks into her face, with some expression of disapproval. The young lady hisses at him: "What do you want? This is not your business, it's a private matter." This is certainly right, but at the same time totally wrong. She is "absent present" (Gergen, 2002), in two places at the same time: in the train and on the phone, in the space constituted by remote communication. The first place is public; the second is private and public at the same time. Only as long as the people who are present pretend not to listen does the situation work.

Today, there is a growing concern that the boundaries are blurring in the other direction; that the private sphere is threatened by intrusive media new and old, by public institutions or the state, and that therefore the private sphere has to be protected. Indeed, much recent research is concerned with the violation of informational privacy by public institutions, by the state and by commercial interests (Solove, 2004), stressing the protection of privacy (Marlin-Bennett, 2004; O'Hara and Shadbolt, 2008).[8] Violations of privacy, in particular violations of informational privacy, by "public" institutions (state, administration, commercial and business) may provoke the individual to control her privacy and so to hide or feign her identity.

2.5. The end of the culture of confession?

Even though it might be useful to interpret media culture as a culture of confession, we have to take into account that "confession" may change its meaning and be transformed when set in the media context. So, what is the fate of the culture of confession when it enters the media? What happens when self-disclosure leaves the therapeutic context and goes public?

There are a few peculiarities of media self-disclosure suggesting that we should distinguish between real self-disclosure and televised self-disclosure (Orrego et al., 2000), or, more generally speaking, between revelation of privacy and mediated confession. Firstly, the self-disclosure threshold in the new media may be so low because in many forms of television programming or the Internet there is no real (reciprocal) partner to whom self-disclosure is addressed. Online-self-disclosure, but also some forms of televised confession, does not involve the same degree of vulnerability as would be the case in personal relationships. The barrier is lower for self-revelation when freed from the constraints of co-presence (Thompson, 2005, p. 38), when there is anonymity or pseudo anonymity and a mediating screen.[9]

In addition, it is not quite clear what *public* means on the Internet, or if there is an audience at all. The anonymity and the absence of social presence is comparable to the "stranger on the train" experience, when strangers reveal themselves to one another because there is no fear of misuse or sanction, and so vulnerability is markedly reduced. Producers and consumers of Internet sites frequently are members of the same community (social network). There is no equivalent to TV where people are exposed to the audience in the studio and/or on the screen.

Televised self-disclosures are often perceived as especially inappropriate behavior which violates norms of good taste and rules of civilized behavior to such an extent that it does not appear to be "real," even though it might be intended to be serious and sincere. On the Internet there never is absolute certainty as to whether people show their real identity or something purely virtual. Especially for adolescents, the Internet is a welcome opportunity for identity experiments (Schouten, 2007). If, for example, one visits websites like the *Internet-Confession-Centre* one finds an odd mixture of true (but anonymous) revelations of more or less bad deeds and of nonsensical chatting or pure dissimulation in order to elicit some responses from other anonymous members of the "confession community." So, virtual identity play (in this case faked confession) may help to find an ideal self, an identity suitable for self-presentation in public. But it has little to do with self-reflection in the traditional (therapeutic) sense. Furthermore, hope for some sort of fame—or, at least, for some public attention may be a mighty driving force for self-disclosure in the media. Despite the possibility of shame, there is hope for success and fame.[10]

Some scholars find, however, that the Internet is getting more and more like real life for younger people, and for example, there seems to be no difference in *impression management* between face-to-face-interactions and online-interactions (Chester and Bretherton, 2007). Misoch (2004) found that at least on private websites people tend to present what they think is their "authentic" self. And for the last decade (in contrast to the 1990s) researchers in psychology are more willing to accept Internet surfing as a normal and adequate means of identity search, communication, and improving personal relationships (Valkenburg and Peter, 2009), and so consider it part of the real world. Those findings are useful in correcting an all too negative picture. Nonetheless, it seems quite clear that there is a transformation in the way private matters come into the public sphere, while the meaning of "public" is being transformed accordingly. The "public sphere" in the Internet seems to be more like an "aggregation of private selves" (Illouz, 2007, p. 78) or a mass of hundreds of unknown friends (Markus, this volume, Chapter 6). While further research is needed, the following remarks are tentative conjectures.

When intimate matters are told in public they begin to lose their character of being authentic and mutate into a kind of *theatrical performance*. What we can see is the social and mediated construction of publicly made intimacy. It is not a sincere presentation of a genuine self; rather, it is an illusion of authenticity at best. Actors in the media play with a role, and so play with the boundary between real self and virtual self. The goal is no longer authenticity, but public attention. Of course, that kind of role playing has to be learned. Thus, there are media coaches, experts for the presentation of feigned authenticity. All this includes the growing importance of images, expressive acts and the body (corporeality). The visual aspects of self-presentation are becoming more important: presentation of the body as representation of the self, self-disclosure as disclosure of intimate parts of the body. This is not surprising when we think of television, as television is image oriented, while the culture of confession has arisen from the world of the word. Parts of the Internet (for example, private webcams) are image oriented too, and there are similarities between *Big Brother* on TV and private webcam sites. But also in the parts of the Internet which are more word oriented there is no longer a confession culture in the above sense. Even when exaggerated and so the Internet is seen as a game with identities and virtual selves (Turkle, 1995), there is, nonetheless, a clear trend toward feigning identities. Online diaries or private webcams, it seems, typically do not show characteristics of the therapeutically informed culture of confession, but present a certain image of the person; they do not have the function of self-reflection (Konert and Hermanns, 2002).

So, which are the new institutions of the mediated culture of confession? Are we shifting from the therapy couch to the chat room? This would imply a transformation from searching for the true self toward searching for an ideal self and a play with identities. Or are we going from therapy to the catwalk and the media theater? This would imply working hard in order to find a visualized self suitable for a voyeuristic public.[11] A third possibility emerges with the rise of group therapy. Internet communities (social networks) may be regarded as media successors of group therapy, while confession in this context will receive a renewed meaning in the sense of proclaiming to belong to a community.

The result of these considerations may be summarized as follows. The culture of reflexive, authentic confession, it seems, is already declining. When the culture of self-reflection and confession begins to penetrate into the public sphere, it is being transformed into a culture of staging or into a culture of feigned identities. In addition, a new form of community peer group confession is on the rise. Self-presentation has been democratized, the old experts for self-reflection and self-recognition (pastors, therapists, counselors, coaches) lose influence. Everybody seems to be able to express himself or herself without professional help. Either way, this is a shift from bourgeois subjectivity to postmodern identities. In the private sphere, however, the culture of self-disclosure, of reflection and intimate communication, remains intact—or so we may hope at least—even though it is threatened by public intruders and scrutinizers. There will remain a claim for protected intimacy (or even solitude, as Markus [this volume, Chapter 6] claims) and for authenticity, which is still very important for the quality of real personal relationships. But it will become harder for individuals to discern what is their (and their communicating partners') "real" self and what is their "ideal" image they want to present (and in the same way, what are "real" personal relationships), when the blurring of boundaries between the private and the public spheres continues.

Notes

1. There is no adequate English equivalent for the German term which was introduced by Alois Hahn (1987). It can, however, be circumscribed as a (discursive) process by which the self becomes the topic of reflection, communication and practices.
2. Of course, the boundary between the private and the public is not identical with the boundary between person and collectivity, or individual and society. Rather, the boundary between private and public is situated within the individual—the individual has a private and a public side, or, in Goffman's terms, a private and a public self.
3. The first two dimensions can be traced back to Georg Simmel, who made a distinction between "quantitative" and "qualitative" individualism, or liberal and romantic individualism.
4. For a detailed discussion of the links between various dimensions of privacy and of individualism, see Arthur Glass, this volume, Chapter 4.

5. It is a permanent task of the (post) modern individual to balance the need to keep something secret with the need to reveal certain aspects of our privacy (Rosenfeld, 2000; Petronio, 2000).
6. As Meyrowitz (2002, 170) admits, it is rather "pushing the boundaries of good taste" than "blurring of the boundary between public and private."
7. What is new is easy to see when we take a look at the history of moving pictures. Meyrowitz (2002, 161ff.) describes the self-regulation of the film industry since the 1920s. The aim was to ban certain "private" things from "public" consumption, including "lustful kissing" or homosexuality or "sex relationships between the white and black race" (p. 163). Thus, many characteristics of private, intimate life were banned from the public screen of the movie theater—a situation which is hardly imaginable today. America, it is said, became a "voyeur nation" (Calvert, 2000).
8. There is, however, the competing value of freedom of the press (Gounalakis, 2000). New technologies enhance the chance to be controlled and monitored continuously, but at the same time, they make life more convenient (for example, Google, the cell phone, and so on).
9. See Joinson and Paine (2007) for an overview of research; see also Joinson (2001), who found significantly higher levels of spontaneous self-disclosure in computer-mediated discussions compared to face-to-face-discussions; visual anonymity increases self-disclosing behavior in the net. Schouten (2007) found that reduced or totally absent non-verbal (visual) cues increase the willingness of self-disclosure, because this increases control over the process of revelation (for example with the technique of Instant Messaging). However, there seems to be a lot of carelessness and imprudence in online self-revelation (Meyrowitz, 2002, 172).
10. The most intriguing aspect of the Clinton/Lewinsky scandal, Meyrowitz (2002, 154–5) says, "is not to be found in the details of the sex play ... but in the manner in which the two primary participants have survived the 'shame' that would once have banished them from public life." In the post-modern era, with its new culture of shamelessness, there is a new trend: "Once-shameful (or guilt-worthy) acts become a source of fame and success" (Meyrowitz, 2002, 155). Instead of committing suicide, Meyrowitz means, those people, "appear as celebrities on talk shows" (Meyrowitz, 2002, 155). Thus, scandals become a source of attention and success (see also Imhof and Schulz, 1998). America has reached, Meyrowitz says, an era of post-privacy, with a culture of shamelessness. See also Bauer (2008) for confession going public (with more examples from politicians).
11. Then, the need for visibility (Blatterer, in this volume, Chapter 5) must become supported by "managed visibility" (Markus, this volume, Chapter 6).

References

Bauer, S. W. (2008), *The Art of Public Grovel: Sexual Sin and Public Confession in America* (Princeton: Princeton University Press).

Boltanski. L. and E. Chiapello (2006), *The New Spirit of Capitalism* (London: Verso).

Bourdieu, P. (1984), *Distinctions* (London: Routledge and Kegan Paul).

Burkart, G. (2007), *Handymania: Wie das Mobiltelefon unser Leben verändert hat* (Frankfurt am Main: Campus).

Calvert, C. (2000), *Voyeur Nation: Media, Privacy, and Peering in Modern Culture* (Boulder: Westview Press).

Chester, A. and D. Bretherton (2007), "Impression Management and Identity Online," in A. N. Joinson, K. McKenna, T. Postmes, and U.-D. Reips (eds), *The Oxford Handbook of Internet Psychology* (Oxford: Oxford University Press), 226–36.

Foucault, M. (1977), *Discipline and Punish: The Birth of the Prison* (London: Allen Lane).

Foucault, M. (1990), *The History of Sexuality: The Will to Kowledge*, vol. 1., R. Hurley (trans.) (London: Penguin).

Foucault, M. (2007), *Security, Territory, Population: Lectures at the College de France 1977–78*, M. Senellart (ed.), G. Burchell (trans.) (New York: Palgrave Macmillan).

Furedi, F. (2004), *Therapy Culture: Cultivating Vulnerability in an Uncertain Age* (London and New York: Routledge).

Gergen, K. (2002), "The Challenge of Absent Presence," in J. E. Katz and M. A. Aakus (eds), *Perpetual Contact: Mobile Communication, Private Talk, Public Performance* (Cambridge: Cambridge University Press), 227–41.

Giddens, A. (1992), *The Transformation of Intimacy: Sexuality, Love and Eroticism in Modern Societies* (Cambridge: Polity).

Gounalakis, G. (2000), *Privacy and the Media: A Comparative Perspective* (Munich: Beck).

Habermas, J. (2002), *The Structural Transformation of the Public Sphere*, T. Burger and F. Lawrence (trans) (Cambridge: Polity).

Haddon, L. (ed.) (1998), *Communications on the Move: The Experience of Mobile Telephony in the 1990s* (Stockholm: COST 248 Report).

Hahn, A. (1987), "Identität und Selbstthematisierung," in A. Hahn and V. Knapp (eds), *Selbstthematisierung und Selbstzeugnis: Bekenntnis und Geständnis* (Frankfurt am Main: Suhrkamp), 9–24.

Hochschild, A. R. (2003), *The Commercialization of Intimate Life: Notes from Home and Work* (Berkeley: University of California Press).

Illouz, E. (2007), *Cold Intimacies: The Making of Emotional Capitalism* (Cambridge: Polity).

Imhof, K. and P. Schulz (eds) (1998), *Die Veröffentlichung des Privaten—die Privatisierung des Öffentlichen* (Opladen: Westdeutscher Verlag).

Joinson, A. N. (2001), "Self-disclosure in Computer-Mediated Communication: The Role of Self-Awareness and Visual Anonymity," *European Journal of Social Psychology*, vol. 31, 177–92.

Joinson, A. N. and C. B. Paine (2007), "Self-Disclosure, Privacy and the Internet," in A. N. Joinson, K. McKenna, T. Postmes, and U.-D. Reips (eds), *The Oxford Handbook of Internet Psychology* (Oxford: Oxford University Press).

Katz, J. E. (2008) *Handbook of Mobile Communication Studies* (Cambridge and London: The MIT Press).

Katz, J. E. and M. A. Aakus (eds) (2002), *Perpetual Contact: Mobile Communication, Private Talk, Public Performance* (Cambridge: Cambridge University Press).

Konert, B. and D. Hermanns (2002), "Der private Mensch in der Netzwelt," in R. Weiß and J. Groebel (eds), *Privatheit im öffentlichen Raum. Medienhandeln zwischen Individualisierung und Entgrenzung* (Opladen: Leske und Budrich), 415–505.
Kraus, W. (2006), "Die Veralltäglichung der Patchwork-Identität," in G. Burkart (ed.), *Die Ausweitung der Bekenntniskultur: Neue Formen der Selbstthematisierung?* (Wiesbaden: VS Verlag).
Lasch, C. (1979), *Haven in a Heartless World: The Family Besieged* (New York: Basic Books).
Ling, R. (2004), *The Mobile Connection: The Cell Phone's Impact on Society* (San Francisco: Elsevier).
Marlin-Bennett, R. (2004), *Knowledge Power: Intellectual Property, Information, and Privacy* (Boulder: Lynne Rienner).
Meyrowitz, J. (1985), *No Sense of Place: The Impact of Electronic Media on Social Behaviour* (Oxford: Oxford University Press).
Meyrowitz, J. (2002), "Post-privacy America," in R. Weiß and J. Groebel (eds), *Privatheit im öffentlichen Raum. Medienhandeln zwischen Individualisierung und Entgrenzung* (Opladen: Leske und Budrich), 153–204.
Misoch, S. (2004), *Identitäten im Internet. Selbstdarstellung auf privaten Homepages* (Konstanz: Universitätsverlag).
O'Hara, K. and N. Shadbolt (2008), *The Spy in the Coffee Machine: The End of Privacy as We Know It* (Oxford: Oneworld).
Orrego, V.O., S. W. Smith, M. M. Mitchell, A. J. Johnson, K. Ah Yun, and B. Greenberg (2000), "Disclosure and Privacy Issues on Television Talk Shows," in S. Petronio (ed.), *Balancing the Secrets of Private Disclosures* (London: Erlbaum), 249–59.
Petronio, S. (ed.) (2000), *Balancing the Secrets of Private Disclosures* (London: Erlbaum).
Rosenfeld, L. B. (2000), "Overview of the Ways Privacy, Secrecy, and Disclosure are Balanced in Today's Society," in S. Petronio (ed.), *Balancing the Secrets of Private Disclosures* (London: Erlbaum), 3–17.
Schegloff, E. A. (2002), "Beginnings in the Telephone," in J. E. Katz and M. A. Aakus (eds), *Perpetual Contact: Mobile Communication, Private Talk, Public Performance* (Cambridge: Cambridge University Press), 284–300.
Schouten, A. P. (2007), *Adolescents' Online Self-disclosure and Self-presentation* (Dissertation, The Amsterdam School of Communications Research).
Sennett, R. (1977), *The Fall of Public Man* (New York: Knopf).
Solove, D. J. (2004), *The Digital Person: Technology and Privacy in the Information Age* (New York: New York University Press).
Thompson, J. B. (2005), "The New Visibility," *Theory, Culture and Society*, vol. 22, no. 6, 31–51.
Turkle, S. (1995), *Life on the Screen* (New York: Simon & Schuster).
Valkenburg, P. and J. Peter (2009), "Social Consequences of the Internet for Adolescents: A Decade of Research," *Current Directions in Psychological Science*, vol. 18, 1–5.
Weintraub, J. (1997), "The Theory and Politics of the Public/Private Distinction," in J. Weintraub and K. Kumar (eds), *Public and Private in Thought and Practice: Perspectives on a Grand Dichotomy* (Chicago: The University of Chicago Press).
Weiß, R. and J. Groebel (eds) (2002), *Privatheit im öffentlichen Raum. Medienhandeln zwischen Individualisierung und Entgrenzung* (Opladen: Leske und Budrich).

3
Images of Intimacy in Feminist Discussions over Private/Public Boundaries

Pauline Johnson

When in the late 1970s Foucault announced that "freedom in the liberal regime is not a ready-made region which has to be respected ... [i]t is something that has to be constantly produced" (Foucault, 2008, p. 65), he was reflecting on a self-misunderstanding at the heart of liberalism that a spirited feminist critique had already begun to disclose. When a nascent feminism tried to put liberal descriptions of "natural" private freedoms to its own uses, it discovered that they depended on repressive gender ideologies. Its response that "the personal is political" sometimes meant attempting to do away with the distinction altogether (Firestone, 1970). For the most part though feminists have recognized that the separation between the private and public spheres is essential to modern individuality and so vital to its own concerns (see Blatterer, this volume, Chapter 5). Rejecting those feminisms that "would abandon the distinction between private and public entirely," Beate Rössler makes the point that "the difficulties associated with the liberal distinction between a public and a private sphere are not so categorical that the distinction becomes problematic *in principle*" (2005, p. 23, original emphasis). The challenge now is to reconstruct private freedoms that promise release from the gendered productions that underpin a liberal faith in their "givenness." My paper critically reviews some episodes in feminist controversies over how to redescribe the freedoms of private life and offers its own contribution.

I begin by identifying two paradigmatic constructions of the task. One approach identifies a normative continuity between the public and private spheres and reflects upon the distinctive way in which these shared commitments are encountered within the private domain. This is an approach that binds the values affirmed by private life to ideals of egalitarian justice. Another affirms normative discontinuities and hopes to secure the boundaries without appealing to naturalizing constructions. This involves an appreciation of the special values that cling to the investments in particular others that shapes the private domain. I suggest that both undertakings have encountered significant difficulties. The search for continuities has been unable to produce a convincing account of distinctive private freedoms and major attempts to outline discontinuities find it difficult to move outside the thrall of naturalizing descriptions.

Problems encountered by the political philosopher have given a job to the sociologist who has moved alongside to suggest a candidate that could take up the normative burden left by the collapse of a liberal faith in ready-made freedoms. Intimate life has seemed to be an appropriate site for considering the produced character of private freedoms. This is so partly because intimacy asks to be evaluated not as a given disposition or innate capacity but rather as a special achieved set of interactions. Also because an appreciation of individuality and subjectivity is central to this claimed distinctiveness (see Markus, this volume, Chapter 6).

I turn, then, to an investigation of two major attempts to reconstruct the private freedoms elaborated in a self-reflexive intimate sphere. Each proposes a quite different negotiation with public commitments. Published in 1992, Anthony Giddens' *The Transformation of Intimacy: Sexuality, Love and Eroticism in Modern Societies* works within a paradigm that hopes to uncover normative continuities. Giddens reflects upon the evolution of a self-fashioning intimacy toward expectations set within a democratic public sphere. More recently, Axel Honneth has become interested in the self-shaping of intimate life in accordance with its own special values (see Blatterer, this volume, Chapter 5). Honneth thinks that distinctive freedoms set in motion by the pursuit of an idealized intimacy cannot form a continuous normative spectrum with commitments set by a democratic public but can only be constantly checked against them (Honneth, 2004 and 2007). I will argue that both attempts to reflect on private freedoms via a reconstruction of the values through which contemporary intimacy understands itself suffer from one-sided accounts of the intimate sphere. Each attempt to resolve the value of the intimate domain under one-dimensional descriptions reproduces problems already identified in the adopted models of normative continuity and discontinuity.

The final part of the paper develops an alternative way of thinking about the values of contemporary intimacy. Endeavoring to peel back distortions that cling to a long-standing preoccupation with resolving its cultural significance, I opt for an account of the intimate sphere as an on-going negotiation between distinct, sometimes competing, ways of valuing itself. It seems to me that this approach to the self-understandings of contemporary intimacy provides useful grounds for a reconstruction of private freedoms that have galvanized contemporary feminism.

A word now on what the paper is not trying to do. A feminist debate about how best to position itself with respect to private/public boundaries has been going on for a long time and the many-forked road has been well chartered by others (Landes, 1998, 2003; Rössler, 2005, pp. 34–42). It's not my intention to attempt to retrace the progress of the debate but rather to excavate some of its underlying issues. This will involve marshalling material from some quarters that don't normally feature much in the way that the debate has run.

3.1. Normative continuities

Carole Pateman's *The Sexual Contract* (1988) offered a telling feminist critique of the idea of a pre-political realm of freedom upon which a liberal construction of a private/public split rested. On this diagnosis, a liberal public sphere drew free and equal men together to defend their paternal power in a private realm that was organized around the subordination of women in marriage. Pateman's radical critique of the sexist practices that propped up the "natural freedoms" protected by a public of men attacked the oppressive gender ideologies that seemed to be inherent within liberal private/public divisions. As Wendy Brown observes, though, "liberalism has become one with modernity rather than a position within it" (Brown, 1995, p. 138; see Glass, this volume, Chapter 4). Nowadays, feminism typically recognizes its indebtedness to the principle of individuality that is built into liberalism's private/public divide and so too accepts that it needs to find new ways of describing our private freedoms. Rössler usefully describes the challenge as a matter of a symbolic "re-filling" of the contents of private freedom once the ideological load carried by liberalism's naturalizing constructions have been exposed (2005, p. 33).

Susan Moller Okin's *Justice, Gender and the Family* (1989) occupied a key place in a feminist attempt to reconstruct our understanding of private freedoms in the wake of its critique of liberalism's faith in their givenness. She insisted that this would require something more than an attempt to "read back" into the private sphere norms that had been forged outside it to guide interactions between autonomous actors in a democratic public. Okin's understanding of what was involved was partly shaped in response to a critique of repressive gender assumptions that seemed to cling to

John Rawls' account of justice. The prejudicial assumptions of Rawls' understanding of justice as the self-regulation of interactions between autonomous subjects who were assumed to have the responsibilities of "heads of households" meant that it could not provide a normative floor for the private sphere. Despite promising beginnings, Rawls' theory as a whole does not, Okin complains, "depart from the liberal tradition's failure to perceive the family as a political institution, to which principles of justice should apply" (Okin, 1991, p. 47). Taking a step back from this search for normative continuities, Okin finds that Michael Walzer's reflections on liberal democratic societies divided into distinct "spheres of justice" had a lot to offer to a feminism keen to reflect upon the special normativities of the private sphere. Walzer's open-ended distributive principle according to which "*[n]o social good x should be distributed to men and women who possess some other good y merely because they possess y and without regard to the meaning of x*" (Walzer, 1983, p. 20, original emphasis), seemed attractive. In the end, though, the "separate spheres" framework only offered a general heuristic that would still need to be filled out with a feminist reflection on the "meaning of x." The particular "goods" that had to be negotiated in a normatively reconstructed private life would have to be filled out. Here Okin encountered difficulties. In the end, expectations invested in public justice still provide the normative framework for Okin's deliberations on the significance of private life. Rawls' persuasion that private interactions acquire their general significance by providing the moral training ground for citizens reappears.

By the early 1990s, Giddens' explorations into the transformations taking place in contemporary intimacies seemed to push the discussion forward in an important way. He described the intentions of *The Transformation of Intimacy* as follows,

> I don't attempt to analyze how far gender inequalities persist in the economic and political domains. I concentrate instead upon an emotional order where women—ordinary women, going about their day-to-day lives, as well as self-consciously feminist groups—have pioneered changes of great, and generalizable, importance.
>
> (Giddens, 1992, p. 2)

Giddens undertakes to reflect upon normative bridges that are being built between the private and the public spheres. On this narrative, intimate life has been transforming itself toward the realization of its own highest potentials as it edges toward a confirmation of commitments outlined in an egalitarian, democratic public sphere. Contemporary intimacy "implies a wholesale democratizing of the interpersonal domain in a manner fully compatible with democracy in the public sphere" (Giddens, 1992, p. 3).

The intimate sphere, Hannah Arendt tells us, emerged out of a struggle to determine the value of a private life whose functionalized significance had been eroded as activities of the domestic sphere were subsumed under the exchange imperatives of the rise of the social (Arendt, 1958). She wasn't so much interested though in exploring how a new private domain made use of expectations invested in intimate life to rebuild its own significance. When Giddens takes the theme up, he begins with an account of the important place of romantic love in shaping the value of the intimate sphere. Propelled by a passionate, unwilled attraction for the other, it seems that a modern individualized romantic love helped to open up a cultural space through which expectations of a new intimacy could appear. A heightened individualizing sensibility gripped this new way of loving and Giddens makes the point that romantic love "for the first time associated love with freedom" (1992, p. 40). Its promise of an "at first sight" compulsive, once and for evermore dedication to the beloved contests the grip of conventional and instrumentalizing bonds and places love at the service of a nascent, self-realizing personality (Giddens, 1992, p. 40). Romantic love presumes that "a durable emotional tie can be established with the other on the basis of qualities intrinsic to that tie itself" (Giddens, 1992, p. 2). The reflexivity of a self-preoccupied romantic love gives it a central role in the emergence of what Giddens has called the "pure relationship" that subordinates itself to no external purposes.

Not just there from the start, romantic love has also pushed the pure relationship along its evolutionary path toward the realization of its own concept. The narrative dynamism and idealization of individuality borne by romantic love establishes the grounds of what Giddens describes as a contemporary "confluent love" (1992, pp. 61–4). He makes the point that this evolutionary development first had to clear away certain aspects of a romantic legacy in order to permit the essentially democratic imperatives of a mature intimacy to flourish. In particular, a self-referring "projective identification" that wrapped the lover up in their own feelings and so blinded them to the concrete particularity of the beloved had to be unseated. "Opening oneself out to the other, the condition of ... confluent love is," Giddens remarks, "in some ways the opposite of projective identification, even if such identification sometimes sets up a pathway to it" (1992, p. 61). This is a self-transformation that encounters losses as well as gains. Confluent love jars with the "forever" and "one and only" promises of romance and insists on the negotiated mutuality of its interactions. "[T]he more the finding of the 'special person' recedes ... the more it is the 'special relationship' that counts" (Giddens, 1992, p. 62). However, Giddens is certain that a self-transforming intimacy that is moving toward the clear and generalizable norms of mutuality and reciprocity between equal partners is on an emancipatory track that reproduces the expectations of civic freedom. The norms of a confluent love articulate the "overwhelming concern with how individuals might best determine and regulate the conditions of their association" that is "characteristic of virtually all interpretations of democracy" (Giddens, 1992, p. 185).

It might seem that Giddens completes a story that Okin began to tell and even resolves its major difficulties. However, problems reappear in this attempt to reconstruct normative continuities between a self-transforming intimacy and the value commitments of a democratic public. For one, Giddens suggests an overly normative account of processes reshaping intimate life. "Projective identification" is, as empirical studies by Eva Illouz and others confirm, no superseded episode in the narrative of intimacy. It continues to make its claims upon "ordinary" and "self consciously feminist" women alike (Illouz, 1997). Indeed, it has been plausibly argued that the romantic construction of love as a "mere feeling," constantly re-energized by a consumer culture, has actually wound back the sober intelligence of a confluent love (Evans, 2003). It seems that our reflections on the cultural significance of intimate life need to make room both for the pull of unaccountable, romantic passion and for the push of expectations of mutuality and reciprocity between equals.

Giddens' account of the transformation of intimacy is not just too normative. From another point of view, it is not normative enough. On his account, a self-transforming intimacy tracks a path confirmed by values shaped outside it. There is no room here for an account of intimate life as a crucible for needs that contest conventions encrusted onto democratic norms affirmed by a liberal public. Rather, the democratic give and take of a confluent love is presented as the normative terminus for an evolving intimate sphere and promises to stabilize the unruly, inchoate passions that set it in motion. Suspicions that this teleological history of progress toward a well-managed intimacy hides some important losses seem confirmed when Giddens recommends "therapeutic works and self-help manuals" as a guide to "accurate accounts of the changes affecting personal life" (1992, p. 64). At odds with his announced intention to reflect on the process of contemporary intimacy toward its own highest cultural potentials, Giddens' evolutionary narrative ends up confirming a framework that is principally invested in the reduction of existential complexity (see Johnson, this volume, Chapter 3).

3.2. Normative discontinuities

The point was made earlier that contemporary feminism has been challenged by the consequences of its own critique of a liberal private/public divide. Claiming for itself the commitment to individuality upheld by liberal bifurcations, feminism nevertheless needs to release itself from the gender ideologies that cling to liberalisms' faith in a ready-made private freedom. Those undertakings to "refill" the contents of private freedoms using the commitments shaped in the public sphere seem destined to authorize only those ways of valuing private life that confirm a pre-set agenda. It seems, then, that we need to revisit descriptions of supposedly ready-made private freedoms and engage with a discriminating evaluation of their worth.

This brings us to consider those feminisms that have sought to rehabilitate *as values* certain frameworks and scales of significance that liberalism has passed off as "natural" feminine dispositions. Beth Elshtain and Sara Ruddick have been at the center of this kind of undertaking (Elshtain, 1981 and 1982). Elshtain is particularly interesting because she consistently evokes the produced character of values silenced by naturalizing ideologies that can now be discussed, evaluated and chosen in a discriminating fashion. Elshtain sees herself as working a conceptual space between several unattractive responses to a troubled liberal divide. She rejects a feminism that seeks to fully politicize the private world and equally repudiates the "privatization" of the public realm "with politics falling under its standards, ideals and purposes" (Elshtain 1981, p. 4). Elshtain is keen also to distance herself from a "rigid bifurcation" between the two spheres "with the private realm conceived instrumentally, treated as a necessary basis for public life but a less worthy form of human activity" (1981, p. 4). Against these options, Elshtain is interested in "retaining but recasting public and private boundaries as part of an effort to preserve each yet reach toward an ideal of social reconstruction" (1981, p. 4).

This is partly a recasting of the defensive character of a liberal public sphere which seeks to confine certain needs and capacities "sexuality, natality, the human body (images of uncleanness and taboo, visions of dependency, helplessness, vulnerability)" to a supposedly naturalized private sphere (Elshtain, 1981, p. 15). However, whereas Nell Noddings

(1984), for instance, is determined to reassert a supposed feminine culture against the muteness to which it has been consigned by a liberal public sphere, Elshtain is convinced that, once the dispositions of modern private life are released from naturalizing ideologies and recognized as cultural achievements, we face the task and the opportunity of assessing their valuable aspects to "reach towards an ideal of social reconstruction." This commitment to a creative appropriation needs to grasp the fundaments of the private sphere as "the realm of particularity." As the "theater of particularity and everyday concrete meaning" this "little world" exudes its own values and imperatives (Elshtain, 1981, p. 305). The "militant's single-mindedness" that draws out only that which makes modern private life "exploitative and unjust" turns its back on the effort that is required to choose what to bring forward from the "taken for granted" to attain recognition as valued human achievements and resources. This kind of "reflective feminism" offers itself as a re-evaluation, not repudiation, of contemporary family life. For, once we affirm, not just as natural attributes but as valuable humanizing achievements, the loving concern for the lives of particular others that is upheld by family ideologies, these idealizations can pose themselves as critical needs that are constantly blocked and distorted by exploitative and unjust contexts. Elshtain makes the point that,

> [t]o attain and affirm an ideal of family life as the locus of humanization is, contrary to certain unreflective radical orthodoxies, to put pressure upon social structures and arrangements, not to affirm them. For to the extent that the public world, with its political, economic, bureaucratic force, invades and erodes the private sphere, it, not the private world should be the target of the social rebel and feminist critic.
>
> (1981, p. 335)

Elshtain is persuaded that the "theater of particularity" must strive to hold its own. Taking up a theme that we already encountered in Walzer, she is convinced that "particular experiences and spheres of social relations exude their own values and purposes and have ends not attainable by or within other spheres" (Elshtain, 1981, p. 334). However, she also gives the point a critical edge and insists that these are not just given attributes demanding protection from domination but the acquired aspirations of particular ways of interacting that require certain kinds of contexts to flourish. Elshtain suggests that ideals and purposes nurtured in personal life can critically interrogate assumptions buried in those descriptions of what counts as freedom that are supplied by a liberal public sphere. We are familiar with the pressure that has been put on liberal accounts of the autonomous citizen by subjects who cannot experience their needs for freedom in the mold supplied by the idea of the self-mastering individual.

A proposal for a reconstruction of the values of private life that seeks to work with the integrity of the "realm of the particular" appeals to Honneth too (2004 and 2007). His contribution promises to take the discussion forward by addressing a significant difficulty in the undertaking that has not been sufficiently registered by Elshtain. Critics make the point that Elshtain needs to address the problem of how a self-critical orientation can emerge from a private domain whose "own values and purposes" are affirmed and whose separate ends "not attainable by or within, other spheres" remain the only frame of analysis (Rössler, 2005, p. 26). Honneth takes the issue up. He insists that we must learn how best to negotiate *between* the untransferable normativities that bind the modern private and public spheres (Honneth, 2004).

Like Giddens, Honneth is keen to reconstruct the values that a modern private sphere, struggling to affirm its importance in the wake of the historical detachment of domestic life from the realm of production, gave to an idealized intimacy. Honneth even finds Giddens' concept of the "pure relationship" useful to describe the normative orientation of new private bonds that are dependent upon feelings alone (Honneth, 2004, p. 148). However, Giddens and Honneth describe the fundamental trends and imperatives of the contemporary intimate sphere very differently. Giddens, we have seen, reflects upon a robust trajectory in contemporary intimate life bent on realizing its own democratic concept. More than a decade on, Honneth does not dispute the claim that transformations within the intimate sphere have seen a pluralization of forms freed from the singular shape of a nuclear family. However, to him, the self-transformations of the intimate sphere remains a story of an embattled domain that can only call upon the resources of love and care in its efforts to respond to the deep social problems that have been dumped upon it. Sorely tested, family life is showing signs of "inner, emotional disintegration" (Honneth, 2004, p.146). Honneth is not much interested in investigating how the intimate sphere might try to make itself equal to its challenges. He reflects, rather, on the way in which these forces threaten the special values and purposes that have shaped the self-understandings of modern intimacy. He agrees, it seems, with Elshtain that we owe it to ourselves and to the future to ensure that we do not permit, "through our silence, things to pass as in a dream" (Elshtain, 1981, p. 353).

Focused on the question of how to best grasp the cultural importance of contemporary intimacy, Honneth sets up a debate between two major paradigms. He is persuaded that Hegel's critique of a Kantian contractual model of marriage has useful insights. In part, the problem for us with Kant's advocacy of the contractual underpinnings of modern marriage is the datedness of its investment in "the central Christian notion that marriage represents a social arrangement within which human beings can satisfy their sexual desires without losing their moral dignity" (Honneth, 2004, p. 150). Thinking for a more secular age, Rawls reintroduces Kant's moral reasoning and argues that the explicit moral regulation of private life sets the necessary grounds of a self-regulating individuality (Honneth, 2007, p. 172). Hegel is concerned, rather, with the particular character of Kant's Christian inspirations and what this affirmation of the contractual grounds of modern marriage supposedly leaves out from an appreciation of its distinctive ethical weight. He puts before us the Old Testament view that "marriage is a completely novel institution insofar as the mutual love of both partners leads to a fusion that ultimately makes a higher-level unity out of two people" (Honneth 2004, p. 150). Honneth, too, is attracted to an "affective model" that finds that "the source of all moral attitudes in the family is not rational insights into rights and duties, but solely the feelings of devotion and love" (2004, p. 153). However, he insists that *both* of these paradigms are needed to make sense of the normativities relevant to modern intimate life. An appeal to the rights of autonomous actors cannot alone guide conduct in the "realm of particularity" where individuals are constantly called upon to restrict their pursuit of their own interests and life plans to attend to the needs of loved ones. By the same token, the conviction that "the source of all moral attitudes in the family is not rational insights into rights and duties, but solely the feelings of devotion and love" has been exposed as a legitimating ideology for all manner of abuses. Honneth is persuaded, then, that the regimes of affection and justice will always constitute a disputed moral field in which contrasting forms of recognition continually collide (2004, p. 154). He is clear, though, that there can be no in principle lines drawn and no charter of trumping claims drawn up. Each intimate unit will have to constantly negotiate "where to set limits to the applicability of universal principles of justice" (2004, p. 160). When love fails as the grounds for communication of needs and family members feel their personal integrity threatened, "rights have to provide a space to which he or she can withdraw for his or her own protection" (2004, p. 155).

The "exit strategy" proposed here is similar to a line of thinking already started by Rawls. It is a proposal for a kind of normative double vision. As a member of a family and as the participant in a web of intimacies, it is expected that individuals will not act as the bearers of formal rights and limit their engagements to contractual specifications. Only if he or she takes the point of view of the citizen can the family member discover the expectations of justice against which patterns of his or her intimate interactions can appear as abuse. As Honneth sees it, individuals "have to be able to lay claims to the principles of universal justice whenever they see themselves as no longer being recognized with the dignity of a legal person in the family community" (2004, p. 155).

There are, as I see it, two major things wrong with this analysis; firstly a descriptive problem. Honneth overlooks the relevance of expectations of dignity and justice to our assessments of the value of our intimacies *as* intimacies. Herlinde Pauer-Struder rightly makes the point that "[i]t would be a strange conception of love that explicitly demands excluding considerations of justice from it. The personal integrity of a person is at stake if she loves someone who treats her in ways that seem deeply unjust" (2004, p. 166). Honneth seems to have taken the criticism on board to an extent and has more lately suggested that recognition of the other as a moral agent can be extrapolated from an ethics of care. Commenting on "the intersubjective relationships of love" he affirms that "here actions are undertaken for the sake of another person whom we have to regard as being morally worthy" (Honneth, 2007, p. 178). It's not clear, though, that this line of thought removes the problem. To be sure, a caring love does not like to feel itself wasted and will normally find some way of approving of the beloved. However, the point is not just that judgment can be accommodated into the little worlds set up by affection and love, rather that the little world has to shoulder different types of normative loads. Rössler finds it hard to see "why needs *and* autonomy, love *and* respect should not always be equally involved in moral issues within family relations" (2005, p. 161). A second, related, criticism is that, by not registering intimate life as a site rent by conflicting descriptions of its value, Honneth has trouble reconstructing contemporary intimacies as the ground upon which critical motivations and needs can appear. To be sure, Honneth recognizes contemporary intimate life as a site where conflicting imperatives are negotiated. However, as he portrays it, these tensions only produce a schizophrenic personality who is split between the egalitarian respect that he or she expects as a rights-bearing citizen and his/her feeling engagements in the "theater of particularity." This account of contemporary intimacy doesn't offer much to a feminism that is interested in reflecting on intimate life as a site able to produce aspirations that could offer a critical interrogation of conventional contexts. The critical interest set by Elshtain's exploration into the distinctive motivations at play in the intimate domain seems to be missing from Honneth's account.

Critical orientations are also compromised in Giddens' reconstruction of the democratic trajectory of a self-transforming intimacy. Giddens, as already noted, offers to reflect upon the agency of "women—ordinary women, going about their day-to-day lives, as well as self-consciously feminist groups" in pioneering changes of "great, and generalizable, importance in contemporary intimate life" (Giddens, 1992, p. 2). However, it seems that we can only recognize these changes as emancipatory gains because they confirm the normativity of interactions upheld by a democratic public. Thus resolved into a normative frame set by the public sphere, there can be no register here of new needs shaped within the intimate sphere. Yet the "theater of particularity" has, as Elshtain insists, not only generated needs for democratic interactions but also produced a range of preoccupations whose claims have been silenced by naturalizing ideologies. Needs for authentic self-expression and the like may well find themselves alienated by the terms in which a democratic public has described generalizable interests. A critical engagement does need to offer itself as a *departure* from expectations of an egalitarian reciprocity between points of view that is set up by a public commitment to building rational consensus. However, we might expect a different account of what *counts* as reasonable interactions only if we recognize the private domain as its own special cauldron of needs and aspirations; including longings for an authenticity that can't be contained within the envelope of expectations set by the ideal of the autonomous, rationally self-mastered self.

Emerging from the attempt to recover significance for modern private life once its functions in productive life had been replaced, the intimate sphere has always chased after descriptions of its value. This heightened and contested self-consciousness means that reflections on how we value contemporary intimacy should help feminism in its efforts to reclaim private freedoms from the sexism of liberal descriptions. Two main approaches have been considered and both seem to offer one-sided accounts of the range of investments we make in contemporary intimacy and neither seems able to cater well for the critical motivations that are essential to feminism. In the next part of the discussion I suggest that the limitations of both approaches can be traced to shortcomings of a long-standing preoccupation with resolving the significance of intimate life under the patronage of a particular value commitment.

3.3. A field of tensions

Intimate life has never been able to rest within a supposition of ready-made meanings and significance. From the beginning, its value has been up for grabs and subject to a lively contest. This struggle can be traced back to a heated dispute started in the eighteenth century between the claims of love and friendship as the two rival templates. Niklas Luhmann tells us that at this time love and friendship began to compete with each other "for the right to shape the code of intimate relationships" (1986, p. 81). On his account, love, not friendship "won the race" in part at least because the former was able to draw upon the "symbiotic mechanism of sexuality" to differentiate itself and this "was not at the disposal of friendship" (1986, p. 82). Taking up the theme of the quest for normative resolution, Theodore Zeldin comments on the impact of nineteenth-century Romanticism. He observes that the "long debate in the eighteenth century as to whether friendship or passionate love held together more firmly" was settled by "the acceptance of the idea that sex was the best guarantor of harmony" (Zeldin, 1994, p. 325).

However, this was only to be a temporary resolution. Today, friendship has strong advocates to be the paradigm through which contemporary intimacies can best make sense of their value. Allan Silver is, for example, convinced that friendship is the "prototype" for contemporary intimacies (Silver, 1996, p. 46). Ray Pahl (2000) interprets our investments in the intimate sphere through a grid supplied by the norms of friendship and Giddens, too, borrows distinctive expectations set by friendships to describe the give and take reciprocity of the "confluent love" that is for him the normative terminus of a self-transforming intimacy. But friendship can't be confident that it has "won the race" in any decisive sense either and love too has its champions. Ulrich Beck and Elizabeth Beck-Gernsheim are persuaded that love has been carried forward as a "secular religion" (1995). They mean that love's promise of a dogmatic little world of feeling advances an interpretation of intimacy that offers to lift the embattled self beyond the chronic uncertainties of the risk society. Honneth is on the side of love also and supposes that a fragile intimate life only has this "emotional state" (2007, p. 167) to hold it together.

The contest between love and friendship to be the normative vessel for contemporary intimacies wouldn't matter a lot if not much could be made of their differences. Indeed, significant contrasts are not easy to spot. Both, for instance, celebrate choice and exclusivity. Like friends, lovers know only freely chosen affections that cannot be mandated. At the same time, Eros does not have a monopoly on passion. Friendships can mean everything to us and can even accommodate sexuality. For all that, Emmanuel Levinas seems to be right when he insists that love does not represent a particular case of friendship and that friendship is not a species of love (1969, p. 265). What, then, is the refractory aspect? Hannah Arendt offers a clue when she observes that friendship does not feel itself "extinguished the moment it is displayed in public" whereas love seems to be violated under the "bright light of the constant presence of others" (1958, p. 51). While friendship and love are both exclusive, private affairs, friendship is worldly, it must be "about something." C.S Lewis puts the difference this way: while lovers "are normally face to face, absorbed in each other," friends go "side by side, absorbed in some common interest" (1960, p. 79). Friendship, then, is a relationship that "must be reciprocated to make sense" (Vernon, 2005, p. 34). Reciprocity and mutuality are its guiding lights. Love, though, knows all about unrequited feeling.

Friendship and love are different but we seem to be captured by an imperative to use one or the other as contemporary intimacy's normative template. We saw that this imperative informs Giddens' narrative of the transformations of intimacy and manifests itself also in Honneth's reflections of the unaccountable feelings that bind the realm of particularity. However, this will-to-rationalize appears to mainly speak to the theorist's interest in securing the importance of intimate life against a potentially deflating inchoateness. Along the way it incurs some costs though, in the first instance against an appreciation of the complexity of the values we give to contemporary intimacies. It seems a good idea, then, to look for a framework that is more able to cope with a mix of values.

It might seem odd to turn first to Hannah Arendt for some suggestions here. After all, her disdain for modern private life, interpreted along Aristotelian terms as a function of natural needs, is well known. Yet alongside this commentary Arendt also refers to the private domain in modern terms as a sphere of intimacy and she is fascinated by its normative complexity and its rich ambiguities. Today, Arendt tells us, we call private life "a sphere of intimacy ... whose manifoldness and variety were certainly unknown to any period prior to the modern age" (1958, p. 38; see Markus, this volume, Chapter 6). She is intrigued also by its double characteristics of innovative cultural potential and frail ineffectiveness. Elaborating itself on ground cleared by modern processes that rolled back the functional place of the domestic sphere, the intimate domain could become the site of a new individuality bent on exploring its subjective potentials. This absence of any rationalizing purposes proved a source of "enormous enrichment" to intimate life and permitted its distinctive experimental ambiguity. Remarking on "how rich and manifold the realm of the hidden can be under the conditions of intimacy," Arendt (1958, p. 72) is struck also by its cultural dispossession. Unlike the private household, intimacy "has no objective tangible place in the world" (Arendt, 1958, p. 39). In the end, Arendt is persuaded that contemporary intimacy cannot provide the grounds through which new ways of thinking and acting can appear and her hopes for a robust individuality go with political action enacted in the public sphere. So, Arendt's hostility to the modern public/private divide takes over. She is not going to be able to help us unpack further the normative complexities of contemporary intimacy.

However, Arendt's appreciation of the rich ambiguities and experimental fluidities of private life under conditions of intimacy sets us looking for a way out of familiar normative molds. We have seen that Honneth has already claimed Hegel to head one paradigm in the contest over the value of intimacy. Hegel, he points out, is drawn to the significance of the involuntary ties of affection that bind the intimate marriage against Kant's account of its contractual underpinnings. However, this reading seems to overlook the significance of observations that Hegel also makes about the normative tensions that have to be negotiated within the affection ties of the intimate marriage.[1] We might be able to use this as the ground for a third paradigm that Honneth fails to contemplate.

Hegel was seemingly intrigued by the expanded meanings that bourgeois marriage had acquired within early nineteenth-century German society (Hegel, 1991). With Arendt and others, he notes that narrowly functional determinations of the value of marriage; securing inheritances, forming commercial alliances and subduing rivalries, were making way for its importance as the site of a new mode of interaction, the sphere of intimacy. Hegel draws particular attention to the ethical significance of the newly voluntary character of the union. Bourgeois marriage is a relationship based on the free choice of two individuals who consent to give up their "natural and individual personalities" and to "constitute a single person." Hegel upholds the enlightened proclamations of the Civil Code of 1804 that stipulated that differences in social strata are irrelevant to the choice of spouse and that the free will and consent of two adults is the only material point of view (Benhabib, 1996, p. 34). As he saw it, the Code provided the political framework for the ethical character of modern marriage. Only if marriage is formed as a voluntary union can it promise to be the grounds of a newly self-conscious subjectivity. The self-awareness that is grounded in and fostered by the chosen character of the marriage anchors the "subjective moment" of the free individual that is, for Hegel, the chief strength of the modern state (Benhabib, 1996, p. 32). So, the ethical union of the bourgeois marriage does not simply draw upon an already constituted subjectivity but promotes its self-recognition and it does so in the most self-contradictory fashion.

Hegel, as we already learnt from Honneth, makes the point against Kant that "marriage is not a contractual relationship as far as its essential basis is concerned" for the "precise nature of marriage is to begin from the point of view of contract—i.e. that of the individual personality as self-sufficient unit in order to supersede it" (Hegel, 1991, p. 203). Hegel goes on to draw up significances that are elided in Honneth's account. The ethical love that is the basis of the modern marriage is, Hegel suggests, "the most immense contradiction" (1991, p. 199). Plato told us that we become what we love and Hegel too observes that in love "... I find myself in another person ... I gain recognition in this person ... who in turn gains recognition in me" (1991, p. 199). However, love cannot be rationalized around its ethical, self-choosing aspect. Love cannot be rationalized at all; it is "a feeling." The puzzle which understanding "cannot resolve" is that love claims to be both the grounds of an ethically self-fashioned subjectivity but it is ethical life in "its natural form." The passionate, unwilled character of love is not simply a corruption of the essentially ethical character of the union but is its condition also. We cannot direct ourselves to love nor can it be arranged for us. Hegel, as we have seen, eschews the crudity of the attempt "still to be found in Kant," to interpret marriage merely as a civil contract (1991, p. 201). However, Hegel is no Romantic and he repudiates also the reduction of love to its "transient, capricious and purely subjective aspects" (1991, p. 201). While the passionate, unchosen nature of love is at once the condition of its unique significance as ethical life in its natural form, this reference to "feeling" can also be the grounds for the destruction of the ethical character of love. Hegel is alert to the dangers of the Romantic reduction of love to passion untempered by the commitments to the self-choosing ethical dimensions of a loving intimacy. He chides Schlegel for advocating a point of view "not unfamiliar to the seducer" when he upholds the freedom and intensity of a love that simply asserts itself as a need (Hegel, 1991, p. 164). So, for Hegel, the natural, unforced ethics of the intimate marriage at once *refers itself* to an impulsive, untutored feeling and is, at the same time, *placed under threat* from the caprice of love. Hegel's own nervous response to this normative instability is to seek to secure marriage within an account of wider social purposes. "Since marriage contains the moment of feeling, it is not absolute but unstable, and it has within it the possibility of dissolution" (Hegel, 1991, p. 203). Accordingly, Hegel invokes the role of marriage in the socialization of children in an attempt to secure the value of bourgeois marriage against the unnerving instability of ties that refer themselves only to an ethics of intimacy.

Hegel was finally unnerved by the prospect of an ethical intimacy seated within and called upon to constantly negotiate a raft of tensions. If the intimate union was to survive, it needed to draw upon its various ethical dimensions and use each as the measure of the excesses of the other. This looked too precarious and Hegel, we saw, turned to the stability of the legal contract. However, we don't have to be so cautious. It might be that an ethics of intimacy, which rests upon the elaboration of distinct normative poles that form the grounds for a mutual and ongoing assessment of each other, can help to push through the stalled "either/or" constructions that we have encountered so far.

We can start to see some advantages if we compare Hegel's account of the complex mix of values that inform the intimate marriage with Honneth's one-dimensional view of an ethics of intimacy. Honneth, we have noted, suggests that respect and justice have no organic presence within an intimate sphere that is bound only by untutored feelings. Only by adopting the point of view of the public actor can we import grounds for weighing up the ethical character of intimate interactions. However, this perspective seems out of step with the dynamic self-reflexiveness of contemporary intimacies. Dissatisfactions with intimacies *as* intimacies appear to speak to a complex set of investments. So, the broken heart is not persuaded that it must rail only at its own folly when love's promise of eternity is snatched away. The loss can also be experienced as a betrayal of reasonable expectations of reciprocity and mutuality knitted into the intimate union by the many threads of contemporary intimacies. The mix can also be complementary and sometimes we experience a blend of values as an emancipatory gain and as a boost for a developing individuality. Kristjansson (2006) offers a one-dimensional account of the modern parent/child relationship identified as a "true" friendship. He is surely right to some extent and expectations of reciprocity and a degree of voluntariness do today construct patterns of expectations between parents and children. However, other values have crucial parts to play as well and an agapic love, full of tender sympathies and care, is tributary also into the flows of parental love. A mix of anxious sympathy and egalitarian respect sometimes leads to emotional trauma but can also have potent ethical effect. How else can we account for ennobling instances when parents are drawn out of their comfort zones to support the unanticipated sexual choices of a loved child? At times it can all be just confusing. Stephanie Coontz reminds us of the degree of ethical uncertainly in the contemporary intimate marriage, full of negative, but devoid of positive, heuristics. Today, she writes, "[m]arried couples no longer have a clear set of rules about which partner should do what in their marriage. But they do have clear set of rules about what each partner should *not* do" (Coontz, 2005, p. 309).

3.4. Conclusion

It might be best to think about the intimate sphere as a site for the multi-directional migration between distinct values that we give to our close personal bonds. The point has been made that this construction of intimacy as a carrier for normative complexity has some descriptive advantages over various undertakings to resolve its meaning. This construction also allows us to reflect upon a dynamic intersection of values at play that can unleash critical and emancipatory tendencies within the intimate sphere. Forced to negotiate an endless pull and push between distinct, sometimes competing, descriptions of its value, intimate life enables ongoing gains in our understanding of what we want from personal life. This happens because one value description can offer itself as the ground upon which we weigh up the impacts of another. This self-conscious weighing up of what matters to us by way of a fulfilling personal life can fuel a critical interrogation of imposed, gender ideologies and inhibiting social contexts.

Octavio Paz calls upon us to heed the "intimate connection between love and freedom" (1996, p. 99). We saw, too, that Giddens pointed out that romantic love made vital contributions to a nascent feminism as it stirred up longings to break though repressive conventions. Yet, Hegel prefigured a sometimes strident feminist critique when he warned that romantic passion could also be used to vindicate the wanton selfishness of the seducer. We don't need to adopt the stance of the rights bearing subject to grasp that sometimes love can turn from plunging us into new vital experiences of subjective depth into crushing our sense of self. We don't always reach for an "exit strategy" but, drawing on the egalitarian and reciprocal norms that are also entwined into contemporary intimacy, try for some judicious reform. Love, too, can have something to say to a grudging give and take reciprocity that might insinuate itself into an unbalanced intimacy.

There are no reliable scripts it seems. However, while this might be a worry for the therapist (see Johnson, this volume, Chapter 8), feminism has constituted itself through its reflection upon the lived impacts of various cultural tensions. Democratic Enlightenment hopes that equal individuals could constitute their autonomous self-rule rationally through interactions of mutual accountability found their way into the private domain. Modern feminism was partly an expression of the critical force of these norms (Johnson, 1994, pp. 25–47). But Elshtain and others need to be heard too. Feminism, it seems, was also galvanized by a Romantic affirmation of untrammeled, feeling subjectivity (Johnson, 1994, pp. 47–68). Certainly it seems that a divided feminism has often too readily offered its allegiance on an "either/or" basis. However, there is, as I see it, more to be gained if a self-conscious feminism situates itself as a reflection on the dynamic processes at work within a living intimate domain in which distinct value ideas are sometimes encouraged by and sometimes checked against each other.

Notes

Heartfelt thanks to John Grumley who read many versions and offered invaluable advice on both my papers included in this collection.

1. Honneth comments that while to him it is clear "how many possibilities or moral lapse and injury are inherent in the experience of love as such," Hegel "saw no basic difficulties here" (Honneth, 2007, 177).

References

Arendt, H. (1958), *The Human Condition* (Chicago: University of Chicago Press).

Beck, U. and E. Beck-Gernsheim (1995), *The Normal Chaos of Love* (Cambridge: Polity).

Benhabib, S. (1996), "On Hegel Women and Irony," in P. J. Mills (ed.), *Feminist Interpretations of G.W.F Hegel* (Pennsylvania: Pennsylvania Press), 25–44.

Brown, W. (1995), *States of Injury: Power and Freedom in Late Modernity* (Princeton: Princeton University Press).

Coontz, S. (2005), *Marriage, a History: From Obedience to Intimacy or How Love Conquered Marriage* (New York: Penguin).

Elshtain, J. B. (1981), *Public Man, Private Woman: Women in Social and Political Thought* (Oxford: Martin Robertson).

Elshtain, J. B. (1982), *The Family in Political Thought* (Sussex: The Harvester Press)

Evans, M. (2003), *Love: An Unromantic Discussion* (Cambridge: Polity).
Firestone, S. (1970), *The Dialectic of Sex* (New York: Morrow).
Foucault, M. (2008), *The Birth of Biopolitics; Lectures at the College de France 1978–79* (Hampshire and New York: Palgrave Macmillan).
Giddens, A. (1992), *The Transformation of Intimacy: Sexuality, Love and Eroticism in Modern Societies* (Stanford: Stanford University Press).
Hegel, G. W. F. (1991), *Elements of a Philosophy of Right* (Cambridge and New York: Cambridge University Press).
Honneth, A. (2004), "Between Justice and Affection: The Family as a Field of Moral Disputes," in B. Rössler (ed.), *Privacies: Philosophical Evaluations* (Stanford: Stanford University Press), 142–63.
Honneth, A. (2007), "Love and Morality: On the Moral Content of Emotional Ties," in *Disrespect: The Normative Foundations of Critical Theory* (Cambridge: Polity), 163–80.
Illouz, E. (1997), *Consuming the Romantic Utopia: Love and the Cultural Contradictions of Capitalism* (Berkley: University of California Press).
Johnson, P. (1994), *Feminism as Radical Humanism* (San Francisco: Westview).
Kristjansson, K. (2006), "Parents and Children as Friends," *Journal of Social Philosophy,* vol. 37, no. 2, 250–65.
Landes, J. (1998), *Feminism, the Public and the Private* (New York: Oxford University Press).
Landes, J. (2003), "Further Thoughts on the Public Private Distinction," *Journal of Women's History*, vol. 15, no. 2, 28–39.
Lewis, C. S. (1960), *The Four Loves* (London: Geoffrey Bles).
Levinas, E. (1969), *Totality and Infinity* (Pittsburgh: Duquesne University Press).
Luhmann, N. (1986), *Love as Passion: The Codification of Intimacy* (Cambridge: Polity Press).
Noddings, N. (1984), *Caring: A Feminine Approach to Ethics and Moral Education* (Berkley: University of California Press).
Okin, S. Moller (1989), *Justice Gender and the Family* (Stanford: Stanford University Press).
Okin, S. Moller (1991), "Humanist Liberalism," in N. L. Rosenblum (ed.), *Liberalism and the Moral Life* (Cambridge: Harvard University Press), 39–53.
Pahl, R. (2000), *On Friendship* (Cambridge: Polity).
Pateman, C. (1988), *The Sexual Contract* (Stanford: Stanford University Press).
Pauer-Struder, H. (2004), "Justice as Pre-condition of Affection and Care. A Comment on Axel Honneth," in B. Rössler (ed.), *Privacies: Philosophical Evaluations* (Stanford: Stanford University Press), 142–63.
Paz, O. (1996), *The Double Flame: Essays on Love and Eroticism* (London: Harvill Press).
Rössler, B. (2005), *The Value of Privacy* (Cambridge: Polity Press).
Silver, A. (1996), "'Two Different Sorts of Commerce' or Friendship and Strangership in Civil Society," in J. Weintraub and K. Kumar (eds), *Public and Private Thought and Practice: Perspectives on the Grand Dichotomy* (Chicago: Chicago University Press), 43–74.
Vernon, M. (2005), *The Philosophy of Friendship* (New York: Palgrave Macmillan).
Walzer, M. (1983), *Spheres of Justice: A Defense of Pluralism and Equality* (New York: Basic Books).
Zeldin, T. (1994), *An Intimate History of Humanity* (New York: Harper and Collins).

4
Privacy and Law

Arthur Glass

Not much will be gained from discussing privacy and its legal regulation in the abstract. Perhaps the need for privacy is an aspect of human nature (Moore, 1984, p. 59ff.) but the form this need takes and the way that law may be used to protect this interest are neither given by nature nor likely to be interestingly the same throughout history. When considering our understandings of privacy and its appropriate regulation we are of course contemplating the world made by us, the social rather than the natural world.

However, by calling our views about privacy social I do not mean to say that they are mere convention, or inherently local to each society or jurisdiction. Our ideas about privacy and its appropriate protection come to us as part of a larger inherited tradition of ideas and practices; a normative context which will both constitute the way we see privacy issues and channel our thinking about the significance of the privacy interests at stake, as well as how these interests might be protected. From the perspective of western law the larger context of understanding I have in mind is, of course, the ideas and social practices associated with the tradition of liberalism.[1]

This liberal conception of privacy is most immediately connected to ideas concerning the nature of the liberal subject and the character of the legal and social institutions created by and inhabited by such a subject. My first task is to describe briefly what is meant by the liberal subject and to note some of these liberal institutions (section 1). In section 2, I delimit within this larger context the subset of ideas and problems that are usually raised in present-day discussions of privacy and law. I then ask what basic values are at stake in these discussions—autonomy, respect for personhood or some other values (section 3). In section 4, I discuss what role law should play in protecting privacy for it is not possible or appropriate for law to regulate all privacy interests. The legal techniques for protecting privacy range from constitutional guarantees of a right to privacy, to statutory schemes, civil actions, and exhortations via privacy principles.

4.1. The liberal self and liberal institutions

The liberal subject as a modern subject demands "the right of the subject's particularity," as it is famously put; a right that is "the pivot and centre of the difference between antiquity and modern times" (Hegel, 1971, p. 84).[2] In more modern formulations this right of subjective freedom is posed as the right of individuals to be self-directed in response to the "practical questions" of life: what sort of person do I want to be? How do I want to live my life? The central idea is that of being one's own person; to work out for oneself and choose one's own good; and in this to be directed by desires and considerations that are part of one's authentic self and not imposed from outside (Christman and Anderson, 2005, p. 3).[3] "The only freedom which deserves the name, is that of pursuing our own good in our own way, so long as we do not attempt to deprive others of theirs, or impede their efforts to obtain it" (Mill, 1989, p. 16).[4] Persons are autonomous if they are able to identify with the desires and objectives that govern their actions. The possibility of personal autonomy assumes the ability to take a self-reflective attitude to oneself and the possibility of living a life of one's choosing. I will return to this idea of personal autonomy below in the discussion of the value of privacy.

As for the institutions and practices inhabited by the liberal subject, let me briefly remind you of the following. You would expect a liberal state to have constitutional structures (separation of powers, checks and balances) that constrain state power and guarantee negative rights in the form of civil liberties (freedom of thought and speech, freedom of association). There should be a legal system that is sufficiently clear, effective and impersonal to secure our independence from and dependence upon others; a legal system that provides an equality of rights and freedoms in that all liberal subjects have an equal claim to these liberal protections.

A distinction will be made between public life, on the one hand, which is the legitimate realm for state action and private life, on the other. State action should be neutral in the sense that it does not favor one view of the good over another. There should be a wall of separation, for example, between church and state. No doubt liberalism does not live up to this claim of neutrality and the boundary between public and private remains publicly contestable. However, the point of the boundary remains (wherever it falls and whoever it benefits at any particular point of time) namely, to safeguard a private arena for individuals to live out their life plans free of state regulation or social interference.

Liberal institutions should enable persons to realize their personal autonomy; but it is not their purpose to make us realize this goal. Liberalism is opposed to paternalism whether in the form of community norms or legislative will. People are the best judges of what is good for them. No external agency should interfere with one's actions with the aim of promoting one's good (Geuss, 2001, p. 92).[5]

4.2. The legal right to privacy

In the organization of its rules, liberal law makes use of the categories of public law (constitutional law, administrative law, criminal law, regulatory law) and private law, the law dealing with private transactions (contract, property, tort, commercial law). That the basic goal behind these laws is individual freedom is reflected in the different default rules operating in the two areas. In the public realm of state activity everything not authorized is forbidden. In the private realm of individual activity, everything not forbidden is permitted. Many laws from either grouping can be connected with our interest in privacy. Laws that keep the peace, stabilize property relations, enforce contracts and so on, have a bearing on our ability to lead private lives. From this perspective many types of legal interests can be called privacy interests (Allen, 2004, p. 26).

However, when we speak of the right to privacy or of privacy law we usually have in mind the following types of problems. Privacy is an important interest said to be at stake in the effort to control personal information, or access to one's home, or freedom from surveillance, or from searches and seizures; as well as protection of reputation and protection of the ability to make personal decisions. It is not always clear what holds together all these uses of privacy in varied legal and social contexts. But the basic idea would appear to be that there should be a legally protected zone "within which physical or cognitive access to me should not be allowed to others not of my choosing" (Geuss, 2001, p. 88). There are some matters, private matters, which are not a legitimate concern of others.

It is not uncommon to separate out different dimensions of privacy. Beate Rössler (2005), for instance, usefully distinguishes between local (or physical) privacy (basically, no wrongful intrusions into the home, or bodily interference), information privacy (no improper dissemination of personal information or illicit surveillance) and decisional privacy (no interference with key personal decisions).[6] These categories are not self-contained; for example, intrusions into the home may result in illicit surveillance, or decisional privacy may be connected to bedroom activities. Nonetheless for purposes of exposition, distinguishing between these three categories makes sense and I exemplify the three categories of privacy with some better known privacy protecting laws.[7] Here we can see immediately which understandings of privacy interest law and moving in the other direction how law's understandings have informed more general ideas about privacy.

Local: Laws that protect the sanctity of the home and bodily integrity by placing limits upon intrusions into domestic or other places (such as workplaces) and protecting the privacy of the body outside of the home by way of laws against assault or unreasonable searches and seizures. Specific laws for specific problems, such as forbidding employers to require workers to disclose information (about mental illness) or submit to tests (HIV testing or genetic testing). Possibly, the availability of a civil action for the wrongful intrusion upon the seclusion of another.

Informational: Laws that protect the privacy of communications (mail, telephones, email), or protect confidentiality, perhaps arising out of particular relationships, (doctor, patient, lawyer, client, and so on). Statutory schemes protecting the collection of personal data (credit information, medical and government records) directed in particular at the problems that this information (collected by the government or the private sector) may be secretly compiled, inaccurate or transferred without consent. Perhaps tort remedies available for the unreasonable public disclosure of private matters (the privacy torts), or more commonly protecting against falsehoods that injure reputation (defamation).

Decisional: The United States Supreme Court has drawn a constitutional right to privacy out of the penumbras and emanations of the traditional guarantees of the Bill of Rights. This right protects against laws that intrude upon decision-making about such matters as contraception, reproduction, marriage, child rearing, health information, sexual practices and intimate personal relationships (Allen, 2004, p. 21).

To give an Australian example, it was by way of the right to privacy set out in Article 17 of the International Covenant on Civil and Political Rights 1966 that a ruling was given by the UN Human Rights Committee that Tasmanian law was found not properly to protect the sexual privacy of homosexuals.[8]

The ways to date in which law has dealt with privacy have come under increasing pressure from at least four distinct sources. First, and most obviously, from technological developments which have changed the nature and range of privacy threats, as have developments in government and business practices. It is now much easier to invade a person's privacy and there is more reason to do so. I have in mind such matters as video surveillance (in shops or CCTV), webcams, nanny cams, radio frequency identification devices (RFIDs), data generated by mobile phones or internet use (the monitoring of browser behavior), the increased accessibility of public records (networked data bases), data matching and data mining, biometric testing, the collection of genetic information, the commercial exploitation of personal information (credit reporting, direct marketing).[9]

Second, liberal law has responded to contestation of the public/private divide as a result of political struggles over women's rights, and to a lesser extent gay rights. These struggles have shifted cultural understandings with regard to family life. The reasons why we protect family life are extended to all kinds of intimate relationships. We are more concerned now than in the past that the private realm may be a place of injustice and that state action may be called for to prevent abuse or exploitation of women or children. And women want their private life protected as they seek employment and take part in public life.[10]

Third, we want more from the state in matters that can potentially affect privacy. We want the state, via law, to "manage" the problems of security, health, crime prevention, welfare fraud, unlawful immigration and so on. The risk to privacy is that the instrumental needs of the state may override our communal understandings of privacy.

Finally, courts and lawmakers have been troubled by the entertainment industry and the intrusive activities through which it feeds its (and our) apparently insatiable appetite for personal information (Lacey, 2004, p. 47). Here the right to conceal comes up against the right to publish and an expansive understanding of public interest in this context will give primacy to free speech over privacy.

4.3. Why do we value privacy?

By calling an interest private we are saying that it is of sufficient importance for the individual and its effect on others of sufficiently little importance for us to reasonably think that there should be no interference or regulation; or possibly, in other contexts, that there should be interference and regulation in order to protect it (Dewey, cited in Geuss,

2001, p. 107). In explaining this importance the need for privacy has been linked to such aspects of human flourishing as the health of family life or the enhancement of intimate relationships (Rachels, 1975).

A more convincing case can be made for personal autonomy as the basic value at stake in privacy claims (Rössler, 2005; see also Kupfer, 1987; Cooke 1999; Roberts 2001). The ideas associated with privacy, it is argued, provide a structure within which a self-determining life is possible and in this way the privacy rules help to protect the possibility of individual autonomy. The value of privacy is that it furthers personal autonomy; it is not the same as autonomy (Rössler, 2005, pp. 71–6; Roberts, 2001, p. 65ff.).[11] If we are to ask effectively the practical questions, of whom we are and what sort of life we want to live, we need a cognitive and emotional space in which we control the access others have to us. We need a private realm in which we can reflect upon our desires and self-descriptions and decide which are authentic or appropriate for us. The privacy rules provide a normative structure in which the more personal aspects of our lives are free from the knowledge and control of others; a space within which experiments in living are shielded from the threat of undue scrutiny and judgment.[12]

From this standpoint, we can revisit the three types of privacy discussed above. Decisional privacy protects our choices about certain intimate matters from the intrusive interference and influence of others. These are our decisions and no one else's. With these types of decisions it is of no significance "whether the reasons decisive for me could also be accepted by everyone else" (Cohen, 2004, p. 55). Informational and local privacy, on the other hand, have a vital but less direct connection with individual autonomy. Informational privacy protects our control over what others can know of us. For control over our self-presentation to others (whether people of our choosing or the world at large) is an intrinsic aspect of enjoying a self-determined life. We cannot interact with others in an authentic way unless we can rely on our reasonable expectations of what they know of us (Rössler, 2005, pp. 116, 129, 140). Local privacy, for its part, protects the possibility and the space for withdrawal and for undisturbed behavior free from the view of others. It protects our inner life from a "public exposure that would cause it to wither, or would require too much distortion" (Nagel, 1988, p. 10).

Linking privacy to the basic value of individual autonomy in this way is for Daniel Solove unhelpful, as the problem is often one of reconciling the right to privacy with another right that can also be grounded in or linked to autonomy (freedom of expression, say, or state security understood as a prerequisite for autonomy) (Solove, 2008, p. 85f.). He gives the example of *Bonome v Kaysen* to illustrate the point that personal information often belongs to more than one person. Here a woman published her autobiography telling of her struggles with severe vaginal pain. She discusses in detail her sexual relationship with her former boyfriend as well as other personal aspects of their life together. For Solove, considerations of autonomy are indecisive as they appear on both sides of the ledger—as her right to discuss her own life and as the boyfriend's right to conceal this information from the world.

However, the point of grounding our need for privacy in autonomy is to give it the appropriate weight in these sorts of contests, which in informational privacy will often be a dispute between freedom of expression and the freedom to conceal. That these rights are ultimately justified as aspects of or prerequisites for the same value, individual autonomy, does not prevent us from reflecting on the relevant concerns and making judgments in concrete cases.

In an interesting discussion Robert Post distinguishes between two different concepts of privacy; privacy connected to dignity and privacy connected to autonomy (Post, 1989, 2001). Privacy as autonomy, as we have seen above, refers to the protective structure needed if we are to have the space to create our own identity. Privacy as dignity refers to how we see ourselves as deserving of respect from others. Here privacy is not based on our right to fashion ourselves against the prevailing social norms. Rather, privacy as dignity assumes that we inhabit a common way of life rich in the obligations of respect that we owe to each other. We see ourselves and others as worthy of respect (Taylor, 1989, p. 15). Specific norms of civility give content to this general obligation and police the boundaries of decent behavior in different contexts. Here the privacy rules can be seen as protecting a notion of personhood that we regard as vital for social life. And the nature of these obligations of respect depend upon the character of the social occasion; compare, for example, the obligations of respect of pupils to teachers, say, with those of surgeons to their anaesthetized patients.[13]

Privacy norms of respect may vary between countries that otherwise share a high regard for the value of personal autonomy. This is nicely brought out by James Whitman who contrasts the different cultural expectations with regard to privacy between Germany and France, on the one hand, and the United States on the other (Whitman, 2004). Whitman sees the Europeans as more oriented to privacy challenges to dignity and to each person's right to informational self-determination. The main enemy here is the media and the market, while in America the focus of anxiety is on state interference with private decision-making. But too much should not be made of these differences for in other contexts (data processing for the purposes of anti-terrorism, for instance) European law protects the liberty of its subjects from state interference better than American law (Bignami, 2007).

The distinction between privacy as autonomy and privacy as dignity is not the distinction between a personal understanding and a social understanding of privacy. Our sense of autonomy and the high value we place on it is as much constituted by the prevailing social norms as our sense of respect. It is because we are autonomous beings that we command equal respect from others. And when we exercise our autonomy we are not able to fashion ourselves independently of the social scripts made available to us (Appiah, 2005, p. 21ff.). Self-fashioning is always shaped by the social material to hand. However, the distinction between privacy as autonomy and privacy as respect brings out how we may consider the privacy norms breached in contexts where no actual harm can be demonstrated to the autonomy of those involved. For example, in the interests of respecting human dignity in ourselves and others we may consider it wrong for someone to freely give up their right to privacy (peep show cases[14]) or think it appropriate to protect the dignity of others who lack autonomy (children, mentally ill patients). According to the prevailing communal norms, there are just some things that should not be done to people, even if they consent or are in no position to know of the hurt.[15]

To make these points more straightforwardly, we can accept that protecting personal autonomy is the most plausible value at stake here while granting that in any concrete discussion of privacy it may not be the only value. In the appropriate context there may well be other concerns—respect for human dignity, interest in limiting the power of officials, preventing the possible illegitimate uses of this knowledge (by the state or others), for example. With all of these matters we are concerned with the need to protect significant aspects of our personhood and with evaluating the gravity of actions that depart from communal norms. Whatever the normative material before us, we do well to remember that "general principles do not determine solutions to moral problems of this kind. They indicate what needs to be justified, where the onus of proof lies and what can count as a justification" (Benn, 1971, p. 13).

4.4. The role of law in protecting privacy

There may be aspects of privacy that we consider valuable (you should not, without consent, read your partner's diary, say) but think that law should play no role in protecting this interest. But if we think that the matter is amenable to legal regulation, the problem is how to translate our understandings of privacy into workable law. For law can be ineffective;[16] alternatively, it can overreach itself and have unintended consequences—"chill" autonomous activity, interfere with legitimate government action, favor and thus privilege one understanding of decent behavior over another.

What we should take into any consideration of law are two points. First, while privacy problems may involve a number of values and concerns its link with personal autonomy is central. We risk undervaluing the privacy interests at stake if we do not appreciate this connection. It is often suggested in privacy analysis, that the problem is not so much recognizing the privacy interest but "its lack of purchase" (Alldridge and Brants, 2001, p. 20). Restrictions on the right to privacy are better evaluated in a context which gives sufficient weight to what is being lost.

The second point is that we need to consider in detail the specific context in which the privacy problem arises. Why exactly do we want to describe this interest as private, what in this context are our purposes and values? For if law is to be effective we need to have a clear eye for the social norms that law will make concrete and to the kind of harm or misuse of information we are attempting to prevent. How likely is it that a particular interference with privacy will actually affect, rather than possibly affect, everyday life (see Rössler, 2004, p. 126f.)? How should we characterize the defendant's actions? There will be differences between communities (and between individuals) as to the degree to which they worry about the potential risks to privacy, from the state or from commercial exploitation; and in the degree to which they find offensive the making public of personal information.

Privacy law is an attempt to craft appropriate restrictions on state powers, impose workable duties on states and others when they obtain private information and make available private remedies for citizens whose privacy has been seriously affected. The qualifiers "appropriate," "workable," "seriously" make it clear that whatever the facts of the matter, at some point judgments have to be made as to the nature and worth of the privacy interest involved and the weight to be given to rival values and interests. These judgments will be made by legal officials in interestingly different contexts.

For example, where there is a constitutional right to privacy the settling of its scope will be done by review courts, potentially against the workings of every day politics. Do we want this? In particular, do we want judges deciding, as in the United States, just which forms of intimacy should be protected by way of the privacy standards? On the other hand, where the community is seriously divided on these issues, that judges are not directly accountable to the electorate may be a very good reason to have them decide these basic questions.

In pursuing the social goals of security, crime prevention, health, minimizing social security fraud or immigration fraud, and the like, the state may adopt measures (electronic surveillance or other surreptitious intrusions) that interfere with local or informational privacy. The legal framework for considering this type of problem will be some form of "proportionality analysis."[17] An analysis that calls for an evaluation of the worth of the end, the nature of the means (are they well crafted or possibly over or under inclusive) and a bringing together of means and ends with the question, is this particular interference with privacy proportionate to the legislative goal? For example, that there should be mandatory reporting of possible child abuse by teachers is seen as proportionate, while medical checks on virginity as a measure against migration fraud is not.

Where there is dissemination of personal information by other persons (often the media), the question is, should law lend its weight to protecting this kind of privacy by providing a private remedy? Any remedy will focus attention upon the degree of transgression from communal norms (would a reasonable person consider this a serious invasion of privacy?) in a context where there may be legitimate public interest in publicizing this type of information. Interference with one's home or one's person (that is, interference with local privacy) will usually constitute a serious transgression.[18] But, outside of this, what is the acceptable use or abuse of personal information about a person? Here law will be interested in such questions as, how was the information obtained? Is the plaintiff a public figure? Is the information already in the public domain? And was it essential to disclose the plaintiff's identity (see Wacks, 2006)?

A modern state needs personal information about its citizens to properly administer national security, tax, welfare, immigration, and so on. And we have an interest in being properly administered. From the point of view of the government agency, it is always better to know more about us rather than less. The problems here are not physical intrusion or the revelation of private secrets but that the data may be misused and so lead to discrimination or the dissemination of false or partial information. The legal response in this area has been privacy codes setting out the operative "privacy principles," based in convention or statute. These codes provide due process safeguards, requiring consent to data collection, rights of review and redress and attempt to limit the data to the lawful purposes of the system (see Rule, 2007, p. 26f.). Sanctions are provided by establishing an office whose role it is to promote and defend these privacy rights. A recurring problem will be the degree to which these schemes exempt the data collection and use by police, tax officers and security agencies. How can individuals check this information (data mining, for example) without undermining any investigation? What should happen to these records after the completion of any investigation?

Information is needed from us if we are to have efficient consumer or commercial transactions. In this area the lawfulness of data collection will turn on whether we have consented to its collection and use. But how realistic is this? If we want to receive credit, open a bank account, take out insurance and so on, how can we not consent? On the other hand, what should we make of the fact that for reasons of convenience we are willing to relinquish our privacy like this on a regular basis (see Rössler, 2004)?

4.5. Conclusion

The liberal tradition values a private realm free from encroachment by government, administrative agencies, commercial intrusions and the pressure of public opinion. Our ideas about privacy are best understood as furnishing a normative structure that assists us to exercise a capacity for personal autonomy. The legal "right to privacy" addresses particular encroachments upon this structure.

I have discussed the legal regulation of privacy by pointing to the variety of questions and judgments that will be made by legal officials in different contexts. But these questions cannot be answered solely on the basis of legal technique. They summon up questions of social morality that should not be left to the lawyers, or other experts. Citizens need to play a role in approving the laws that govern them and ultimately this is the source of justification for particular laws that protect forms of intimacy, restrict state action that threatens privacy or penalize particular abuses of personal information. Legitimating these measures calls for an exercise of self-government in the political rather than personal sense.

Liberal democracy needs autonomous citizens to decide questions of privacy, as well as many other matters. However, if our privacy is threatened, so too is our personal autonomy and then we are not well-placed to properly participate as members of the political community. In other words, there is an important link not just between notions of privacy and personal autonomy but between privacy and political autonomy.[19]

Notes

1. Liberalism has its opponents and it comes in different forms. But especially when put in general terms, as I do here, it remains the prevailing way we think about politics and law. "Much as we might regret it, we are in fact living in a time and place in which we really do not have any effective general framework for thinking about politics apart from liberalism" (Geuss, 2001, 114).
2. Though, of course, for Hegel this right can only be fulfilled within a particular social and institutional context.
3. Personal autonomy is to be distinguished from Kantian autonomy—the capacity of the moral subject to give oneself the moral law and to be guided by these objective moral principles. The questions of what we should do, how we should live are not answered out of moral criteria and indeed may oppose these criteria. Further, while it is put in individualist terms, all that is required of liberal subjects is that they are sufficiently self-reflective to distinguish their view of the good from reasons that should apply to everyone else. In other words, persons who have accepted the religious or traditional way of life they were raised in can still be said to exercise personal autonomy.
4. "The ruling idea behind the ideal of personal autonomy is that people should make their own lives" (Raz, 1986, 369).
5. "Paternalism is despotic ... because it is an insult to my conception of myself as a human being determined to make my own life in accordance with my own (not necessarily rational or benevolent) purposes" (Berlin, 1969, 157).
6. Solove (2008) uses different terminology but makes similar distinctions.
7. Here, as elsewhere, I limit myself to the common law world and Western Europe.
8. *Toonen v Australia* 1994. The European Convention of Human Rights 1950 provides that everyone has the right of respect for their private and family life, their home and their correspondence (Art. 8).
9. Privacy is also threatened by a different kind of commercial pressure—subliminal advertising, spam emails and cold calling (phone marketing).
10. Feminists and others point to the ideological nature of the public/private distinction and how it can work against the interests of women and others. But, for the most part, these criticisms do not question that privacy (properly understood), and personal autonomy are valuable for all persons.
11. The need to maintain this distinction between a precondition for the ideal and the ideal itself is the basis of the criticism by Rössler and others that *Roe v Wade* (the abortion case) was not about protecting relationships via the privacy rules (and thus not a case about privacy) but it was directly about a woman's right to self-determination.
12. Here we see the advantages of this approach over accounts of privacy which offer a definition of privacy in terms of limited access (for example, Gavison, 1980). As a neutral definition, limited access does not explain why we value privacy, and privacy understood as limited access can only extend to decisional privacy metaphorically.

13. As Post (2001, 2093) makes clear, where the goals of the social structure are different, so too are the norms of respect.
14. A ruling of the German Administrative Court, upheld by the Constitutional Court, banned erotic dancing within a slot machine booth as a denial of the dancer's dignity (discussed in Klein, 2002, p. 158).
15. In the tort of unreasonable intrusion upon the seclusion of another the plaintiff does not have to show actual harm and in the tort of unreasonable publicity given to another's private life the issue is serious breach of communal standards, not harm to the plaintiff. For elaboration of these points see Post (1989).
16. It could be said that while we have more regulation of privacy, more privacy codes, we have less privacy. But the same could be said of road safety, where we have more regulation but more accidents. The answer is not to repeal the laws.
17. The law itself may add an additional structure. For example, Article 8 of the *European Convention on Human Rights* sets out the types of reasons that would be justification for interfering with the right to privacy. These are only laws necessary for national security, public safety, the economic well-being of the country, the prevention of crime, the protection of health or morals, and the protection of the rights of others.
18. The privacy tort of unreasonable intrusion into seclusion of another is less likely to be restricted, as with the other privacy torts dealing with informational privacy, by notions of legitimate concern to the public.
19. This connection is the theme of papers by John Christman, Richard Dagger, Rainer Forst, Bert van den Brink, Gerald F. Gaus and Jeremy Waldron in Christman and Anderson (2005).

References

Alldridge, P. and C. Brants (eds) (2001), *Personal Autonomy, the Private Sphere and the Criminal Law* (Oxford: Hart Publishing).

Allen, A. (2004), "Privacy in American Law," in B. Rössler (ed.), *Privacies: Philosophical Evaluations* (Stanford: Stanford University Press), 19–39.

Appiah, K. (2005), *The Ethics of Identity* (Princeton: Princeton University Press).

Benn, S. (1971), "Privacy, Freedom and Respect for Persons," *Nomos*, vol. XIII, 1–26.

Berlin, I. (1969), *Four Essays on Liberty* (Oxford: Oxford University Press).

Bignami, F. (2007), "European Versus American Liberty: A Comparative Privacy Analysis Of Antiterrorism Data Mining," *Boston College Law Review*, vol. 48, 609–98.

Christman, J. and J. Anderson (eds) (2005), *Autonomy and the Challenges to Liberalism* (Cambridge: Cambridge University Press).

Cohen, J. L. (2004), *Regulating Intimacy: A New Legal Paradigm* (Princeton: Princeton University Press).

Cooke, M. (1999), "A Space of One's Own: Autonomy, Privacy, Liberty," *Philosophy & Social Criticism*, vol. 25, no. 1, 23–53.

Gavison R. (1980), "Privacy and the Limits of the Law," *Yale Law Journal*, vol. 89, 421–71.

Geuss R. (2001), *Public Goods, Private Goods* (Princeton: Princeton University Press).

Hegel, G. W. F (1971), *The Philosophy of Right* (Oxford: Oxford University Press).
Klein, E. (2002), "Human Dignity in German Law," in D. Kretzmer and E. Klein (eds), *The Concept of Human Dignity in Human Rights Discourse* (The Hague: Kluwer Law International), 145–60.
Kupfer, J. (1987), "Privacy, Autonomy, and Self-Concept," *American Philosophical Quarterly*, vol. 24, no. 1, 81–9.
Lacey, N. (2004), "Interpreting Doctrines of Privacy," in B. Rössler (ed.), *Privacies: Philosophical Evaluations* (Stanford: Stanford University Press), 40–51.
Mill, J. S. (1989), *On Liberty*, S. Collini (ed.) (Cambridge: Cambridge University Press).
Moore, B. (1984), *Privacy: Studies in Social and Cultural History* (New York: Pantheon Books).
Nagel, T. (1988), "Concealment and Exposure," *Philosophy and Public Affairs*, vol. 27, no. 1, 3–30.
Post, R. (1989), "The Social Foundations of Privacy," *California Law Review*, vol. 77, 957–1010.
Post, R. (2001), "Three Concepts of Privacy," *Georgetown Law Journal*, vol. 89, 2087–98.
Rachels, J. (1975), "Why Privacy Is Important," *Philosophy and Public Affairs*, vol. 4, 323–33.
Raz, J. (1986), *Morality of Freedom* (Oxford: Oxford University Press).
Roberts, P. (2001), "Privacy, Autonomy and Criminal Justice Rights: Philosophical Preliminaries," in P. Alldridge and C. Brants (eds), *Personal Autonomy, the Private Sphere and the Criminal Law: A Comparative Study* (Oxford: Hart Publishing), 49–78.
Rössler, B. (ed.) (2004), *Privacies: Philosophical Evaluations* (Stanford: Stanford University Press).
Rössler, B. (2005), *The Value of Privacy* (Cambridge: Polity Press).
Rule, J. (2007), *Privacy in Peril* (New York: Oxford University Press).
Solove, D. J. (2008), *Understanding Privacy* (Cambridge Mass: Harvard University Press).
Taylor, C. (1989), *Sources of the Self* (Cambridge: Cambridge University Press).
Wacks, R. (2006), "Why No English Common Law Privacy Tort," in A. Kenyon and M. Richardson (eds), *New Dimensions in Privacy Law* (Cambridge: Cambridge University Press), 154–183.
Whitman, J. Q. (2004), "The Two Western Cultures of Privacy: Dignity Versus Liberty," *Yale Law Journal*, vol. 113, 1151–221.

5
Social Networking, Privacy, and the Pursuit of Visibility

Harry Blatterer

The emergence of information technology as a means of mass communication in affluent societies during the 1990s immediately gave rise to optimistic as well as skeptical voices. Those who saw in the Internet a potential for the advancement of democracy from the ground up (Castells, 1997) were opposed by others who feared the extension of government surveillance into ever deeper niches of everyday life (Lyon, 1998). Those who marveled at the social and political possibilities for decentered and/or disembodied identities (Plant, 1993; Poster, 1995; Chandler, 1998) were reminded by others of less salutary possibilities such as increased loneliness (Kraut et al., 1998) and the possible eventual redundancy of human labor (Castells, 1998). Amid these discourses privacy took center stage. While growing Internet use around the globe has served to subdue both the overly optimistic and the unduly skeptical, the issue of privacy continues to exercise the public imagination. At issue is a simple fact: usage of the technology leaves traces of personal information that can be used by other parties for their gain, and potentially to the detriment of the person to whom that information pertains, but which that person no longer owns. Sociological arguments as to why people would be willing to part with personal information, even though the potentially harmful consequences are largely known, invariably center on the need for self-presentation in highly individualized societies; in societies, that is, where traditional identity markers have lost their once determining force (Schroer, 2006). Taking as its starting point individualism rather than individualization, a more negative explanation links the mass development of public self-disclosure to the cultural normalization of a narcissistic personality type (Derber, 2000). In what follows I suggest that the public disclosure of private information is not only embedded in a culture that supports the pursuit of attention for its own sake or in an insatiable need for self-referentiality, but that the need for and pursuit of visibility is an *a priori* motivation whose expression is enabled—rather than caused—by available technologies. That pursuit of visibility, so I argue, is in tension with the need for privacy. And that tension is particularly evident on social networking sites such as *Facebook* and *MySpace* because these sites can only exist as long as people are willing to freely share personal information; as long, that is, as they are willing to give up some of their privacy in order to maximize their publicity, their visibility. I address this tradeoff in section 1. In section 2, I sketch the connection between human visibility in the sense of our biological and cognitive capacities and our social "second nature" with reference to several writers. Hans Blumenberg's phenomenological anthropology shows our visibility to be of momentous consequence for our humanness. Visibility is equally fundamental to our social constitution in Axel Honneth's conception where it underpins the intersubjective granting or withholding of social recognition. A discussion of Honneth's ideas is followed by comments on some of Hannah Arendt and John Thompson's thoughts on visibility and political power. Finally, in section 3, I reiterate and reflect on my hypothesis that there is a significant tension between the need for privacy and the need for visibility as well as on that tension's potential consequences for our collective autonomy.

5.1. The privacy/publicity tradeoff

Central to my discussion is what Beate Rössler (2005) calls "informational privacy," one of three dimensions of privacy she identifies in her analysis: "I speak of *informational* privacy when people claim the right to protection against unwanted access in the sense of interference in personal data about themselves, in other words access to information about them that they have no desire to see in the wrong hands" (Rössler, 2005, p. 9, original emphasis).[1] Like all forms of privacy, informational privacy too is worth protecting because there is a "functional correlation between privacy and freedom," that is, between privacy and the kind of autonomy that allows someone to "ask herself the question what sort of person she wants to be, how she wants to live, and if she can then live in this way" (2005, p. 17). This freedom to self-determination depends on subjective capacities as much as on given social conditions including—crucially—a separate and protected private realm. The separation of the private and the public spheres "expresses the notion—fundamental to liberalism—of the protection of individual freedom and the autonomy of persons in the face of inadmissible interference or regulations on the part of the state" (2005, p. 10).[2] From this perspective, behaviors and practices that jeopardize informational privacy also jeopardize the kind of autonomy that constitutes a cornerstone of liberal democracy. Emerging trends in online interaction are well worth interrogating if only to fathom the potential consequences for changes in public conceptions of autonomy, changes that are to a significant extent contingent on and manifest in everyday practices.

The emergence of so-called social networking sites in the mid-1990s, but particularly with the rapid growth of sites such as *MySpace* and *Facebook*[3] (launched in 2003 and 2004 respectively), heralded a decisive leap in the distribution and availability of personal data, leading researchers to speak of an "unprecedented phenomenon of information revelation" (Acquisti and Gross, 2006, p. 37). Now concerns about privacy, which at first centered on new possibilities for governments to undertake surveillance of the population, began to include voluntary disclosing behavior on the part of users. Indeed, it is this voluntarism—the preparedness to willingly publicize personal information—that appears most puzzling. So, we might ask: why do members of social networking sites voluntarily part with personal data even though that information is potentially retrievable by others who can use that information out of context and against their best interests? This is an interesting question also because it is common knowledge today that employers are increasingly vetting prospective employees' social networking pages, that the owners of these sites trade personal information with other businesses (see Solove, 2007a), and that therefore Sun Microsystems CEO Scott McNealy's words, "You have zero privacy. Get over it" (Sprenger, 1999), were more prophetic than many at the time would have wished to believe. It thus appears that individuals are not only leaving traces of personal data inadvertently, but also that they willingly forgo some of their claims to privacy even with full knowledge of the possible consequences. Voicing her concerns about both the inadvertent and deliberate compromising of informational privacy, Rössler (2005, p. 120) warns of the possibility that this "may result in certain forms and dimensions of self-determined and authentic behavior not only becoming substantially less practicable, but also being conceived less relevant, less crucial, less intrinsic to a rewarding life." Importantly, such changes are apt to affect more than individual conceptions of privacy; they may also affect "the idea of liberal democracy itself, which is dependent upon autonomous subjects who are aware of and who value their autonomy" (2005, p. 120). Online interaction on social networking sites raises such potentials especially clearly, because here the *deliberate* disclosure of personal data is a necessary component of networking interaction. To illustrate I will now turn to some research findings concerning the privacy-publicity nexus.

5.1.1 Privacy and social networking

Attitudes to privacy in online interaction are differentiated along generational lines:

> There is a generational divide that is as strong today as the divide that existed between kids and their parents over music in the 1950s. ... People older than 25 years think of everything they do on their computer as being private unless they share it, where people younger than that think of everything they do on a computer as public unless they choose to make it private. This is a fundamental difference.
>
> (Veen cited in Galvin, 2008, p. 23)

Research into usage of social networking sites by young people suggests a range of meanings attributed to privacy in the online context. Corresponding both to Rössler's "local" and "informational" privacy's dimensions, Livingstone (2008) shows that for teenagers the online realm represents a space of their own in which they can interact away from the adult gaze. Under those perceived conditions of privacy, teenagers may divulge information that previous generations may have regarded private to hundreds of often barely known others (Livingstone, 2008, p. 404). Likewise, Govani and Pashley (2006) found that 80 per cent of users in their study did not read *Facebook's* privacy policy. Forty per cent of users were aware of *Facebook's* policy concerning sharing data with third parties. And while people may have known about available privacy settings less than half made use of them. Importantly, this barely changed after the researchers alerted students to the possible dangers and pitfalls. Another more recent college-based study corroborates these findings and shows that the majority of students opt not to take advantage of the privacy settings that *Facebook* offers, and instead are content to use the publicity maximizing default settings (Kolek and Saunders, 2008).

Privacy compromising behaviors are to a significant degree structured by the technology. One example is social networking sites' very broad definition of user categories. Thus, while individuals' notion of "friends" may be highly differentiated, sites such as *MySpace* and *Facebook* operate with the simple binary friends/all users. According to Livingstone (2008, p. 405), this "fails to capture the varieties of privacy that teenagers wish to sustain." Here, Livingstone refers to teenagers' need for control over access to information, so that a user may be "public to his friends, but private to his parents" (2008, p. 405). In a similar vein, asked to reflect on the public nature of his *Facebook* profile, a respondent in another study had this to say: 'Well, it is sort of public ... but it is not the general public—it is like your public, the people that you hang around with' (West et al., 2009, p. 624). These kinds of findings lead to the conclusion that among young people "notions of what is private and what is public are fuzzy and there is no clear-cut public/private dichotomy" (West et al., 2009, p. 625).

There is then reasonable cause to believe that attitudes to privacy are changing, and that this is particularly the case among a cohort of young users for whom online communication is the norm. Whether this construal of the public/private divide indicates a "level of sophistication ... with nuanced understandings of concepts ['public' and 'private']" on the part of young people (West et al., 2009, pp. 624, 625) is arguable. For the lack of control over personal information at bottom equals an insufficient level of informational privacy.[4] I suggest that this does *not* constitute a blurring of the public/private divide. Rather, this "fuzzy" notion indicates a redrawing of the boundary between the two realms. That redrawing, which is a consequence of everyday interactions via the technology, cedes a greater portion of the private terrain to those who want to collect information about persons for commercial and other purposes and so diminishes the terrain of privacy available to those who provide information.[5] *Prima facie*, this is a paradoxical situation because all active members of social networking sites are simultaneously collectors and providers of personal information. But this ought not to distract from the reality that private users potentially as well as actually transfer information to businesses, prospective employers and government agencies. Giving users the benefit of the doubt, and thus assuming there exists reasonable awareness of social networking sites' ownership of personal information, and following evidence that this knowledge barely increases circumspection regarding online behavior (Govani and Pashley, 2006), we can conclude that there is a willingness to trade a significant part of informational privacy for publicity. With the rise of social networking sites this tradeoff has become a mass phenomenon. After all, the sites exist by virtue of this tradeoff and despite any "privacy dilemmas" single individuals may face (Lahlou, 2008; see also Barnes, 2006).

None of this addresses the question why people mostly err on the side of disclosure; why they accord relatively greater value to disclosure than to informational privacy. Starting from the premises that individuals do not "naturally" engage in the kind of disclosing practices at issue here (Burkart, 2006b, p.17), and that technology alone cannot determine social action (Smith and Marx, 1994), I want to now go on to offer one among a range of possible explanations and so turn to the topic of visibility.

5.2. Online disclosure and the pursuit of visibility

When considering online disclosure of personal information, the sociological literature offers several connected strands of analysis of which I will mention only some. Although Erving Goffman (1959) mostly analyzed face-to-face encounters, his insights have received renewed attention in research of online interaction. Because in this area the difference between "the real" and "the virtual" is of continued interest, Goffman's elaboration of "impression management" finds particularly strong resonance (Miller, 1995; Whitty, 2008). With a focus on macrosocial processes, disclosing practices can be traced as part of an overall trend of individualization whereby ever more aspects of life and self are made subject to individual decision making and responsibility. The demise of traditional ways of life and the pluralization of often competing normative understandings of a successful life, in addition to the increasingly mediated nature of interaction, render the project of the self "a reflexively organized endeavour" (Giddens, 1991, p. 5). All manner of presentation of self in the public domain—from TV chat shows and confessionals to online blogs, the styling of personal homepages and profiles on social networking sites, and so on—can be fruitfully contextualized in the modern problem of self-identity that emerges as individualization processes gather speed (Burkart 2006a; also this volume, Chapter 2). From this perspective, public disclosing practices have been envisaged as a "struggle for attention" that is motivated not so much by the question "who do I want to be?" but is driven by self-presentation as an end in itself (Schroer, 2006).[6]

These acts of self-presentation, then, presuppose a particular orientation to self, an orientation that has overcome norms of modesty prevalent in earlier phases of western history. To that end, the emergence since the end of the nineteenth century of what Eva Illouz (2008) has called "the therapeutic persuasion" has lent cultural legitimacy to an expressive objectification of the self. A successful life is a project built around the self as an analyzable and remediable entity. Failure to partake in the therapeutic discourse may attract the suspicion of a lack of self-care and/or "emotional intelligence" and thus of a predisposition to psychological and relational dysfunctionality (see also Ehrenberg, 2004).[7] In a sense, the cultural ground has long been prepared for public displays of "the *private psychological* self," something that is especially prevalent in online contexts (Illouz, 2007, p. 78, original emphasis). Critiques of disclosing trends that tend to be critical of the therapeutic cultural drift frequently reduce them to a symptom of a rampant individualism embedded in a "culture of narcissism" (Lasch, 1978) where exhibitionistic self-promotion becomes part of a normalized repertoire of late modern identity formation (Derber, 2000; Gaynes, 2009; Rosen, 2004, pp. 158–92). With what follows I want to distance myself from that perspective, but also from the view that such trends betoken an erosion of "interhuman bonds" (Bauman, this volume, Chapter 1), and add a different dimension to the debate.

5.2.1 Visibility: Social fact, pursuit, and virtue

As a fact of anthropogenesis, our visual cognitive capacities and our visibility to others intertwine and affect the constitution of individuals and social environments alike. In his elaboration of a "phenomenological anthropology" Hans Blumenberg (2006) charges our visibility to those who share our environment with a fundamental significance for our very humanness. Enabled by a bipedal erect posture, increased visibility is both an advantage and a risk. We are exposed to others—friends and foes—who are exposed to us. And so our visibility makes us experts not only at self-presentation but also at self-concealment; opacity and visibility go hand in hand (2006, p. 789). This, in turn, significantly determines our orientation to self, to the world, and even to what may lie beyond it. Having attained a horizon in the literal sense, we have come to expect the unknown to cross that (literal and then metaphorical) horizon at any moment; it has enabled us to imagine and orient ourselves to that which is absent and even to substitute it with other media (for example, money). Blumenberg's thought provoking, expansive *Beschreibung des Menschen* cannot be done justice here, but it can sensitize us to visibility being *more* than a desire for its own sake driven by individualism and technological innovation. It is but a small step from here to a consideration of visibility's role in the mutual accordance of respect.

For Axel Honneth (1992), respect—or in his terms, following in the German philosophical tradition, "recognition" (*Anerkennung*)—is a fundamental human need. With modernity, that need is no longer subject to "honor" bound to individual positions in the social hierarchy; its provision becomes increasingly institutionalized. The law, work and intimacy are the three spheres in which, according to Honneth, the "institutionalized recognition order" (Fraser and Honneth, 2003, p. 138) is reproduced and constantly reconstructed through intersubjective processes. Individuals are not only accorded recognition for the realization of normative societal ideals, but in so doing they express their recognition of institutional and cultural arrangements. And because they are accorded legal rights, they are also able to challenge the existing normative order. So, beyond the contradictions of class based interest—the earlier centerpiece of critical theory—lies the granting and withholding of social recognition as a driver of social change, be it on the level of face-to-face interaction or in our interactions with the most abstract institutions and processes. Importantly, the conditions of recognition that obtain in various social environments have consequences for individuals' self-orientation, because from this view the very modern question "who am I?" cannot be divorced from the question "who am I in the eyes of others?"

In his work on invisibility, Honneth (2003) takes "the eyes of others" very seriously indeed, and elaborates the affirmation of another's visibility as no less than "the elementary form of all social recognition" (2003, p. 119).[8] Seeing and being seen—the central marker of difference between us and other life forms in Blumenberg—for Honneth serves also as a means to differentiate person from person, to accord respect to some and withhold it from others. The disrespected, those on the margins of society, are rendered socially invisible to those who determine their status. The examples of the servant in whose presence master and mistress know no shame, of the black person who feels *looked through* rather than *looked at*, ignored rather than acknowledged, illustrate our "capacity to show our disregard to persons who are present by behaving as if they were not" (2003, p. 112). Visibility and invisibility are then reliant on our cognitive capacities but go beyond them as means of social differentiation and distinction. Like Blumenberg, who accords our visibility developmental primacy over reasoning, so Honneth accords "priority" to social recognition over cognition, because "it is the prominent status of gestures and facial expressions with which we demonstrate to one another in general a motivational readiness to be guided in our actions by the moral authority of another person," so that our potentially injurious acts of treating another as if invisible "is the result of a *deformation* of the human capacity for perception with which recognition is connected" (2003, p. 126, original emphasis). Both Blumenberg and Honneth affirm the centrality of visibility as a determining fact of our humanity, our sociality.

For Hannah Arendt too visibility is central to our shared humanity. The human *political* condition depends on our "plurality," which enables us in the first place to act in concert for our freedom. But to act in concert means to do so openly, visibly, in public where "everything ... can be seen and heard by everybody" (1958, p. 50). For Arendt, a well functioning public sphere needs both plurality and visibility, because plurality without visibility equals a society in which people exist side by side, without facing one another, bereft of a basic precondition for mutual recognition, to invoke Honneth's conception. Visibility without plurality on the other hand is akin to panopticism (Berger 2009).[9] For Arendt, then, visibility is a prerequisite of free political activity, while its obverse, invisibility, is the condition of loneliness and oppression.

In John B. Thompson's account (1995, 2005), Arendt's prerequisite becomes institutionalized. Thompson makes the connection between visibility as a constitutive aspect of our political condition and the uses of various communication media through modern times. At issue is what he refers to as "mediated visibility" (2005, p. 31). Mediated visibility is as much a tool for political power, as it functions as a resource to call to accountability those who wield power. But not only did the development of electronic communications media transform the relationship between political incumbents and their constituency, it opened the way for the presentation of self in the public domain to become a social phenomenon at large; it ushered in what he calls "'the society of self-disclosure': a society in which it was possible, and indeed, increasingly common for ... individuals to appear before distant audiences and lay bare some aspect of their self or their personal life" (2005, p. 38). The influence of that technology thus augurs a qualitative transformation of the public domain, which "has become a complex space of information flows in which words, images and symbolic content compete for attention as individuals and organizations seek to make themselves seen and heard" (2005, p. 49). This intensifies dramatically both the possibilities of political visibility but also of obscurity and so mobilizes "struggles for visibility" in the public domain.

There is a further aspect to the pursuit of visibility that I want to flag at least: its moral content, or what we might call *visibility as virtue*. The open and willing making visible of self—for all the potential dissimulation—can also be construed as a mark of innocence, integrity, honesty. An illustrative example here is what has been called "the most common retort against privacy advocates": I've got nothing to hide (Schneier cited in Solove, 2007b, p. 747). Especially in the context of increased powers of surveillance vested in the post 9/11 state, people on balance are willing to trade in increasing areas of their privacy for a perceived increase in security (Steinhardt, 2003;

Rosen, 2004). But the "nothing to hide argument" (Solove, 2007b) is also marshaled by *Facebook* users in order to justify their relative nonchalance concerning online privacy issues (Govani and Pashley, 2006, p. 8). So it is not only in the specific case of the privacy/security tradeoff, but also in the more general case of the privacy/publicity tradeoff that this argument for disclosing behavior is iterated. In the absence of dedicated research it is debatable whether or not there is a link between a politically and media driven "politics of fear" (Altheide, 2006) in the post 9/11 environment and a greater willingness to disclose personal information voluntarily and online. But it is likely that as privacy became a more immediate security concern, people became also more amenable to disclosing information about themselves (Günter, 2005). In this context it is also worth pursuing the generational differences in attitudes to privacy alluded to above, especially if we consider that a new generation of citizens is coming of age in an era when tighter government control is fast becoming a taken-for-granted fact of life not only in the United States but in many other jurisdictions (Rosen, 2004). For now I want to go on to reflect on the link between the pursuit of visibility, privacy and autonomy.

5.3. Visibility and the value of privacy

The ubiquitous usage of social networking sites has enabled the pursuit of visibility in its various social forms and this has, in turn, prompted a shift of the boundaries between the public and the private spheres. Because we are conscious of our seeing and being seen we are inclined to present ourselves openly or disguise ourselves; to take advantage of the technological means for dissimulation and/or authentic self-presentation. In fact, in times in which there are plural criteria for social recognition the need for the validation of authentic selves remains undiminished. Sites such as *Facebook* and *MySpace* offer avenues to garner recognition for our lives—for milestones and achievements as much as the more mundane aspects of our existence, but also for the very fact that we participate fully in the latest trends. Choosing not to do so is (at least in certain circles) tantamount to choosing the kind of invisibility that may severely curtail one's possibilities for social interaction, for "connectivity" in Maria Markus's terms (this volume, Chapter 6). Political interaction too has increasingly moved online. Politicians are taking full advantage of "the new visibility" (witness Barack Obama's presidential campaign and *Facebook* presence). To be sure, reticence concerning one's visibility in the public arena may be equated with having something to hide, particularly in societies where political rhetoric and practice are oriented toward the trading in of some privacy for a perceived increase in security. As a consequence, the need and desire for visibility are in significant tension with our need for privacy.

While the value of privacy may indeed lie in its connection with liberal notions of autonomy, on the level of routine interaction such considerations are likely to be far from people's minds. This does not mean that autonomy doesn't matter. In fact, the freedom to freely disclose personal information to a specific as well as an abstract public may well be conceived as part of the freedom to build a life of one's own. Young people, for example, may use social networking sites in their struggle for autonomy during a phase of the life course that is highly—and increasingly—monitored by adults. From a perspective that accords vital importance to the preservation of a distinct private realm, the problem is not so much that single individuals are electing to share personal information with little thought for the possible consequences, but that this has emerged as a *collective*, everyday form of interaction. As an individually negotiated but collectively shared set of practices this trend has the potential to change the normative understanding of privacy from the ground up; to change reasonable expectations about what constitutes informational privacy and so weaken its legal defensibility (O'Hara cited in Kleinman, 2010); and, finally, to make disclosing behavior the default position *per se*.

Against those concerns we might argue that they do not consider what exactly is being traded in for what. For while people today are willing to divulge the kinds of personal information they were once at pains to keep from public view, they rarely open their private lives in total to full public scrutiny. This is said to call for a more differentiated understanding of privacy (Solove, 2007b). But it also raises the question whether a more differentiated (second order) understanding of privacy—such as that suggested by West et al. (2009) in their research on young people's non-dichotomous view of what counts as public or private—adequately *explains* differentiated understandings in everyday life, or whether this amounts to no more than a theoretical *mirroring* of privacy compromising trends which are then simply and all too easily subsumed under the rubric of "agency." On that view, people's uncertainty about the meaning of privacy is interpreted as a more sophisticated understanding of the term. However, that development can just as well be read as symptomatic of an inability to connect individual behavior to potential consequences for societies at large. And on *that* view we are confronted with the paradox that the exercise of autonomy in terms of self-presentation undermines individuals' control over personal information. Here the need for visibility plays an important role: as a fact of our anthropological constitution; as fundamental to the human need for social recognition; as a condition for effective political participation and as connoting the virtues that pertain to openness of self, it is in tension with the need for informational privacy. This, at least, is my hypothesis; its validity awaits testing in much needed empirical research. That research ought to take seriously, and so begin from the premise, that normative understandings of privacy, and so the real conditions of our autonomy, are significantly shaped by mundane routine actions and interactions. There is, finally, neither a need to be alarmist about a devaluation of privacy and threats to autonomy nor is there cause to celebrate new forms of public-private negotiations. But as the history of the unfinished struggle over privacy shows—a struggle that has furnished many, but by no means all, with better control over their lives—it pays to remain watchful over its meanings, borders and potential futures.

Notes

My interest in visibility and privacy was sparked by discussions with Maria Markus. I thank Bernard Leckning and Sveva Magaraggia for their very insightful and helpful comments.

1. The other two dimensions are "decisional" and "local" privacy, which Rössler defines as follows: "I speak of *decisional* privacy when we claim the right to protection from unwanted access in the sense of unwanted interference or of heteronomy in our decisions and actions. ... I speak of *local* privacy in a completely non-metaphorical sense when we claim the right to protection against the admission of other people to spaces or areas (Rössler, 2005, 9, original emphases; see also Arthur Glass, in this volume, Chapter 4).
2. At the same time the liberal conception of the public-private divide is thoroughly gendered and thus inherently contradictory (for an analysis of the feminist critique see Rössler, 2005, 19–41).
3. Initially *Facebook* was primarily used by high-school and college networks and so mainly facilitated communication in a limited context and known environment. This partly explains students' relatively relaxed attitudes to privacy. However, today *Facebook* is globally available and is the third largest site on the Internet with approximately 300 million users (www.facebooklogin.net, 2009).
4. In Rössler's language, there is a lack of "access" to control over personal information, whereby "access" is broadly defined as underpinning all dimensions of privacy (2005, 7–9).
5. The spatial metaphor used in this instance is not intended to detract from the cogent argument that rather than a clearly delineated domain, privacy is best envisaged and discussed in terms of its different dimensions (Rössler, 2005, 20; for a similar point see Solove, 2007b).

6. Markus's point that a reduction of visibility to *connectivity* precipitates a reduction of public engagement to *publicity* advances the argument considerably (this volume, Chapter 6).
7. For a critical engagement with therapy culture and its sociological literature, see Pauline Johnson (this volume, Chapter 8).
8. For a nuanced discussion of visibility see Maria Markus's contribution in this volume (Chapter 6). Markus distinguishes between "classical" and "managed visibility." The former refers to intersubjective processes of recognition based on capacities and achievements; the latter to actors' strategic eliciting of acknowledgment of their mere presence.
9. On Arendt and visibility see also Markus's chapter in this volume (Chapter 6). I have not dealt here with Michel Foucault's connection between visibility, power and control. There is ample literature that does so in the context of contemporary forms of self-disclosure as well as online surveillance (for example, Thompson, 1995). For a nuanced comparison of Foucault's visibility as power and Arendt's visibility as freedom see Gordon (2002). For reasons of economy I cannot discuss here the most salient examples of political claims for visibility: the assertion of a diverse range of sexualities and gender practices against the extant heteronormative order, and claims for recognition on account of various ethnic and racial identifications (see, Alcoff, 2006).

References

Acquisti, A. and R. Gross (2006), "Imagined Communities: Awareness, Information Sharing, and Privacy on the Facebook," *Lecture Notes in Computer Science*, vol. 4258, 36–58.

Alcoff, L. (2006), *Visible Identities: Race, Gender, and the Self* (New York: Oxford University Press).

Altheide, D. L. (2006), "Terrorism and the Politics of Fear," *Cultural Studies—Critical Methodologies*, vol. 6, no. 4, 415–39.

Arendt, H. (1958), *The Human Condition* (Chicago and London: Chicago University Press).

Barnes, S. B. (2006), "A Privacy Paradox: Social Networking in the United States," *First Monday*, vol. 11, no. 9, 4 September, http://firstmonday.org/htbin/cgiwrap/bin/ojs/index.php/fm/article/view/1394/1312, date accessed 11 November 2009.

Berger, B. (2009), "Out of Darkness, Light: Arendt's Cautionary and Constructive Political Theories," *European Journal of Political Theory*, vol. 8, no. 2, 157–82.

Blumenberg, H. (2006), *Beschreibung des Menschen* (Frankfurt am Main: Suhrkamp).

Burkart, G. (ed.) (2006a), *Die Ausweitung der Bekenntniskultur: Neue Formen der Selbstthematisierung?* (Wiesbaden: VS Verlag).

Burkart, G. (2006b), "Einleitung," in G. Burkart (ed.), *Die Ausweitung der Bekenntniskultur: Neue Formen der Selbstthematisierung?* (Wiesbaden: VS Verlag), 7–40.

Castells, M. (1997), *The Power of Identity*, vol. 2, *The Information Age: Economy, Society and Culture* (Massachusetts and Oxford: Blackwell).

Castells, M. (1998), *End of Millennium*, vol. 3, *The Information Age: Economy, Society and Culture* (Massachusetts and Oxford: Blackwell).

Chandler, D. (1998), "Personal Home Pages and the Construction of Identities on the Web," http://www.aber.ac.uk/media/Documents/short/webident.html, date accessed, 20 November 2009.
Derber, C. (2000), *The Pursuit of Attention: Power and Ego in Everyday Life* (Oxford: Oxford University Press).
Ehrenberg, A. (2004), *Das Erschöpfte Selbst: Depression und Gesellschaft in der Gegenwart* (Frankfurt and New York: Campus).
Fraser, N. and A. Honneth (2003), *Redistribution or Recognition? A Political-Philosophical Exchange* (New York: Verso).
Galvin, N. (2008), "Too Much Information," *The Age*, 9 October 2008, 23.
Gaynes, R. (2009), "Facebook Takes Narcissism to New Level," http://www.columbiatribune.com/news/2009/may/10/facebook-takes-narcissism-to-new-level/, date accessed, 25 November 2009.
Giddens, A. (1991), *Modernity and Self-Identity: Self and Society in the Late Modern Age* (Cambridge: Polity).
Goffman, E. (1959), *The Presentation of Self in Everyday Life* (New York: Doubleday).
Gordon, N. (2002), "On Visibility and Power: An Arendtian Corrective of Foucault," *Human Studies*, vol. 25, no. 2, 125–45.
Govani, T. and H. Pashley (2006), "Student Awareness of the Privacy Implications When Using Facebook," http://lorrie.cranor.org/courses/fa05/tubzhlp.pdf, date accessed 5 November 2009.
Günter, K. (2005), "World Citizens between Freedom and Security," *Constellations*, vol. 12, no. 3, 379–91.
Honneth, A. (1992), *Kampf um Anerkennung: Zur moralischen Grammatik sozialer Konflikte* (Frankfurt am Main: Suhrkamp).
Honneth, A. (2003), "Invisibility: On the Epistemology of 'Recognition,'" *Aristotelian Society Supplementary*, vol. 75, no. 1, 111–26.
Illouz, E. (2007), *Cold Intimacies: The Making of Emotional Capitalism* (Cambridge: Polity).
Illouz, E. (2008), *Saving the Modern Soul: Therapy, Emotions, and the Culture of Self-Help* (Berkeley: University of California Press).
Kleinman, Z. (2010), "How Online Life Distorts Privacy Rights for All," http://news.bbc.co.uk/2/hi/technology/8446649.stm, date accessed 12 January 2010.
Kolek, E. A. and D. Saunders (2008), "Online Disclosure: An Empirical Examination of Undergraduate Facebook Profiles," *NASPA Journal*, vol. 45, no. 1, 1–25.
Kraut, R., M. Patterson, V. Lundmark, S. Kiesler, T. Mukopadhyay, and W. Scherlis (1998), "Internet Paradox: A Social Technology that Reduces Social Involvement and Psychological Well-Being?, *American Psychologist*, vol. 53, no. 9, 1017–31.
Lahlou, S. (2008), "Identity, Social Status, Privacy and Face-Keeping in Digital Society," *Social Science Information*, vol. 47, no. 3, 299–330.
Lasch, C. (1978), *The Culture of Narcissism* (New York: Basic Books).
Livingstone, S. (2008), "Taking Risky Opportunities in Youthful Content Creation: Teenagers' Use of Social Networking Sites for Intimacy, Privacy and Self-Expression," *New Media and Society*, vol. 10, no. 3, 393–411.
Lyon, D. (1998), "The World Wide Web of Surveillance: The Internet and Off-World Power-Flows," *Communication and Society*, vol. 1, no. 1, 91–105.
Miller, H. (1995), "The Presentation of Self in Electronic Life: Goffman on the Internet," *Embodied Knowledge and Virtual Space*, http://ess.ntu.ac.uk/miller/cyberpsych/goffman.htm, date accessed 10 December 2009.

Plant, S. (1993), "Beyond the Screens: Film, Cyberpunk and Cyberfeminism," *Variant*, vol. 14, no. 2, 14–17.

Poster, M. (1995), "Postmodern Virtualities," *Body and Society*, vol. 1, no. 3–4, 79–95.

Rosen, J. (2004), *The Naked Crowd: Reclaiming Security and Freedom in an Anxious Age* (New York: Random House).

Rössler, B. (2005), *The Value of Privacy* (Cambridge: Polity).

Schroer, M. (2006), "Selbstthematisierung. Von der (Er-)Findung des Selbst und der Suche nach Aufmerksamkeit," in G. Burkart (ed.), *Die Ausweitung der Bekenntniskultur: Neue Formen der Selbstthematisierung?* (Wiesbaden: VS Verlag), 41–72.

Smith, M. R. and L. Marx (1994), *Does Technology Drive History? The Dilemma of Technological Determinism* (Cambridge: MIT Press).

Solove, D. J. (2007a), *The Future of Reputation: Gossip, Rumor, and Privacy on the Internet* (New Haven and London: Yale University Press).

Solove, D. J. (2007b), "'I've Got Nothing to Hide' and Other Misunderstandings of Privacy," *San Diego Law Review*, vol. 44, no. 1, 745–72.

Sprenger, P. (2009), "Sun on Privacy: Get Over It," http://www.wired.com/politics/law/news/1999/01/17538, date accessed 25 November 2009.

Steinhardt, B. (2003), "Does Privacy Have a Future After 9/11?" *Journal of Contingencies and Crisis Management*, vol. 11, no. 1, 32–6.

Thompson, J. B. (1995), *The Media and Modernity: A Social Theory of the Media* (Stanford: Stanford University Press).

Thompson, J. B. (2005), "The New Visibility," *Theory, Culture and Society*, vol. 22, no. 6, 31–51.

West A., J. Lewis, and P. Currie (2009), "Students' Facebook 'Friends': Public and Private Spheres," *Journal of Youth Studies*, vol. 12, no. 6, 615–27.

www.facebooklogin.net (2009), http://facebooklogin.net/biographies/mark-zuckerberg-has-a-net-worth-of-2-billion/, date accessed 20 November 2009.

Whitty, M. (2008), "Revealing the 'Real' Me, Searching for the 'Actual' You: Presentations of Self on an Internet Dating Site," *Computers in Human Behavior*, vol. 24, 1707–23.

6
Can Solitude be Recaptured for the Sake of Intimacy?

Maria R. Markus

This paper deals with one particular aspect of personal life in late modernity: the devaluation of "solitude."[1] It seeks the explanation for a dramatically expanding phenomenon: people's willing exposure of some of the most intimate aspects of their lives to total strangers. This search leads to an investigation of two recent cultural trends: the striving for "visibility" and "connectedness" (or "connectivity"). These concepts are analyzed in some detail and illustrated with a few empirical examples. I argue that they transform what has been previously understood as "personal relationship" into that of "connectivity" and reduce the meaning of the "public" to "publicity." I suggest further that when connectivity and visibility become dominant, the space for solitude narrows. Thus, the argument will progress to a brief elaboration of the concept of solitude and its importance for relationships of intimacy. Solitude is not loneliness and it is not isolation, it does not cut persons off from the outside world. Rather, it is a shelter from external noise in which reflection and self-reflection become truly possible, autonomy gains its meaning, and relationships can flourish. Solitude, I argue, empowers people to face the world on their own terms.

6.1. Privacy, disclosure, and modernity

In May 2008 *Cleo* magazine published (in the sealed section) a series of interviews with young couples from various professional backgrounds (including a plumber and a carpenter, a pilot, a teacher and some students) concerning their sexual practices, like frequency of intercourse, favorite positions during intercourse, favorite body parts of the partner, aids used, openness to threesomes and the like. The interviews were accompanied by quite tasteful nude photographs of the couples involved. Taking into account the nature of the magazine and its commercial aspects, there is nothing particularly remarkable in this case; at its core, however, it converges with a number of examples from other magazines, television talk shows, and of course the Internet with its various blogs and networking sites, pointing toward a social trend that deserves, I argue, consideration.[2]

The curious aspect of this and similar cases when we look at them from the sociological point of view is: what can possibly prompt the couples—in this case seemingly in love with each other—(or various individuals in other cases) to sacrifice their privacy and the intimacy of their relationships and to go "public"? Does this imply that intimacy (including sexual intimacy) today does not need a shelter of privacy; that the latter has become somehow obsolete for our intimate life to thrive? The commercial aspect of this particular case aside, what could possibly be the gain of such an exposure for the persons involved?[3] Eva Illouz in her *Cold Intimacies*, speaking about Internet dating sites, observes that "[t]he Internet makes the private self *visible* and publicly displayed to an abstract and anonymous audience, which, however, is not a public ... but rather an aggregation of private selves" (2007, p. 78, my emphasis).[4]

Needless to say that, as I have pointed out earlier, it is not just the Internet that can provide visibility of that sort. So perhaps the key for understanding such voluntary exposure of some of the most intimate aspects of one's life to strangers and, thus one of the reasons for relinquishing one's privacy, is seeking *visibility* and through that covertly asking for validation, affirmation, or some kind of approval (occasionally perhaps even for some sort of absolution) in respect of one's life choices, in this case in sexual matters.

There would be nothing particularly new in such a striving, except that in the past this sort of a feedback has been sought and received from a close friend (not for nothing called confidant or confidante), a priest, a therapist or counselor and the like, all under the veil of privacy or even secrecy. The novel aspect of recent developments is that now such disclosures have crossed the boundaries of the private and appear in a public or at least in a semi-public territory, opening personal/intimate stories to "an abstract and anonymous audience."[5] It is here that visibility is sought. Whether it is provided (that is, whether it is rewarded by recognition) and in what form, is another matter to which I shall return later on. The emphasis on the "abstract and anonymous" nature of this public well reflects its novelty and the difference from the public sphere as discussed for example by Habermas (1989) or from the public spaces provided by communities of one sort or another.

This anonymity comes largely from the fact that the members of this audience are mostly strangers to each other and to the person telling her or his story. It is thus not surprising that members of this public have nothing much in common. There is no common ethos or common purpose among the recipients of such disclosure-spectacles. While it may provide publicity, it does not really function as a public.

It is perhaps worthwhile to note here that the tendency for this type of self-disclosure is often combined with the strong objection not just against an uninvited gaze of others but also against much lesser transgressions of privacy, like for example taking photos of children at various school functions without obtaining the permission of all involved and so forth. At the same time, the people involved often do not recognize or at least do not acknowledge that by speaking about or showing some very intimate aspects of their lives, they actually radically relinquish control over their privacy and no longer have any power to influence the interpretations or utilization of the information thus disclosed.

The concept of privacy is, of course, a complex one. Most of the writers of whatever political and theoretical persuasion would agree that privacy is socially constructed and thus in different societies and in different times it can have different meanings and different things can be branded as private or public. At the same time, it is also widely acknowledged that some sort of differentiation between the levels of openness and exclusivity (thus a public versus a more private aspect) of various social relations or activities are a constant accompaniment of human history. In premodern societies, however, these divisions are almost invariably unstable and complicated by the fact that many, if not most, of the relationships in such societies are of a personal nature, independently of whether they are public or private.

With nascent modernity a whole array of new processes has been unleashed, leading to a gradual separation and consolidation of the two spheres. These transformations have included the autonomization of the political and economic structures, changes in the material and spatial conditions of everyday life, increasing individualization and, last but certainly not least, the development of new attitudes and new norms of civility. From the second half of the last century, however, what can be observed is a gradual problematization and relativization of this division at least partly due to the conscious striving of various social movements, especially the feminist critique of this dichotomy.

What today is accepted by many feminists and non-feminist writers is that the concept of the private is gradually moving away from its meaning as what is being "hidden and withdrawn" toward "what pertains only to the individual" (see, for example, Seligman, 1998). Thus the most widely endorsed understanding of the private nowadays is mostly related—in one way or another—to an agent's control over a realm of his or her life ensuring a certain level of personal autonomy and including also the right to publicity.[6] In Iris Marion Young's formulation, "privacy should be defined as that aspect of persons' lives that any individual has a right to exclude others from" (1987, p. 74). She interprets the feminist slogan "the personal is political" not as a denial of the distinction between the public and the private but, on the one hand, as a demand that "no social institutions or practices should be excluded a priori as being the proper subject for public discussion and expression" and, on the other hand, that "no persons, actions or aspects of a person's life should be *forced* into privacy" (Young, 1987, p. 74).[7]

I am in principle in agreement with these propositions and certainly accept the point about avoiding "forcing anyone into privacy." I would, however, add that no less important a requirement—congruent with the above mentioned understanding of privacy as the agent's control over their own affairs—is that no one ought to be forced "out of their privacy" into the public arena by an uninvited "outing" of his or her sexual preferences or other aspects of their intimate life. Being in control should mean just that: being able to decide which aspect of one's life a person wishes to expose for others to know and to see, and which they wish to keep "private," that is, for themselves or for those explicitly chosen by them.

Returning, however, to the question of visibility, let us see what it actually means, what it involves, what the main motivations for seeking visibility are, and what the implications of achieving it are.[8]

6.2. Visibility and the question of recognition

Hannah Arendt, analyzing the development and modern transformations of the public and the private realms, made an emphatic point about the importance of visibility, which is ensured above all by appearance in public, understood by her mainly as the political sphere. The ability to be seen and heard provides the individuals with "ontological security." According to Arendt, this can be achieved only in the public arena, where "the presence of others who see what we see and hear what we hear assures us of reality of the world and ourselves" (1958, p. 50). Not everything, however, can directly appear in public: "there are very relevant matters which can survive only in the realm of the private," writes Arendt (1958, p. 50). Recognizing that in the modern age there has been accomplished an "enormous enrichment of the private sphere through modern individualism," she argues that "even the greatest forces of intimate life" can appear in public only after "being transformed, deprivatized and deindividualized" through the newly emerged sphere of the "social" (Arendt, 1958, p. 51). Whatever critical comments we can make in respect of Arendt's concept of the social, it is relevant to the process of the transformation of both spheres: the private (including the intimate) and the public, and to the shifting of the boundaries between them, so relieving to a degree the rigid dichotomy of the private and the public.

One such transformation is discussed in this volume by Günter Burkart who points out that "[w]hen intimate matters are told in public they begin to lose their character of being authentic and mutate into a kind of *theatrical performance*" (Chapter 2, original emphasis), or—in other words—are "transformed into a culture of staging" (Chapter 2).[9] Burkart makes, however, another important comment as well. Namely, that such a transformation does not mean that the need for real intimacy disappears altogether from the private sphere. Needless to say, this latter point is valid for all the trends analyzed here, which are just that—dynamic trends and not all-encompassing, fixed (new or old) arrangements.

However, does Burkart's main point mean that all the quests for visibility are just "theatrical performances," lacking any authentic meaning, searching not for peer recognition of the person's social validity, but are rather attempts at a narcissistic showing off? Such a generalized conclusion will not stand if only because there are different ways and motivations in searching for visibility and thus also for providing recognition, or denial thereof, as the case may be.

For the sake of the present discussion, we can reduce the varieties of visibility to two basic types: firstly, there is a "classical" form of visibility, which is connected to recognition, that is a result of some sort of achievement, be it in science, arts, sport, economic life, helping others, or even just coping with serious adversities in one's life. In such cases the standard of achievement is often internally defined and is not directly dependent on social expectations or on external award of any kind, its value being in the achievement itself.[10] Secondly, an increasingly prominent place is occupied today by "managed visibility" constructed by self- or other-promotion that is often unrelated to any particular skill, talent, or achievement. This creates a variety of sometimes iconic (or, in some other cases, just mini) celebrities, depending on their promoters and possible combination with some sort of achievement.

In principle, only the first type of visibility is able to generate a genuine *recognition as social validation*, which has its corresponding mode of relating to oneself in "self-respect" and/or "self-esteem" (depending on the concrete form of recognition) (Honneth, 1995, 2003; see also Markus, 2001). At the same time, without being accompanied by recognition, visibility is indeed only a spectacle, resulting at best in a taking notice, that is "cognition" in Honneth's vocabulary. Such a visibility can hardly provide a firm basis for establishing any meaningful relationships, while, at the same time, the relation to oneself generated by it can easily be quite deceptive. The two types of visibility, however, cannot be separated so neatly. This is due mainly to the role of the mass media in creating and sustaining a celebrity culture in which it has an obvious stake. In this process of manufacturing celebrities, even when built upon some real achievement, this latter is often either lost or at least overshadowed by the trimmings of celebrity, independently or even against the achiever's wishes, creating an ambivalent aspirational model. Of course, the construction of celebrity is far from being always positive. Scandals sell and so the "disclosures" of true or—again—manufactured aspects of celebrities' lives, including the unearthing of various hidden secrets of their intimate relationships, belong to this process. The so-called Clinton affair or, very recently, the publicity surrounding the golfer Tiger Wood's marital infidelities well illustrates this point.

My concern with celebrity culture and mechanisms of its working is, however, limited here only to its providing an aspirational model for numerous mini-celebrities and their self-presentations through *Facebook*, *MySpace*, or other Internet sites, in various chat-shows or reality television and through other media. There are at least two notable aspects of those self-presentations: one is the combination of the attempts to show oneself as a unique individual while simultaneously mimicking standardized patterns of desirability and success (see also Illouz, 2007, p. 82), provided above all by the "culture of celebrity." The second, in which I am primarily interested here, is the density of the mediated connections, their frequency, accompanied often by the detachment of their users from the people around them, for which there is abundant—if mostly anecdotal—evidence. It is especially spectacular, when we include into our considerations such forms of communication like cell phones and emails.[11] While these latter have a somewhat different character as they still function mainly "from person-to-person," due to technological innovations there is a considerable (and increasing) overlap and blurring of the boundaries between these and the previously mentioned

Internet sites. The formerly separate modes of mediated communication are increasingly merging. This is not denying that a certain functional differentiation between them still exists. So, for example, emails often serve business purposes, or indeed provide ways of maintaining genuine relationships. But neither do I wish to deny that Internet connections also serve various other purposes beyond self-presentation, including scholarly debates, focus groups, or even organization of political actions. This latter is especially present in countries with no autonomous political sphere and a number of authors include this topic in their analyses (for example, Castells et al., 2007). Investigation of these issues, however, goes far beyond the scope of this paper.

Returning thus to our discussion, what seems to go at least some way in explaining the density of mediated communications is that seeking visibility for many people means above all just "being connected."[12] Social validation is thus equated here with the *number* of people who know *about me* rather than actually know me. This seems to be the driving force behind striving for more and more connections and obtaining more and more "friends" on *Facebook* or on *MySpace*, who—if needed—can be purchased from *uSocial.net* for just 20 cents per piece, or even cheaper—"conditions apply" (Thompson, 2009). This is quite enlightening in respect of the possible nature of such connections. We can safely assume that most of them cannot and do not develop into any meaningful, let alone intimate, relationships, including friendships. After all, the concept of a "friend" loses its meaning when it relates to possibly hundreds of people. Most of these connections are more like the ones between Sennett's strangers, who "meet, interact, and depart as strangers."[13] And yet many people are almost obsessively hooked to their cell phones or to the screens of their computers as if there were no life beyond these, ignoring often other real people that actually surround them. We can observe this in family settings, in restaurants, or even at bus stops. So the question "why?" remains. If indeed, as I have argued earlier, visibility as social validation cannot be truly satisfied through connections, orientated predominantly by the "culture of celebrity," what kind of particular human needs or desires can such an amorphous connectivity address? What are the fears and anxieties that the security blanket of connectivity silences or at least alleviates?

6.3. Contingency, intimacy, and solitude

As argued by many authors, but perhaps most overarchingly by Zygmunt Bauman, in the background of these insecurities and anxieties, there is a clearly observable tendency of accelerated development of virtually all social processes in modernity.[14] The social transformations connected to it certainly could not be evaluated in merely negative terms. They do open a considerably wider scope of choices for an individual, thus allowing a greater degree of personal autonomy in leading one's life. At the same time, however, they also place a heavy burden of constant decision making and the responsibility for these decisions on the shoulders of each individual, without reliable social support and with all the social ties becoming more fragile and temporary. In Bauman's works, the present human condition is represented by the metaphor of *liquidity* in which nothing can hold its shape for any substantial period of time. Contingency and uncertainty have become an organic part of the social reality we live in. While in some sense this tendency characterized modernity from its very beginning, or at least from the eighteenth century on, today such acceleration takes an unprecedented speed and form, further deepening people's insecurities and making them reluctant to organize their personal lives, intimacy included, on the basis of long-term commitments. But even when commitment extends only "until further notice" (Giddens, 1992, p. 63) the relationships built upon it are still more difficult both to sustain and to dissolve than most of the virtual connections. As Bauman puts it: "In a network, connecting and disconnecting are equally legitimate choices," so such connections are "easy to enter and to exit," "you can always press 'delete'" (2003, p. xii). In a somewhat more nuanced way, Illouz observes that while the Internet creates unprecedented possibilities for sociability and relationships, at the same time, it "empties them of the emotional and bodily resources" (2007, p. 111). In any case, the depth of engagement in non-virtual relationships, especially intimate ones, surpasses as a rule the intensity of the virtual connections, making the latter easier to manage. It is not to deny that occasionally the connections so initiated develop outside the network into real relationships, meaning "a close and continuous emotional tie to another" (Giddens, 1992, p. 58).

However, intimacy itself did not escape the impact of the above discussed social transformations, and the concept today holds many meanings explored by various authors. And obviously we can find even more differentiation on the practical level of people's everyday lives and their self-understanding. I cannot go here into any detailed discussion of either and will provide only a brief summary of some of the most consequential for my further discussion of aspects of intimacy today.[15]

Intimacy in a very general sense means "closeness," but it is not just a physical proximity, imposed by living conditions or expressed in mere physical or exclusively sexual contacts.[16] It is emotional, spiritual, intellectual and bodily closeness as a *chosen form of life*. Ideally, intimacy provides a space for mutual disclosure, recognition, communication, and for an innovative formation of the relationship, according to partners' preferences and on the basis of mutual trust and respect. This is a complex task, which is made even more complex by what Illouz calls the mixing of "two repertoires: one of private and spontaneous emotionality and one of public and political equality" (2008, p. 129). The further complication came from the infiltration of the private sphere by the activity of various experts, who—in the form of counseling, therapy, sexual education, therapeutic prescriptions and many other types of advisory activities—introduce covertly a systemic logic into everyday life, thus limiting individuals' creativity in the process of constructing and shaping their intimate relationships. This also often orients people toward an overzealous guarding of the boundaries of the self which diminishes the willingness for mutual "caring" and "taking responsibility" in intimate relationships. "Caring" is indeed in many respects a key issue for intimacy, although it is not always recognized.

According to Reiman, it is "the context of caring which makes the sharing of personal information significant" (1984, pp. 305) for intimacy. He rejects as too narrow the view that "intimacy is both signaled and constituted by the sharing of information and allowing of observation *not shared with or allowed to the rest of the world*," branding it as a "market conception of personal intimacy." A similar point is made by some other authors like, for example, Julie C. Inness (1992, p.78ff.), who defines intimacy as drawing its value and meaning from the agent's love, care, or liking which leads to relationships characterized by consent, fairness and mutuality.[17] I ought to mention here also Stephanie Dowrick, whose concept of "caring" is perhaps even more appealing as it includes the idea that because of such caring about our partner in the intimate relation, we might prioritize our immediate interest in favor of the other. She opens her discussion of intimacy by stating that "Intimacy ... is a matter of tuning into someone else's reality, and risking being changed by that experience" (Dowrick, 1995, p. 183). While it has been brought about by the expansion of emotional individualization and the striving for freely chosen companionship, intimacy—once in existence—intensified and further enriched the emotional household and the sensibility of individuals, making such tuning to the other possible. It is thus not a type of relationship one *enters* into but one that emerges and exists only in, and through, the interactions of the partners, who in the process mutually shape their selves that are not given once and for all, and thus cannot be just "revealed" in the process of communication. We can agree with Dowrick that intimacy can be understood as "knowing the other," but there is another indispensable side to this knowledge, namely the knowledge of oneself and the ability to choose, to follow and to reflect upon the direction in which our self is expanding, changing or just to enjoy our own company. This is *solitude* or "alonetime."

Solitude has a long history and originally has been directly connected to religious life as an inner unity with God. Gradually, however, it becomes valued not just by its ascetic value but also as a kind of pleasure in its own right. The influence of the Reformation, combined with a number of other social transformations, is clearly connected to the emergence of a new attitude toward solitude and self-reflection. Both, being reinforced by the pleasures of solitary reading as the result of the progress of literacy and printing, also opened the way to the idea of "shared solitude," that is, intimacy. The importance of solitude for a truly intimate relationship is beautifully expressed by Rilke in one of his letters to Paula Modersohn-Becker: "I consider this to be the highest task of the union of two people: that each one should keep watch over the solitude of the other" (Modersohn-Becker, 1998, p. 270).

But while the two are closely related they are not the same. Our capacity for solitude exists, as noted by Dowrick, "on the continuum with our capacity for intimacy" (1995, p. 140). She formulates the "paradox" of solitude and intimacy in the following words:

> I cannot be "together" with you unless I have some sense of my own separateness and autonomy. I can't be my own self with you if I am bound to you in dependency. When our togetherness enhances my life but my life does not d epend on it—I can be together with you and still be myself.
>
> (Dowrick, 1995, p. 140)

Solitude, which should not, but often is confused with loneliness,[18] is thus a time for self-knowledge and self-reflection that allows us to connect to others in a better way. "All through life we take in and make use of bits and pieces of information that feed ourselves, and in the deciding of what we take in and expand on exists a personal freedom" (Buchholz, 1997, p. 115). Solitude allows us to maintain and to live with this freedom.

Solitude, however, needs space, and not just, or even not above all, physical space. In this respect we are mostly well endowed. Most of us (at least adults) have a house, or at least an apartment, sometimes quite a big house, a private bedroom and often our private computer. Despite that, or perhaps even because of that, we often experience loneliness and isolation, but not solitude. This latter could well be facilitated by such external conditions; it cannot, however, just emerge out of them. For solitude is a willful state of mind, which can be brought about only by our interest in our own inner self and its relation to the world outside us and in our being prepared to make our own decisions and to take the responsibility for those decisions without necessarily relying on the approval of experts or of hundreds of unknown "friends," which—as I have argued earlier—does not amount to genuine social recognition. Of course, the resources needed for such independence are unequally distributed throughout society. They are differentiated along various lines: generational, financial, ethnic, gender, and so on. Provision of such resources in employment, education, health and other areas is a task that any decent society should consider as one of its main objectives.

Notes

Many thanks to my fellow editors, Pauline Johnson and Harry Blatterer for their help and encouragement; to Mira Crouch, Michael Pusey and Martin Krygier for their sympathetic comments; and above all to Gyorgy, who not only read and commented on all the consecutive versions of the paper, but with whom "being together always leaves a space for being myself" and gives a special meaning to intimacy.

1. My discussion refers above all to the "developed," affluent part of the world with high standards of living and advanced processes of individualization. While, due to uneven development and to the impact of various globalizing processes, some of its propositions could well be valid for the less affluent countries as well, this is not a subject of my considerations here.
2. Numerous examples could be brought here from such television shows like, for example, *Dr. Phil* or *Oprah*, where often very intimate details of people's lives are discussed not just as a basis for providing certain general information for the broad audience, but as a form of a public confession and counseling, Vivianne's case cited in Bauman's article in this volume (Chapter 1) also illustrates this point.
3. One of the women involved, the primary school teacher, has even lost her job as a consequence of her participation (see Glanville, 2008).
4. Needless to say that this is not the "public sphere" as analyzed, for example, by Habermas (1989), in which the private individuals (that is, individuals holding no office) constitute a public body expressing and debating matters of *general interest*. Neither does it mean that a similarly functioning public sphere (or rather perhaps spheres), mediated by modern communication technology, do not exist anymore. This is, however, not an issue I wish to deal with here.

5. According to Burkart (this volume, Chapter 2) under the conditions of such anonymity the barrier for self-revelation and the degree of vulnerability are lowered.
6. This is, for example, the argument of J. C. Inness (1992, see especially pp. 41–2, 48). One can encounter in the literature some more elaborated typologies of the multidimensionality of the private like, for example, the one proposed by Beate Rössler (2005), followed to a degree by Arthur Glass (this volume, Chapter 4).
7. A similar point is also made by Jean Cohen (2002, especially 116–24).
8. For some further important aspects of the concept of visibility see Blatterer (this volume, Chapter 5).
9. Illouz (2007), by the way, makes a somewhat similar point.
10. I have dealt with this issue in one of my earlier papers, where I have examined women's possibilities and limitations to follow the socially accepted standards of achievement (Markus, 1987).
11. Steven Johnson (2009) introduces some data on the number of visitors at some of the most popular Web sites. According to this data, in April 2009 *Facebook*, for example, had 71.29 million visitors, which showed a growth of 217 percent, in comparison to the same period a year earlier. The number of visitors at *MySpace* was somewhat lower: 54.60 million and showed some comparative decline of 7 per cent. Twitter with, at that stage, a considerably lower number of visitors (17.10 million), had at the same time grown during this period of time by a rather dramatic 1,298 percent. McCulloch (2009) cites Reuters data regarding ownership of cell phones, that establishes it at more than 3.3 billion owners, that is, roughly half of the world's population. She also refers to the 2006 Survey by the Queensland University of Technology, showing that in Australia the number of cell phones exceeds the population.
12. William Deresiewicz (2009) makes some interesting observations concerning the relation between visibility and connectivity, both generated by what he calls "the great contemporary terror of anonymity."
13. This is Andreas Wittel's (2001)—I think right—interpretation of Sennett's thesis. Wittel himself, as well as some other authors (especially from within the industry), have a much more positive outlook not just on the potential but even on the reality of the Network's sociality.
14. Zygmunt Bauman analyzes these trends again and again in several of his works like, *Liquid Modernity* (2000), *Liquid Love* (2003), *Liquid Times* (2007), and many others. Some important social implications of such acceleration are discussed also by James Gleick (1999), Rosa (2003), and perhaps with a somewhat different emphasis by Heller (1985).
15. I have dealt with some of these issues in more details in my paper, "Lovers and Friends: 'Radical Utopias' of Intimacy?" (Markus, 2010).
16. On this point I disagree with Rössler, who in her otherwise very important book, includes in her understanding of intimacy relationships in which "love, care and liking" are not involved, like for example a relation with a prostitute, which—here I agree—also requires a protection of privacy (2005, 70).
17. What I find problematic in Inness' argument is that it does not differentiate clearly between privacy and intimacy. While defining privacy as control, this is discussed exclusively as a protection of various forms of intimacy.

18. There is a recent and growing body of literature elaborating on this particular issue, mainly, however, in the context of investigating the phenomenon of loneliness (for example, Gierveld, 1998).

References

Arendt, H. (1958), *The Human Condition* (Chicago: The University of Chicago Press).
Bauman, Z. (2000), *Liquid Modernity* (Cambridge: Polity).
Bauman, Z. (2003), *Liquid Love* (Cambridge: Polity Press).
Bauman, Z. (2007), *Liquid Times* (Cambridge: Polity Press).
Buchholz, E. S. (1997), *The Call of Solitude: Alonetime in a World of Attachment* (New York: Simon and Schuster).
Castells, M., M. Fernandez-Ardevol, J. L. Qui, and A. Sey (2007), *Mobile Communication and Society: A Global Perspective* (Cambridge: MIT Press).
Cohen, J. (2002), *Regulating Intimacy* (Princeton: Princeton University Press).
Deresiewicz, W. (2009), "The End of Solitude," *The Chronicle of Higher Education*, January 30, http://chronicle.com/article/The-End-of-Solitude/3708, accessed 18 January 2010.
Dowrick, S. (1995), *Intimacy and Solitude* (New York: W.W. Norton & Company).
Glanville, B. (2008), "The Teacher Takes Legal Action Against Nude Photo Sacking," *AM: News and Current Affairs*, ABC Radio, May 9, http://www.abc.net.au/pm/content/2008/s2240616.htm, accessed 5 October 2008.
Giddens, A. (1992), *The Transformation of Intimacy: Sexuality, Love, and Eroticism in Modern Societies* (Stanford: Stanford University Press).
Gierveld, J. J. (1998), "A Review of Loneliness: Concepts and Definitions, Determinants and Consequences," *Review in Clinical Gerontology*, vol. 8, 73–80.
Gleick, J. (1999), *Faster: The Acceleration of Just About Everything* (New York: Pantheon).
Habermas, J. (1989), *Structural Transformation of the Public Sphere* (Boston: MIT Press).
Heller, A. (1985), "The Dissatisfied Society," in *The Power of Shame* (London: Routledge and Kegan Paul), 300–15.
Honneth, A. (1995), *The Struggle for Recognition: The Moral Grammar of Social Conflicts* (Cambridge: Polity Press).
Honneth, A. (2003), "Invisibility: On the Epistemology of 'Recognition'," *Aristotelian Society Supplementary*, vol. 75, no. 1, 111–26.
Illouz, E. (2007), *Cold Intimacies: The Making of Emotional Capitalism* (Cambridge: Polity Press).
Illouz, E. (2008), *Saving the Modern Soul* (Berkeley: University of California Press).
Inness, J. C. (1992), *Privacy, Intimacy and Isolation* (New York: Oxford University Press).
Johnson, S. (2009), "How Twitter Will Change The Way We Live," *Time*, 15 June, 28.
Markus, M. R. (1987), "Women, Success and Civil Society," in S. Benhabib and D. Cornell (eds), *Feminism as Critique* (Cambridge UK: Polity Press), 96–109.
Markus, M. R. (2001), "Decent Society and/or Civil Society," *Social Research*, vol. 68, no. 4, 1011–30.

Markus, M. R. 2010, "Lovers and Friends: 'Radical Utopias' of Intimacy?" *Thesis Eleven*, no. 101, 6–24.
McCulloch, J. (2009), "Switching Off," *Sunday Life*, 29 March, 15–16.
Modersohn-Becker, P. (1998), *Paula Modersohn-Becker: Letters and Journals*, G. Busch and L. von Reinken (eds), (Evanston: Northwestern University Press).
Reiman, J. H. (1984), "Privacy, Intimacy, and Personhood," in F. D. Schoeman (ed.), *Philosophical Dimensions of Privacy* (Cambridge: Cambridge University Press), 300–16.
Rosa, H. (2003), "Social Acceleration: Ethical and Political Consequences of a De-Synchronized High-Speed Society," *Constellations*, vol. 10, no. 1, 11–22.
Rössler, B. (2005), *The Value of Privacy* (Cambridge: Polity).
Seligman, A. B. (1998), "Between Public and Private," *Society*, vol. 35, no. 3, 30–6.
Thompson, A. (2009), "What Price a Friend? Just 20 Cents on Facebook," *The Sun Herald*, 13 December, 3.
Wittel, A. (2001), "Toward a Network Sociality," *Theory, Culture & Society*, vol. 18, no. 6, 51–76.
Young, I. M. (1987), "Impartiality and the Civic Public," in S. Benhabib and D. Cornell (eds), *Feminism as Critique* (Cambridge UK: Polity Press), 56–76.

7
The Erotic Imaginary, Autonomy, and Modernity

John Rundell

7.1. Love's owl of Minerva

Modernity holds out both a promise and a loss for love. The promise is contained in modernity's horizon of freedom, a horizon from which love can be viewed as a movement in the social relations of intimacy from singular or mutual enslavement to mutual autonomy. From the position of love's loss, there is a perception that in the modernity of this *fin de siècle* love is in deep crisis, along with all other forms of associations that humans establish with each other and with nature. Cultural images of love, or at least of intimate life, emphasize broken marriages, unhappy and temporary heterosexual and homosexual relationships, emotional dysfunction or collapse, loneliness and despair. Left to themselves, the men and women who inhabit the sphere of intimacy appear to be bereft of the necessary emotional resources that enable them to come together for any length of time. The contemporary experience is, thus, not of love. Love is the catch all phrase for relationships bereft of love, or of solitary individuals who mourn love's loss, often in the inarticulable void of grief.

There is another side that dovetails with this apparent sorry story and experience about love—the side through which love is culturally understood and represented. It is assumed that prior to the contemporary predicament, the subject's experience of love was located in a language or an emotional culture of love that pre-conditioned and gave meaning to the experience of love in a way which ensured that this experience could be commonly understood and mutually shared. It is assumed that this culture of love has either died from exhaustion through over-use, or has been commodified and commercialized to the extent that its meaning has been thinned to the four-lined rhyme of a St Valentine's card. Love is celebrated *en masse*, not as an event, but as a memory.

What emerges in this portrayal is a double-sided picture that, from the side of subjects, paints a portrait of emptiness and grief, and from the side of culture, paints a landscape of one-dimensional forms in tones that glide into one another. Love's owl of Minerva has spread its wings at the fall of dusk, that is, at the end of love's long day. The night, as the conventionally understood time for love, now brings solitude filled only with unfulfillable longing. Bereft of significant meaning and experience, erotic love in the third millennium and in the shadow of the second one, is now a stranger. In other words, the "experience" of love has no great points of reference or orientation under which it can be gathered and conveyed as a culturally shared, reproducible and thus ongoing experience (D'Arcy, 1954; de Rougemont, 1983; Lewis, 1990). It is a shallow, mobile culture and experience, and the suffering that it creates is treated as a pathology by professionalized therapeutic experts.[1]

However, this reading of the formation of modern love, and the image of modernity that stands behind it, short-circuits a more complex set of theoretical and historical reflections concerning the status of love, the forms of association it refers to, and the long history of its transformation. In its long durée, though, the occidental culture of love was neither continuous nor homogenous. It is more accurate to view this culture as a field in which at least five interpretations of love competed and coalesced. These cultures of love were (or are) the Platonic-erotic, the philial, the Christian-agapeic, the medieval-courtly and the modern-romantic. When one speaks of love as a cultural form in the West, it is usually the conjunction and association of the Platonic, the medieval courtly and the Romantic that is referred to under the more general term of the Eros tradition. It is this tradition and its more modern Romantic current that the above set of images lean on, and still speak to us, even as a series of echoes.

Before interrogating the problem of love in modernity and the images that abound in this opening narrative, let us begin by looking at what I will term the erotic imaginary, a particular dimension of the internal life of the subject as he or she moves to embrace the possibility of the other.

7.2. The erotic imaginary and its forms of intimate sociability

Love is an active state. According to Simmel, for example, the subject imputes love and the subject brings "the other" into love. In other words, this movement takes the form of two dynamics—an innerly creating one, and an externally directing one. In terms of love's imputing innerliness, Simmel takes as his point of reference Kant's *Critique of Pure Reason* in which Kant argues that there is an internal transcendental capacity through which the diversity of empirical experiences is synthesized according to the rules of the faculty of understanding. Simmel bypasses the idea of reason, but utilizes the Kantian idea of *a priori* synthesis. According to him, it is the capacity for synthesis that makes love active. Erotic love is the *activity* of synthesis itself, of the reorganization of these two diverse elements into a "homogenous erotic fact" around which other diverse feelings, emotions, and sensations can be linked and united under its very name (Simmel, 1984, p. 157). Erotic love cannot be analyzed in terms of these elements; only in terms of *the activity* of the synthesis. The synthesis gives rise to the attitude of love, and it is this aspect that is common to all of the elements.

This means that for Simmel love cannot be reduced to logic or reason. One cannot give reasons for being in love; nor can the principles of reason or rationality explain what love is. Love cannot be viewed as deriving from ends or purposes. It is not goal directed behavior, and thus using another for one's own purpose is anything but love. Love cannot be based on a naturalistic economy of the drives in which it is reduced to libidinal urges and the pursuit of sexually directed outcomes. Nor can love be reduced to or derived from the principles of practical reason with its emphasis on the good, whether this occurs in the Platonic, the Christian or the Kantian traditions. According to Simmel, erotic love cannot be viewed as coming under the auspices of norm-oriented behavior, that is, behavior geared to social ideals and the criterion of the ought and the good. Erotic love is not a moral maxim.

Although this is far as Simmel gets in his discussion on the constitution of erotic love, a discussion he leaves far too abruptly, it posits that love is an outer-directed synthesizing activity, created by a subject who initiates his or her love. Love is viewed in its own terms. However, it remains unclear in Simmel's account what initiates the outward directing synthesizing activity. If, for him in his Kantianism, love is the synthesis of sentiment and sensuality and yet cannot fall under the faculty of reason, this begs the question as to what in the human subject does the creating and synthesizing of the all-too-human condition of love.

In Kant's work, although not in Simmel's, there is the suggestion of a non-reasoning force that both creates and synthesizes, a force he posits in transcendental terms. Kant terms this non-reasoning force the faculty of the imagination, and it is this that points toward the creative interiority of the human being. In his reflections on the productive imagination Kant moves beyond the idea that the imagination is empirically formed to one in which images become possible as an *a priori* creation. In other words, Kant (1978, p. 165) posits a dynamic, productive imagination as "the faculty of representing in intuition an object that is not itself present." Kant's notion of the productive imagination suggests that love is an active creation, the origin of which resides in the creative imagination.[2] This is in contrast to Simmel who views it as an active *a priori* synthesis that shares homologous structural affinities with reason.

Castoriadis' work represents a radicalization of Kant's basic insight regarding the creative activity of the productive imagination. For Castoriadis, the interior world of the human being—its psyche—exists, ontologically speaking, in a state of ongoing representational activity that knows neither space, time, logic nor symbolic order. In this sense it is a world unto its own, an "unlimited and unstable flux, a representational spontaneity" that created meaning out of itself, for itself (Castoriadis, 1997, p. 151). For him, the representational pleasure of the radical imagination takes over from organ pleasure and becomes the defining characteristic of the human animal. Moreover, at this level, the psyche is indifferent to what is created and what form it takes. Throughout his work, Castoriadis is at pains to emphasize and draw out this primary dysfunctional aspect of the human animal. The power of the creative flux also indicates the imagination's irreducibility to a category of either *aesthetic* creation, or functional psychological organization.

Nonetheless, unless the psyche remains closed (or wishes to remain so, as is the case of psychosis), the world of the social enters it as a co-extensive condition. In other words, with the social world entering it, the subject thus enters a world with others, and one in which common, shared understandings might be possible. The co-extensivity of the world, of the social in the life of the subject, constitutes the breaking up of the enclosed, autistic world of the psyche, where meaning creation is now given the representational coherence necessary for life in society. For Castoriadis, this break-up or pulverization of the psyche represents the necessary alteration in the history of the subject (Castoriadis, 1987, pp. 300–29; 1997, p. 201).

To be sure, Castoriadis emphasizes the break-up of the imaginary core of the psyche in terms of the processes of initial socialization, and the creation of possibilities for political autonomy. However, the creation of love is also another possibility, as it is indicative of another kind of fracturing—one that involves not simply others, but an other who is viewed with particularity and intensity. This fracturing is also different to narcissistic self-alteration. The self-alteration of the psyche through love entails that an other has become significant for it. The move toward the other in terms of an outwardly directed imaginary self-alteration means that the other becomes significant for the self beyond itself. This movement is a very *specific* creative and productive dimension of the human imagination that pushes outward (Castoriadis, 1997, p. 207). The psyche's creation of loving significance toward another also entails that it is an open question who the other may be, and how, erotically, it may be expressed because it is a creation *ex nihilo* and does not belong to a natural economy and is indeterminate.

The openness that love creates needs to be concretized in real or potentially real terms as a *relationship* between lover and beloved. Hegel, for one, uses the experience of love as an ideal-type in order to establish the dialectic of openness in relational terms. Hegel's image of love is one in which the self-generating and creating imagination is located in the specific social space of intimacy in a way that not so much transposes the imaginary force, but transforms it to recognize otherness. As such it becomes its own truth (Hegel, 1983, p. 101; Rundell, 2001, pp. 74–81).

If love as a relational form is established at all, each participant brings his or her own particularity to the specific social space of intimacy. Intimate sociability begins from a position of tension and incommensurability between social actors. From this perspective, love is a form of improbable relating that attempts to constitute an intimate space and establish a very specific type of intensive social relation (Simmel, 1984, p. 164; Luhmann, 1986).

The beloved is a subject who exists outside the lover's imaginary life. He or she can say "yes," "no," or "maybe," the results of which can be joy and exhilaration, hurt and untold suffering, or confusion and despair. The concretization of love—like love itself—cannot be taken for granted. As such, when two people become lovers they cross a fundamental bridge. Up until this point they are unknown to each other. They are strangers. By so crossing this bridge, they embrace not only their strangeness to one another but also their mutual strangeness as to one another's imaginings, dispositions, habits, and needs, notwithstanding social conditions and arrangements that attempt to gloss these over and minimize them. This mutual strangeness is even more acute when the boundary is crossed in settings that are either forbidden or completely unknown. This is especially the case in the meta-narratives of *Tristan and Isolt* and *Romeo and Juliet*, for example, where love is also a mis-communication or a series of misunderstandings that cannot, in this context, be "normalized." Hence, it is not only the recognition of otherness that is crucial here, but also the recognition of the difference that the other brings to it, a difference that is external and remains so.

Furthermore, the relation of love between two people presupposes a dimension of exclusivity or particularity, in the sense that the love relation becomes *the* point of reference. This exclusivity may generate an inequality on the part of those who are excluded from this relation who may express themselves through an emotional economy of envy and resentment (Hegel, 1983, p. 105). Creating love entails that the open-endedness of this type of meaning-making is always in danger. Subjects in love exist in a field of tensions between closure and openness, success or failure, familiarity and strangeness, inclusivity and exclusivity. This is what makes love so unstable.

Love—or what now can be termed the erotic imaginary—is a creation of an imaginary life that synthesizes sexual desire and direction, intense feelings and emotions, bestows meaning and creates a relation in terms of the specificity of otherness. Moreover, this loving specificity is created as an outward movement beyond the singularity of the enclosed imagination. Love is neither impersonal nor detached, but is an involvement with the uniqueness of the other, the other as a unique person. In this sense, love is indicative of a particular opening of the psyche and a particular opening to another. The important point about love is that it is an externalizing mediation of a specific world relation that forces the self to give up its dream of independence (Hegel, 1983, p. 107).

The erotic imaginary creates a synthesis of different aspects of the human condition which, in the context of their modulated and pluralized state, stand in tension with one another. Intimate sociability becomes the site in which sexuality, bestowal, sensuousness, passion, and care for the other or *agape* are aligned and expressed in specific ways under the umbrella of the erotic imaginary. Each aspect brings different dimensions to this space, dimensions that have been variously emphasized and stylized in each of the different cultural traditions of love. Sensuousness is the capacity of human beings to enjoy one another through the immediacy of the senses, that is, to reside in its kingdom through the erotic cultivation of touch, taste, smell, sight, and hearing in either immediate or mediated ways (Singer, 1987, vol. 3, p. 376). Passion is different to sensuousness in that its own power is to cause those in love to yearn for one another, to crave each other's presence, and to express this yearning in explicit or symbolic terms in art, literature or music, for example. At both of their extremes, one can either be totally consumed by erotic love, or starved because of its absence (Singer, 1987, vol. 3, p. 376). However, neither sexual desire nor amorous emotion can account for the moment at which attraction and attachment entails self-subsumption. A particular regard emerges, which concerns the benevolent welfare of the other person, and is placed under the umbrella of the erotic imagination. This benevolent welfare is often altruistic, compassionate, non-possessive and self-sacrificial, and in a different tradition and language is termed care or *caritas* (Singer, 1987, vol. 3, p. 375). In other words, it involves the regard of care toward the other, and enables the subsumption of dissatisfaction.

Moreover, the erotic imaginary and its site of intimate sociability also creates its own temporal horizons; all or none of which may sit well with one another as they combine life's finitude with the infinitude of love. Those narratives, which emphasize love's disruptive, libidinous, and sensuous dimensions, signify, often to the point of idealization, love's first temporal horizon—falling in love. The paradigmatic works of the occidental Eros tradition such as *Tristan and Isolt, Romeo and Juliet,* and *The Sorrows of Young Werther* concentrate on love's first temporal horizon, its episodic, volcanic, and disruptive dimensions that loosen passion and even madness from reason. This is what gives love its great drama.

Nonetheless, two other quite different and independent temporal horizons of the erotic imaginary may or may not become interdependent with its ecstatic dimension. These other temporal horizons may be termed, following Singer's (vol. 3, 1987, p. 383–9) work, "being-in-love" and "staying-in-love." "Being-in-love" re-unites and even re-integrates the extra-temporal dimension of the erotic imaginary with the rhythm of everyday life and the forms of sociability through which it is also constituted. "Staying-in-love" may well be termed the long durée of a life traveled together, and may involve not only other aspects of the life cycle, for example bearing and raising children and care in old age, but also the whole range of emotional economies from joy and delight and pride, to anger, anxiety, and displeasure. Moreover, historically, it has not always been part of the world of intimate sociability, only the household (Singer, 1987, vol. 3., p. 383, 386–7).

From this perspective, then, the erotic imaginary is articulated within a modulated, pluralized field of intimate intersubjectivity in which its delights and dramas range across both the nature and experience of its specific sociability, as well as its imagining economy. Thus far, then, love—or the erotic imaginary—has entailed a double experience—it is a particular imaginary state with its own form of intensification, and a particular form of intersubjectivity with its own modulations and temporal rhythms for those subjects who are and may remain in love.

7.3. The cultural complex of modern love

Creating love may or may not be successful. Initiating or consolidating intimate sociability may or may not occur. Communicating this eroticized state and interacting in a way that is mutually understood has to be solved in order for love to be realized and to blossom. The problem is solved when eroticized communication and interaction—the "yes," the "no," the "maybe"—make a particular topic that can be shared, often ritually, by the participants. Love requires historically specific social creations or social imaginaries so that the emotions, actions, and experiences of love are socially communicable (Bergmann, 1987; Castoriadis, 1987). This also entails that these social or cultural articulations of love become increasingly differentiated, emotionally and culturally from other domains, languages, and styles of life. For example, historically, the erotic imaginary and its site of intimate sociability became differentiated from the warrior style of life with its emotional economy of violence, the world of the household with its obligations toward the life cycle, and the citizen style of life with its emotional economy of temperance, notwithstanding the intersections between them.

In other words, the erotic imaginary once it was instituted as a social imaginary signification, became a cultural pattern of meaning and a social site with its own practices through which specific patterns of intimate and amorous interactions between social actors could be meaningfully articulated and conveyed. At the level of culture, the erotic imaginary became institutionalized as the specific social imaginary for eroticized sociability. As such, those who participate in the culturally instituted erotic imaginary historically create and release a cultural surplus, for example, in the form of lyric poetry, love letters, and love songs (Norton and Kille, 1971; Bergmann, 1987).

One of the contextual features for the development of the erotic social imaginary in modernity is a generalized transformation from stratified societal differentiation to functional social differentiation. In this particular reading, function rather than rank defines social location and each social function becomes more complex and differentiated from one another. As each becomes an autonomous sphere differentiated from others and with its own code or form of understanding, it has to learn to solve problems which it, itself, confronts (Luhmann, 1986, pp. 1–7).

The open nature of modernity as a social form that contests and dismantles older bounded social contexts also meant that the erotic imaginary, too, becomes freed from traditional customary arrangements. The modern erotic imaginary initially leaned on and then supplanted the Platonic-Christian tensions and distinctions between body and soul, this and otherworldly existences. It can also be seen as a parallel development to the chivalric-Tristan version of courtly love with its knightly idealization of the lady. The modern erotic imaginary became a complex and tension-ridden field, especially as it became instituted as a social imaginary. Three aspects emerge as the significant dimensions of the modern erotic imaginary: the notion of autonomous subjectivity; an expressive dimension, which concentrates on an anthropology of feelings and emotions; and love as an engrossing unity, which has been interpreted as an impassioned combination of love and sexual desire in marriage. In this latter context there is an internal tension between images of mergence and separateness, a tension that is at the core of interpretive conflicts concerning the nature of the modern erotic imaginary.

A tension emerged within the modern erotic social imaginary around two images of subjectivity that it deployed: the autonomous and the expressive. Both deployed the image of autonomy articulated by the Enlightenment, and summed up by Kant in his famous dictum "to have the courage to use your own understanding" (1978, p. 54). The modern erotic imaginary transposes Kant's dictum into "have courage to create one's *own* love." The autonomous and the aesthetic-expressive currents constructed subjects, as well as humankind generally, as being released from living with metaphysically construed social, moral, and ethical constraints. The limit is thus viewed as being self-constituting and self-imposed, if imposed at all. Limits were open to constant challenge, conflict and change, but only from the inside (Taylor, 1975, pp. 3–50).

It was one that was also fraught with danger, though. The modern erotic imaginary enabled social actors to break social contexts and boundaries, as the older forms of the erotic imaginary did before it. "Falling in love" is an explosive, disruptive, and ecstatic state that leaves the lovers often suspended outside time, outside the rhythms, demands, and constraints of everyday life. The difference between falling in love within the courtly tradition and the modern one was that the latter required no magic spells and potions to unleash its form of enchantment. Yet, this history of the autonomization of erotic love is longer than what the Romantic tradition might suggest, and is parallel to that of the courtly tradition. The love between Abélard and Héloïse is transgressive in a different way to that of the love between the fictionalized Tristan and Isolt told by both Béroul and Gottfried von Strasbourg (Ferrante, 1973; Béroul, 1998; Wailes, 2001).[3] In both the medieval and courtly versions, the forbidden love that occurs between Tristan and Isolt required magic as the medium for it to be initiated. Love's contingent dynamic through which Tristan and Isolt transgressed the codes of chivalry and rank belonged to a transcendent world beyond the lovers themselves. Once there was retribution, in this case through death, the rhythm and order of the world was restored, love was again subordinated to custom.

In contrast, and notwithstanding the retributive justice metered out to Abélard, the love between Abélard and Héloïse required no magic and belonged to their own erotic imaginings and their self-understanding, an understanding articulated in what was to become their paradigmatic letters (Radice & Clanchy, 1974). In *La Nouvelle Héloïse* Rousseau (1968) fictionalizes their erotic dialogue again in letter form, a form that becomes synonymous with self-declaration and thus self-formation. Rousseau, thus, integrated the early modern Renaissance experience of Abélard and Héloïse into the vocabulary of modernity itself. The autonomous self in the form of Rousseau's Saint Preux created and unleashed it. So did the new Julie. Love, autonomy, creativity and a restlessness, which broke limits and went beyond them, went hand in hand (Rousseau, 1968).[4] In other words, love was a radicalized opening, not only at the level of the psyche, but also at the level of the cultural and social possibilities of a modernity that originates in the twelfth and thirteenth centuries. Against this background, modern eroticized autonomy made love a this-worldly possibility, and eventually became both proto-democratic and proto-feminist (Vogel, 1986; Singer, 1987, vol. 2, pp. 22–3; Johnson, 1995). Love's excitement broke social rules and contexts as lovers who viewed themselves as autonomous subjects pursued a love that was often forbidden because it crossed boundaries anchored in social custom, rank, vocation, sexual orientation, or even gendered identity.

There is another image of the modern erotic imaginary that is more aligned to the self-construction and self-understanding of expressivism: the engrossing self. In this context, the modern erotic imaginary continues the Platonic and neo-Platonic traditions in which there is a search for purity and complete satisfaction in interpersonal love that transcends ordinary sexual experience in a way that enables the lover to embrace the Divine. The modern erotic imaginary *qua* expressivist love alters the transcendent moment in a particular way—the divinity is no longer the reference point, rather the beloved is the one with whom the lover is engrossed.

For Medieval Christian love, which combined both erotic and agapeic dimensions, as well as for the Lutheran-Protestant affirmation of ordinary life in which marriage was based on friendship, God was still the highest point for love (Nygren, 1982; Singer, vol. 1, 1987, p. 296). With the expressivist emphasis on aesthetic creation erotic love is redefined as a desire for something unknowable and beyond limits, unconformable and uncontainable to empirical experience. Love is sublime.

It was, thus, possible for the expressivists to argue that erotic love was the "god" that was to be pursued. The expressivist lover, who is also viewed synonymously with Romanticism, seeks love itself, which is defined as an unknown. He or she becomes engrossed in it. As Singer notes, "Romantic love is a search for a new, unknown, infinite alluring but inherently imperfect object of desire which becomes less and less imperfect as we progressively and successfully merge with it" (1987, vol. 2, p. 295). It is in this sense that love is blind, not in the courtly sense of being bedazzled, or in the realist sense of being deluded away from objectivity, but because there is no goodness prior to love, and therefore nothing prior "for it to see or contemplate until it creates its own perfections" (Singer, 1987, vol. 3, p. 295). Hence, for the expressivist, engrossed lover the erotic imaginary is the creative experience for the subject; or to put it slightly differently, Romantic love articulates not simply an aesthetic, but an erotically expressive one into which one throws oneself. It is this that gives to it its secular-sacred power. It is through this that the social actor interprets his or her ultimate autonomy.

As indicated, this expressivist image of being engrossed takes place in a non-religious context. It occurs in a combination of two worlds that had hitherto stood in tension with one another—the intimate sphere, which is re-socialized, and the sphere of domesticity and everyday life. It is assumed that in the family they are united. It is also assumed that in the family form selfhood, love, and life are united in an engrossing manner, and the vicissitudes of the world-in-general are held at bay (Vogel, 1986). This conjunction of intimacy and domesticity means, though, that there is a double experience of both re-sacralization and secularization. The origin of the modern intensification of the family belongs here as it dovetails with the creation and interpretation of the erotic imaginary in its expressive form. Love-as-engrossment attempted to solve, at the level of society, the double-sided tension between re-sacralization and secularization that is constitutive of the intensified intimate domesticity, one of the hallmarks of modernity. In the age of the modern differentiation of social imaginaries, the experience of love, in contrast to medieval culture where marriage, sex, and love remained relatively differentiated, is paradoxically an experience of de-differentiation (Mitterauer and Sieder, 1982, pp. 71–92; Luhmann, 1986).[5]

For Romantic expressivism, at least, marriage, love, and sexual life—as metaphors for union—coexist as the concrete expressions of the more abstract condition of a yearning for spiritual involvement, of being engrossed in love. Moreover, this engrossed existence with another also represents the unification of those dimensions of life which modern rationalism had supposedly separated: reason and imagination, thought and feeling, body and matter, nature and subjectivity. The man and the woman, sanctified in marriage form the unification of autonomy and Romantic expressivism. The completeness is love itself which will perfect all imperfections and compliment all deficiencies (Shelley, 1927, p. 578; Singer, 1987, vol. 2, pp. 288, 411–27).

From a dimension of relative encirclement and enclosure, which this engrossed condition represents, the modern erotic imaginary is more than an intense erotic association between autonomous subjects. It is an engrossed blending together of loved and beloved, within a particular social setting, the family. In other words, engrossed Romantic-expressivist love can be viewed as an intense sociality of the "being-in-love" type, which is constituted and expressed in an ecstatic simultaneous state of self-suspension and involvement in another outside oneself, which is supposed to endure across all of the temporal horizons of love, and within only one social sphere. However, this intense sociality can occur to the point where all dissimilarity is lost, and can undermine the condition of love as a relational form. Intense sociality can be viewed as either intensely pleasurable—the emphasis on the combination of love, sexuality, and marriage in expressivist-Romanticism's renewed utopic eroticism—or intensely painful because it is experienced as an entrapment, or a loss of, and violence toward, the self. In this way, erotic, engrossed expressivism over-rides and annihilates the principle of autonomous selfhood, as Goethe (1989) portrayed Werther's own self-understanding, suffering and suicide.

These counter-positions of the autonomous and expressivist-engrossed subjects still linger to fuel the assessment of erotic love in the twenty-first century in the midst of the structural transformations and changes in life-experience that have occurred in the intimate sphere. The modern erotic social imaginary is part of a more general cultural shift of modernity and occurs along two interrelated fronts—one pertaining to the language of erotic love itself, the other to the recognition of the human being *qua* subject. The assumed "death" of love is part of a general shift from metaphysically and transcendentally constituted worldviews to post-metaphysical ones constituted by both autonomous and expressivist-Romantic cultural currents. As my opening remarks suggest, this shift has been interpreted from the vantage point of a pessimism, the genealogy of which has deep roots in the expressivist-Romantic tradition. Moreover, these transformations are seen as inseparable from the family, its intensification, and the development of its modern pathologies of both mergence and violent separation because of this. This is set against a historical background of both the devolution of the family as the site for socialization and education, moral and legal sanction, protection, and now leisure, and its emergence as a contested domain for all forms of intimacy.

In the context of a modernity that is pluri-centered, and in which each of its centers has its own long history, the expressivist-Romantic claim of reconciliation in either optimistic or pessimistic terms has been given up. Left with what Beck and Beck-Gernsheim (1995) suggest is "the normal chaos of love," the erotic imaginary of a modernity remains at the intersection of solitude, isolation, sexual intimacy, emotional intensity, and everyday life where the family is no longer a presumed "natural" or historical unit. It is an intersection at which *all* of the modalities and temporal horizons of the erotic imaginary are located and juggled in ways that may or may not combine, especially in marriage and family life. Thus, the modern erotic social imaginary is a signature tune in which subject formation continues to occur by being both affirmed *and* disrupted, especially when the value of autonomy is at play. It also competes with the other social imaginaries and temporal horizons of modernity. This also entails that the internally differentiated temporal horizons of intimate sociability—or times of love—become more acute. Instead of a love lived across a life-time, if one also includes parent-child relations, there may well be many loves, and many love-times. In the light of all of this, it is more accurate to speak of post-metaphysical and post-utopic erotic love, rather than post-erotic love, where both autonomy and relationality become more, rather than less, pressing.

This means that the particular tragic drama, which was characteristic of the grand narratives of the Eros tradition, is now also absent. In our current modernity, the erotic imaginary is brought into the world of everyday life by subjects who are initially strangers to one another, and is subject to all of modernity's tensions and conditions, to intensification, diremption and alienation, to autonomization and democratization. Notwithstanding its tension-ridden social condition, the erotic imaginary remains an internal dimension at the level of the subject. If modernity is an epoch in which there is a differentiation of cultures, forms of life, and functions, it is also an epoch in which there is an acute diremption between the worlds of the psyche and the social-historical. In between are possibilities. Including those of love.

Notes

For Danielle, again. This chapter is a rewritten version of an essay titled "Eros and Imagination. Love and Modernity" first published in *Divinatio*, vol. 14, 5–27, 2001. I would like to thank Danielle Petherbridge, John Friedmann, and Peter Beilharz for their comments on earlier drafts of the original essay.

1. These images have a genealogy that is articulated in de Rougemont (1983) *Love in the Modern World*, which becomes a paradigm for this current. See also D'Arcy (1954), Lewis (1990), Singer (1987), and Luhmann (1986). Anthony Giddens (1992) views the contemporary state of intimacy simply in transactional terms. See also Singer's (1987, vol. 3, 370–2) discussion of de Rougemont.
2. Kant does not take the step from a discussion concerning the productive imagination to that of love. For him, love falls under the umbrella of practical reason.
3. Although Singer (1987) views courtly love as a watershed in the history of European love and provides some (but not all) of our foundations of the more romantic notion of love, he criticizes de Rougemont, for one, of conflating courtly and romantic love, and is skeptical about its terminology.
4. To be sure, in *Nouvelle Héloïse* Rousseau constructs another preferred sociability, that of intimate friendship. Arguably, Friedrich Schlegel's *Lucinde* also belongs to this current, notwithstanding his own version of the Romantic-expressivist paradigm.
5. With the invention of objectivistic forms of knowledge love is viewed, for example, sociologically as part of the history of the family or psychoanalytically from the vantage point of the sexual history of the species.

References

Beck, U. and E. Beck-Gernsheim (1995), *The Normal Chaos of Love*, M. Ritter and J. Wiebel (trans) (Oxford: Polity Press).

Bergmann, M. S. (1987), *The Anatomy of Loving: The Story of Man's Quest to Know What Love is* (New York: Columbia University Press).

Béroul (1998), "Tristan," in N. J. Lucy (ed. and trans.), *Early French Tristan Poems* (Woodbridge: D.S. Brewer), 12–199.

Castoriadis, C. (1987), *The Imaginary Institution of Society* (Cambridge: Polity Press).

Castoriadis, C. (1997), *World in Fragments* (Stanford: Stanford University Press).

de Rougement, D. (1983), *Love in the Western World* (Princeton: Princeton University Press).

D'Arcy, M. C. (1954), *The Mind and the Heart of Love, Lion and Unicorn: A Study in Eros and Agape* (London: Collins).

Ferrante, J. M. (1973), *The Conflict of Love and Honor: The Medieval Tristan Legend in France* (The Hague: Mouton).
Giddens, A. (1992), *The Transformation of Intimacy: Sexuality, Love and Eroticism in Modern Societies* (Oxford: Polity Press).
Goethe, J. W. von (1989), *The Sorrows of Young Werther* (London: Penguin).
Hegel, G. W. F. (1983), *Hegel and the Human Spirit* (Detroit: Wayne State University Press).
Johnson, P. (1995), "The Quest for the Self: Feminism's Appropriation of Romanticism," *Thesis Eleven*, vol. 41, no. 1, 76–93.
Kant, I. (1978), *Critique of Pure Reason* (London: Macmillan Press).
Lewis, C. S. (1990), *The Allegory of Love* (Oxford: Oxford University Press).
Luhmann, N. (1986), *Love as Passion: The Codification of Intimacy* (Oxford: Polity Press).
Mitterauer, M. and R. Sieder (1982), *The European Family* (Oxford: Basil Blackwell).
Nygren, A. (1982), *Agape and Eros* (Chicago: University of Chicago Press).
Norton, D. L. and M. F. Kille (1983), *Philosophies of Love* (New Jersey: Rowan and Littlefield).
Radice, B. and M. T. Clanchy (eds) (1974), *The Letters of Abelard Heloise* (London: Penguin).
Rousseau, J. J. (1968), *La Nouvelle Héloïse: Julie or The New Eloise* (University Park: Pennsylvania University Press).
Rundell, J. (2001), "Imaginary Turns in Critical Theory: Imagining Subjects in Tension," *Critical Horizons*, vol. 2, no. 1, 61–92.
Schlegel, F. (1971) *Friedrich Schlegel's Lucinde and the Fragments* (Minneapolis: University of Minnesota Press).
Shelley, P. B. (1927), "Love's Philosophy," in T. Hutchinson (ed.), *The Complete Poetical Works of Percy Bysshe Shelley* (London: Oxford University Press).
Simmel, G. (1984), *Georg Simmel on Women, Sexuality, and Love* (New Haven: Yale University Press).
Singer, I. (1987), *The Nature of Love*, vols 1–3 (Chicago: Chicago University Press).
Taylor, C. (1975), *Hegel* (Cambridge: Cambridge University Press).
Vogel, U. (1986), "Rationalism and Romanticism: Two Strategies for Women's Liberation," in J. Evans (ed.), *Feminism and Political Theory* (London: Sage), 17–46.
Wailes, S. M. (2001), "Passion as a Form of Communication in Gottfried von Strasbourg's Tristan," *Essays in Medieval Studies*, vol. 18, 31–42.

8
What's Wrong with Therapy Culture?

Pauline Johnson

"No I have not sought counseling nor do I intend to seek it. I am a grown man. I am not receptive to being counseled. I am beyond the reach of counseling." Professor Lurie, main character in J. M Coetzee's *Disgrace,* fronts a university committee set to investigate complaints about his sexual relationship with a student in "the wrong spirit" (Coetzee, 1999, p. 49). Neither an admission of guilt nor an appeal to the compulsions of Eros will satisfy the committee that demands that Lurie make his damaged self available for therapy. Refusing to give the committee a confession that, it can tell, "comes from his heart," Lurie has no stomach for what has been termed in the sociological literature "therapy culture." Typically this sees the ideologies that underpin clinical practices escape from a distinct and functionally specific role to merge with and extend their impact across wider cultural institutions (Furedi, 2004, p. 17). This has involved a shifting vocabulary of ends and means that is underpinned by a constant undertaking to relieve complexity with the helpful offer to manage our subjectivities for us.

Sociologists have been divided over what to think about the rise of therapy culture. They are usually agreed though about its cultural dominance. Frank Furedi observes that "[f]rom birth, marriage and parenting, through to bereavement, people's experience is interpreted through the therapeutic ethos" (2004, p.12). Eva Moskowitz (2001, p. 1) even refers to therapy as an "American cult." According to some, there's not much to complain about. Therapy culture sidesteps the prescriptive closures of the religious world-view and offers only to train up self-understandings required to make one's way in a confusing contemporary world. Anthony Giddens is enthusiastic about the "emancipatory" promise of these "texts of our time," many of which "point towards changes that might release individuals from influences which block their autonomous development" (1992, p. 64). Others are wary of benign appearances and suspicious of the "therapeutic emotional style – which has dominated the American cultural landscape throughout the twentieth century" (Illouz, 2007, p. 6). However, therapy culture has proved a slippery customer and the critical literature has encountered problems in spelling out its reservations in any systematic way. In this paper I want to explore difficulties in some major attempts to justify critiques of therapy culture and I will look into ways of describing its costs.

Formed in the image of the "helping professions," therapy culture is a frustratingly elusive target that confesses to no particular agenda of its own. A seeming open-ended responsiveness to needs that are brought to it means that critiques that weigh in to defend apparently neglected aspirations find it hard to make themselves stick. It could be, then, that a critique based on a "counting the costs" approach is the wrong way to go. Following up on a trail of skepticism about the normative demands of critical theory, Eva Illouz proposes some alternatives to a search for a normatively grounded critique of therapy culture. I will argue, though, that a critical reception can't avoid the demand to justify itself via an account of the cultural sacrifices that are involved. Justification of a critical attitude first requires an interrogation of therapy cultures' claimed ideological open-endedness. While it is able to move agnostically *between* different ways of describing our individual freedoms, it seems that the curing intentions carried by the therapeutic framework construct these values in quite particular and limited ways. In the final section of the paper I will argue that therapy culture describes our freedoms in terms that diminish their rich cultural potentials. In particular I will suggest that a therapeutic framework employs impoverished constructions of the values of rational autonomy and authenticity and obscures the possibilities for creative intersections between them.

A further note on the objectives of the paper might be helpful. Richard Sennett (1974) warned us some time back that once a confessional, therapeutic imperative took hold, the public arena as a forum for issues that had been *selected* for society wide scrutiny and debate would be endangered. However, vital as it is, the issue of collateral damage to a viable public sphere that is brought on by a dominant therapeutic culture is not what I have in mind. I am interested, rather, in exploring difficulties confronted by sociological critiques in spelling out what the rise of therapy culture has cost our understandings of modern individuality.

8.1. Difficulties for normatively grounded critique

It's not too difficult to see why sociologists might have been challenged by the task of spelling out the costs of what Christopher Lasch described as the rise in the post-World War II period of a "psychiatric imperialism" that seemed to be determined to minister "to all of society as the patient" (1977, p. 98). After all, this undertaking offered itself as a benign, caring response to the damaging failures of harsh liberal ideologies that had sheeted all ethical responsibility for the well constructed life home to the autonomous subject. Liberal divisions between private and public life had seemed to depend on the self-confidence and resourcefulness of ethically independent personalities. However, this faith in personal resources was badly shaken by economic upheavals and the trauma of world war and further undermined by the bureaucratization of social and cultural life in the postwar years. In this context, therapy culture, which offered to draw up neglected dimensions of the self and creatively connect these with a reforming social agenda, seemed a welcome revival of the narrative of a powerful self (Zaretsky, this volume, Chapter 10). Private freedoms now seemed to be about teachable "life skills." With this break out of a therapeutic reconstruction of private life came the first round of its critical reception.

Originally published in 1966, Phillip Rieff's *The Triumph of the Therapeutic* articulated the main themes of the early critiques. Rieff despised the "narcissistic" preoccupations of a culture of complaint that championed "the instinctual Everyman twisting his neck uncomfortably in the starched collar of culture" (1996, p. 8). As he saw it, a therapeutic regime that promoted the appetites over a supposedly repressive ego would actually only deliver the self up to an infinitely manipulatable quest for well-being (Rieff, 1996, p.13). Rieff (1996, p. 50) reminded us that individual life is "a delicate personal achievement" and he insisted that a discriminating ego must play a central part. Rieff, and after him Lasch, wanted to reinvest the ego with the task of crafting a life that reflected chosen, individual priorities. They saw this as a rear guard action in defense of a reasoning ego that was under attack from a culture tuned into the dreamy narcissism of an instinctual self (Zaretsky, this volume, Chapter 10).

Today all this sounds somewhat odd. We are now familiar with a therapeutic regime that wants to cure us of "anything in the psyche that escapes or subverts our rational control" (Illouz, 1997, p. 293). For a new generation of critics, the ideal of the rational self-chooser cannot, as Rieff and Lasch supposed, be the grounds upon which we measure the cultural losses of a therapy regime. It seems that therapy culture has now installed itself as *champion* to the rationally self-determined life. Later on in my discussion I want to expose therapy culture as the vessel for a determinate set of interests that imposes itself on the value ideals that it appropriates. For now though I want to consider the way in which shifting descriptions of the ends taken up by a triumphant therapeutic culture has seemed to pull the normative rug from under some of its main critiques.

We have seen that Rieff backed the arbitrating capacity of the rational ego to interrupt the lazy seductions of a therapy industry. However, some years later Michel Foucault (2006) described therapeutic culture as a generalized set of techniques aimed at the production of a rationally self-directing individuality. To grasp what this switch in its objectives meant, we need to appreciate the reshaping of therapy culture in accordance with a new sense of its cultural importance. Early on therapeutic culture had positioned itself as support to a Romantic "stand in" for a lost confidence in a liberal belief in the spontaneous powers of the private individual. As a liberal reliance on private freedom as a "ready made region that has to be respected" (Foucault, 2008, p. 65) came under pressure from inhibiting social conditions, efforts were made to re-describe the spontaneous resources available to a self-realizing individuality. This re-description of freedom as a state of being seemed set to rescue the ideal from the demands of a rational, self-directed life. However, this attempt to reconfigure the ready-madeness of private freedom turned out to be a challenge to the ideal as well. The attempt to manufacture support for the "instinctual Everyman" only underlined that there could be no redemption for the idea of "ready-made" private freedoms. Therapy culture emerged, then, as an enthusiastic advocate of the post-liberal conviction that freedom "is something that has to be constantly produced" (Foucault, 2008, p.65). Therapy culture might now make itself available to any of the struggling cultural aspirations delivered to it.

Main themes in Nikolas Rose's 1990 study *Governing the Soul: The Shaping of the Private Self* drew attention to changed objectives of a maturing therapy culture. Far from chastising its seeming neglect of the rational, arbitrating ego, Rose describes therapy culture as a regime that uses the techniques of a consumer society to distribute the ideal of the rational, self-choosing individual. A therapeutic culture is now charged to reconstruct confidence in competencies that had been assigned to the ego. Rose tells us that to "[s]elves unable to operate the imperative of choice" therapy culture offers to "restore the status of the choosing individual" (1990, p. 228). He evidently regards this promise with some suspicion. In the therapeutic regime, "[e]very aspect of life, like every commodity, is imbued with a self-referential meaning: every choice we make is an emblem of our identity, a mark of our individuality, each is a message to ourselves and others as to the sort of person we are, each casts a glow back, illuminating the self of the he or she who consumes" (Rose, 1990, p. 227). More recently, Illouz has posted a critical response to the "banality" of therapy culture's offer to provide a "cognitive and emotional 'tool kit'" that is supposed to help "disorganized selves manage the conduct of their lives in contemporary polities" (2008, p. 241). She is particularly struck by the flattening of "our emotional imagination and experience" that is required by the advice industry.

The theme of cultural losses that is evoked here seems to call for an explicit account of the sacrifices that are involved. However, as already indicated, therapy culture will not let itself be easily convicted. The "tool kit" is able to offer itself as a support to any type of existential needs that are handed to it and so seems to disarm charges that it has neglected important cultural potentials. Rieff underlines the supposedly open-ended responsiveness of a triumphant therapeutic. Therapy, he tells us, "is no attempt to enforce conformity but apparently part of a profoundly emancipatory project of learning to be a self" (1996, p. 238). Declining the role of ambassador to any particular worldview, therapy culture constantly renews its relevance by its offer to code the contents of our own longings for emancipation. It is, we have seen, equally at the service of the longings for self-realizing authenticity and to aspirations for a self-mastering reason.

It is not just the capacity to embrace different objectives that has troubled the search to ground a critique of therapy culture. Criticism has also been robbed of a certain type of normative foundation by the part therapy culture has played in ousting a liberal appeal to the ready made character of private freedoms. Now that this liberal conviction has lost cultural traction we tend to be unmoved by critiques that focus on a therapeutic manipulation of value ideals. Therapy's bundle of life skills appears only as one mode of the "limitations, controls, forms of coercion" (Foucault, 2008, p. 65) that have been called upon to construct self-understandings of self-choosing individuality. We cannot, it seems, easily convict therapeutic culture for the repressive artificiality of its programs designed to help us "learn to be a self" (Ebert, this volume, Chapter 9). Rose takes the importance of the loss of this particular normative foundation much to heart and finally opts for an uncritical reconciliation with a triumphant therapeutic. *Governing the Soul* ends up denouncing the "paranoid" attitude of some social theorists who are supposedly blind to "the central feature of these new apparatuses and techniques"; namely, to the "pluralization of the agencies and mechanisms of regulation of the internal worlds of institutions, families and individuals" (Rose, 1990, p. 257). This is an accommodation that acknowledges no distortions or cultural sacrifices. The reality, we are told, is that modern selves have come to live the project of modern freedom "in terms of identity, and to search for the means to enhance that autonomy through the application of expertise" (Rose, 1990, p. 258).

Recent sociological commentary on therapy culture has tended to return to a more avowedly critical stance. Frank Furedi (2004, p. 204), for example, insists that, due to its dependence on "the fatalistic premise of the vulnerable self," therapy culture has produced a "passive sense of the self" in which "the experimenting and transformative role of the individual is all but extinguished." And Stjepan G. Mestrovic describes a "postemotional society" as a "new phase of development in which synthetic, quasi emotions become the basis for a widespread manipulation" (1997, p. xi). Such observations seem to again challenge the critics to tell us about the cultural goods that are supposedly denied or distorted. This requirement is frequently not followed up though. Mestrovic (1997, p. xv–xvi), for instance, asserts that the task of describing "escape routes" from therapeutic manipulations is not essential to a critical investigation.

Something of an exception to a contemporary "hands off" approach to self-reflexive critique, Illouz has proposed some interesting ways of exploring what's wrong with therapy culture. I disagree, though, with her ongoing conviction that a critical reception of therapy culture can appeal to an immanently critical posture and so avoid discussing the cultural potentials that are being sacrificed. Illouz has always hoped that we might identify therapy culture's shortcomings by theorizing its own "ambiguous, contradictory properties" (Illouz, 1997, p. 287). *Consuming the Romantic Utopia* (1997) locates a major tension between the value commitments and the purposes embraced by a consumerist therapy culture. She observes that the self-reflexive and "rational attitude to the self" advocated by a therapeutic mindset offers a communicative channel to contemporary needs for "self direction, self-knowledge and egalitarian self-assertion." However, she also remarks on competing imperatives that encourage people "to conceive of themselves as a list of preferences and needs" (Illouz, 1997, p. 287). While therapeutic culture promises to help put us in charge of our lives, it does so by its package of "life skills" and psychological codes. Illouz is confident at this stage that a resistance to these scripting imperatives will leak through. For, "as we try and control our lives through the rational management of our relationships, experiences that transcend rationalization become more elusive and our longing for them all the more urgent" (Illouz, 1997, p. 287). Here Illouz brings in results of some interviews to demonstrate that people continue to signify their not yet extinguished subjectivities via their personalizing receptions of cultural scripts. She makes the point that this kind of active reception is the luxury of a privileged class. It is available only to those who are "somewhat released" from the demands of "effort, work, and routine" (Illouz, 1997, p. 181). However, it is not clear that this empirical study is able to supply the ground of a general critique. The significance of the empirical material seems to depend upon, but is actually unsupported by, an account of longings that seem to encounter consumer scripts as a repressive limit. Indeed, the personal touches that Illouz discovers in certain privileged receptions could even be a symptom of the endless adaptability that Horkheimer and Adorno famously recognized as vital to the hegemonic ambitions of a consumer culture: "Something is provided for everyone so no-one can escape; differences are hammered home and propagated" (2002, p. 97). In any case, the resistant power that Illouz discerns in her early writings proves very weak. A decade later she is persuaded that longings for a creative interplay with the commodifying stream have been extinguished.

Published in 2008, *Saving the Modern Soul: Therapy, Emotions and the Culture of Self Help* further develops Illouz's reflections on the grounds of a systematic critique. Here she identifies major internal tensions between the professed emancipatory investments of a therapy culture, which "fosters a form of sociability based on communication" while encouraging "a strong individualism based on enlightened self-interest," and its institutional purposes that aim at securing "the self within a network of social relations" (Illouz, 2008, p. 103). Describing this always-present tension as a "sociological puzzle," Illouz advocates an immanently critical approach that seeks to evaluate the therapeutic "from within its own horizons of propositions and claims" (2008, p. 20). However, immanent critique requires that we are able to demonstrate potentials in the values advocated by a given framework that are held back or distorted by its own competing purposes. So if the sociological puzzle is to become the ground for an immanent critique, Illouz has to spell out the entailments of the self-directing individualism advocated by therapy culture that appear to be contested by its practical, curing purposes. A slightly earlier study titled *Cold Intimacies: The Making of Emotional Capitalism* (2007) perhaps helps us understand why Illouz is not prepared to support her critical posture with an account of alienated cultural potentials. Illouz once more draws our attention to internal tensions in the "therapeutic emotional style" (2007, p. 6). Remarking on its emancipatory investments, she points out that therapy culture joins with feminism to insist on a new kind of accountability in our interactions. A rationalization of intimate relations has transformed their "emotional texture" introducing expectations of equality and freedom into this domain (2007, p. 30). But there are losses too, for this rationalization "instills a procedural quality to emotional life which makes emotions lose their indexicality, their capacity to orient us quickly and unself-reflectively in the web of our everyday emotions" (Illouz, 2007, p. 38). Under the therapeutic regime "emotions are increasingly disembedded and disentangled from concrete and particular actions and relationships" (Illouz, 2007, p. 38). Illouz goes on to note that, over the last decade, the commodification of emotions that bundles them into readily communicable forms has been pushed forward under the penetration of Internet technology into the private domain.

There is a clear continuity here with the proposal for an immanently critical challenge to a colonizing therapeutic ethos that Illouz talked about in *Saving the Modern Soul*. *Cold Intimacies* contrasts this idea of critique with a rejected idea of "pure critique" that "subsumes culture in the political sphere" and becomes "to a large extent the counting of the ways in which culture either emancipates or represses, delivers 'trash' or 'treasure'"(Illouz, 2007, p. 92). Illouz (2007, pp. 94, 111) finds links between the straitjacket, rationalizing imperatives of the therapeutic and the colluding "banal" proposal by traditional critique to reduce cultural to political life. This latter contributes to a "hyperrationality" whose abstract generalizations are necessarily blind to the particularity of an irreducibly concrete private life (Illouz, 2007, p. 111). Drawing on Michael Walzer's idea of the untranslatability of norms upheld by distinct value spheres, Illouz suggests that rationalizing descriptions of private life can only result in distortions of the profoundly individual ties and subjective feelings that bind the intimate sphere. She is convinced that alienations produced by this colonization (from both critical and therapeutic imperatives) will see us retreat into private worlds, that, held together "by self-generated fantasies," appear as "sterile" and "disconnected from reality" (Illouz, 2007, pp. 113–14).

There are some problems here. Firstly, to suggest that contemporary intimacy is all about particularizing bonds and personal feelings that will invariably encounter rationalizing descriptions as alienating intrusions seems to sacrifice the lived complexity of contemporary intimacy. Surely Beate Rössler (2005, p. 161) is right when she underlines the centrality of a rationalizing interest in respect for the other in the bundle of norms that underpin expectations we have of the intimate interaction. Illouz's undifferentiated account of the alienating impacts of rationalizing descriptions of private life depends on an oversimplified, one-sided account of the intimate sphere. It also seems to depend upon sliding together distinct therapeutic purposes and critical theory interests. Therapy culture only promises to redress the emotional deficit of the damaged life. Far from an alienating imposition upon particular narratives of a concrete private life, therapy culture, as Furedi (2004) forcefully reminds us, is today dedicated to unblocking an inchoate, anxious privacy via a healing public confession. It seems that we will need to rely on a critical theory that is interested in reflecting on ways of valuing cultural potentials to unearth the alienations that might be involved here.

8.2. Distortions of therapy culture

The apparent adaptability of therapy culture must take considerable credit for smoothing the way to its cultural dominance. Therapy culture has not felt called upon to establish that a rational attitude toward life is better than a romantic, sentimental one, nor that we owe it to ourselves to live authentically in accordance with internal existential imperatives. We have seen that as soon as an alternative way of identifying our freedoms is represented as its repressed, excluded other, the therapeutic is able to rise to the challenge and to make itself over as advocate of the apparently neglected ideal. In the following I want to interrogate therapy culture's pretensions to open-ended agendas and to identify the ideological closures that are carried by the generalization of norms and expectations forged in a clinical environment. A therapeutic interest does not just respond to aspirations and needs presented to it but constructs these in a particular, limited fashion. I will focus on dimensions of the values of rational autonomy and authentic subjectivity that are obscured by therapeutic appropriations.

Positioning itself as guide to an existentially dissatisfied self, the therapeutic is, as already underlined, at odds with a liberal faith in a ready made, private freedom. However, this confidence in the spontaneous resources of the private individual was always headed for trouble. As it sought to generalize itself as a universal principle, the absence of the social conditions required to realize it would inevitably attack a complacent faith in the individual's capacities for self-realization. Therapy culture seemed to offer a response that might help to contain the implications of a crisis of confidence in spontaneous freedoms. Self-esteem, resilience, reflective goal-setting are some of the psychological codes that might be learned to resurrect diminished private powers. However, this attempt to respond to the crisis of faith in untutored private freedoms smuggled through important dimensions of the old liberal framework. In particular, preoccupied only with restoring a healing equanimity to the dissatisfied individual, a therapeutic intervention could not elaborate the grounds upon which we might reflect on the worth of certain renderings of our aspirations to freedom.

The therapeutic model imported ways of thinking about problems of private life that were forged in the clinic outwards to describe cultural dimensions of the issues. By contrast, Agnes Heller and Ferenc Feher adopt a sociological perspective on a society-wide problem. They describe ours as "the dissatisfied society" (Heller and Feher, 1988) and neither liberalism nor its critical descendents were ever likely to be able to help us adequately grasp the challenges it entails. Heller and Feher offer a structural diagnosis of contemporary dissatisfaction. It is, they maintain, sited at the intersection of an "unbridgeable discrepancy between expectations" about open-ended, contingent futures and the hard necessities imposed by the "facts of life" (Heller and Feher, 1988, p. 19). A modern experience of incapacity in the face of desires that are born of abstract hopes and the limiting realities of our particular circumstances and personal talents cannot, they insist, simply be disavowed. We need to make ourselves equal to the task of grasping our freedoms and quelling debilitating dissatisfactions in the dissatisfied society. Heller and Feher elaborate important discriminations about modes of negotiating contemporary dissatisfaction that are overlooked by a therapeutic interest.

In particular, Heller and Feher distinguish between wants and needs as the two distinct modes of negotiating discontents set in train by a modern discrepancy between open aspirations and limiting concrete circumstances. As long as we limit our interest in self-determination to the selection from available options we negotiate dissatisfaction through our wants. Chasing up on our wants promises to supply us with a way of grasping our self-determination from the maelstrom of possibilities because we seem to fashion ourselves through the selections we make. This act of self-choosing does not depend upon any prior scheme of values able to direct the selections we might make. Heller and Feher are persuaded, though, that we cannot hope to achieve satisfaction in the dissatisfied society via the existential cycle set in train by the pursuit of wants. Rather than an exercise in self-determining autonomy, the attempt to fashion ourselves through choices between already determined goods comes to be experienced as an alienating *external* determination. A self-choice through the selection among the ready-to-hand can be felt as an alienating determination of the self because it refers back to no rationalizing purposes and so invites no creative interventions. The failures that are encountered here can, according to Heller and Feher, reignite the search for a way of negotiating dissatisfaction that calls upon a higher level of self-reflection. We feel ourselves engaged in a self-determining freedom only as we interpret our found contexts as a field of potentials that can be realized in accordance with our own reflected upon descriptions of their worth. Here the self does not experience itself as simply a categorical will obliged to fill itself with contents that are borrowed from an arbitrary selection. Rather, the need for self-determination posits a rationalizing interest that sets the individual out on the path of ongoing evaluations about the finest potentials in their contexts and themselves. In this way, the need for self-determination leads the self outwards to an interest in elaborating descriptions that can identify the worth and value of certain possibilities. The self-determining individual is accordingly brought into dialogue with others by his or her commitment to discover what is best in themselves and in their concrete circumstances.

Perhaps the importance of the contrast between wants and needs might be illustrated via a consideration of options in the self-interpretation of contemporary feminism. Feminism, it seems clear, is both a symptom of and a response to the dissatisfied society. Certain generalized expectations about the capacity of private individuals to choose their own futures come up against the conventional limits ascribed to gendered personalities and their contexts. As long as this dissatisfaction is dealt with in the mode of wants, feminism limits its image of liberation to the choice between available expectations. According to Heller and Feher's critique, this means that a newly self-choosing femininity will actually find itself again trapped by externally imposed descriptions. It also means that the project of self-determination is inflected with descriptions of capacities imported through the ideal of the rational, self-governing individual. Therapy culture has, we have seen, attempted to fill these out by means of certain approved psychological codes—resilience, self-affirmation, self-esteem and the like. Still gripped by the imperatives of the dissatisfied society, feminism has continued to assert itself as a need for self-determination. This ongoing need has partly been felt as an endless discussion about those potentials in gendered experiences and ways of doing things that ought to be developed in chosen futures.

Illouz has several times stressed the common ground between a feminist and a therapeutic interest in the pursuit of a self-determining autonomy. It seems that both insist on the rational, self-chosen life and each seeks to reconstruct liberal borders between the private and the public that have held scrutinizing interventions at bay. However, this proposed identification underplays the importance of its curing intentions in limiting the way in which therapy culture is able to think about the task of a rationally autonomous individuality. As Furedi points out, for the therapeutic imperative "[f]eeling good becomes an end in itself" (2004, p. 73). The job is done so long as the individual feels satisfied that he or she has been equipped with the bundle of competencies required by the rational self-chooser. This shortfall in the way in which therapy culture understands the ideal of autonomy, which is about feeling good and in charge (not weighing things up for oneself) is what Barbara Ehrenreich (2009) is on about in her recent book *Smile or Die: How Positive Thinking Fooled America and the World.*

Heller and Feher do not, it needs to be said, collude with a liberal disdain for the need for "crutches" that might help us to reduce the complexity of living in the dissatisfied society. They also acknowledge that the commitment to a rationally self-determining life faces many blockages. This attitude can falter before the seeming intractability of circumstance and the preset choices described by a consumer culture offer easy seductions. The blockages might even be a result of our own pathological reactions to circumstance. Therapy culture, as Katie Wright (2008, p. 332) stresses, has played an important role in legitimating the public expression of private pain and, in this way, has helped to make "the speaking of the hitherto unspeakable" possible. However, the point also needs to be made that, as long as the therapeutic model is allowed to set the communicative pathways through which private needs seek public recognition, the vital deliberative aspect of our freedom, in which we strive to reflect upon those aspects of our privacy that might be enriched and supported by an exploration of their generalized significance, is jeopardized.

So far I have argued that therapy culture sets up an interpretive grid that reduces the aspiration to rational autonomy to bundles of competencies. However, the point has also been made that, only interested in stemming debilitating dissatisfactions, therapy culture does not offer itself as advocate to any particular ways of thinking about our private freedoms. Sometimes it positions itself not as the champion to the rationally self-governed personality but as friend to the struggling "inner voice" of an authentic self. Again I want to draw upon a "counting the costs" approach to reflect upon the ways in which the therapeutic diminishes the potentials of any value that it appropriates.

Charles Taylor's (1992) *The Ethics of Authenticity* allows us to backlight limitations of the version that has been appropriated by therapy culture. Observing that an ethic of authenticity is "something relatively new and peculiar to modern culture," Taylor points out that "authenticity" made its appearance in the eighteenth century as the historically new persuasion that each person is endowed with "a moral sense, an intuitive feeling for what is right and wrong" (1992, pp. 25–6). This was a displacement of earlier moral authority that referred only to publicly available powers for the determination of right ways of living and acting. From now on the individual's inner subjective voice would have to be consulted. Taylor's description of the cultural territory occupied by a modern ethics of authenticity reflects upon the intersection of two major ways of thinking. In the first instance, the reference to the claims of a subjective depth builds upon the priority granted to the self-responsibility of each individual by the "individualism of disengaged rationality, pioneered by Descartes" (Taylor, 1992, p. 26). However, authenticity is also "a child of the Romantic period, which was critical of a disengaged rationality and of an atomism that didn't recognize the ties of community" (Taylor, 1992, p. 25). We have seen that some episodes of therapy culture have taken up the ideal of authenticity as part of its struggle against the claim of a disengaged, instrumentalizing reason. In this sense, it has placed itself within what commentators like Taylor and Lionel Trilling (1972) have identified as authenticity's "subjective turn." They want to show that this attempt to reduce authenticity to a mere appeal to the legitimating power of each individual's "inner voice" drastically reduces its complexity and creative importance. It seems that we need to review the one-sided narrative that has tended to construct our thinking about an ethics of authenticity.

Maeve Cooke reflects on the ideal of authenticity as a bid to confer categorical power on an "inner voice" that claims the authority of a natural moral order. To her, authenticity remains deeply contaminated by its appeal to "natural" moral grounds "with which it has been intimately bound up from the beginning" (Cooke, 1997, p. 265). However, this seems to reduce the complexity of the ideal. The modern appeal to an ethics of authenticity did not just register an ongoing faith in the moral authority of nature. Actually, it signified the effort that must now be made in a historicizing and individualizing age to reassert secure moral guidance for action. As a relativizing modern imperative became ever more insistent, the assurance of a moral floor set by nature seemed to carry ever less weight. Released from a supporting naturalizing ideology, the categorical force of the appeal to the authentic imposed itself on the contemporary individual as imperative to follow one's own lights (whatever they may be). As Irving Singer (2009) reminds us, the strident injunctions that took off in the 1960s and 70s to "do our own thing" could be felt as a burden, not just as a call to liberation. Here again a hoped for ready-made freedom came up against a lack of supporting resources to produce an existentially dissatisfied individual (Zaretsky, this volume, Chapter 10). Rieff, Adorno and others identified this as the fertile grounds for the appearance of a therapy industry armed with its reassuring "jargon of authenticity" (Adorno, 1972). The critics hated the sacrifice of individuality that, as they saw it, would swamp a merely feeling self. "Without judgment," Adorno tells us, an ethics of authenticity "hands down the judgment of tradition" (1972, p. 44).

Rather than turning our backs on the idea of authenticity, it seems more appropriate to try and redeem it from limited interpretations. Trilling (1972, pp. 76–7) reflects upon the creative cultural potentials of a dialectical, as opposed to subjectivist, understanding of authenticity. As he sees it, authenticity is not best understood as a defensive proclamation by a feeling subjectivity. Trilling supposes rather that the significance that the authentic "inner voice" claims for itself opens the self to dialogue with others. Taylor is on the same track when he tells us that the ideal of authenticity requires "openness to horizons of significance for otherwise the creation loses the background that can save it from insignificance" (1992, p. 66). Even the tortured Rousseau realized that the authentic self could not just secure its moral authority by an appeal to nature. Trilling and Taylor suggest, then, that a dialectical understanding of authenticity grasps the creative potentials of a subjective "truth" as it seeks to elaborate its significance within a world of already established values. Illouz cuts this potential short when she identifies the longing for authenticity with the entrapment of the self in the sterility of the "self-generated fantasy." Far from contesting the limits of rationalizing therapeutic imperatives, this account of the authentic seems to confirm therapy's hold as it responds to its offer of an effective communicative channel.

8.3. Conclusion

Taylor encourages us to reclaim a dialectical account of the authentic life. We ought, he says, "to be trying to lift the culture back up closer to its motivating ideal" (Taylor, 1992, p. 73). He means this as a practically important goal that would allow us to better appreciate the scope for creative action that is opened up when we seek to get the best out of descriptions of our freedoms. The healing imperatives that a culturally dominant therapeutic model brings forward from the clinic shift this center of interest. Because the therapeutic demands that ideals must be resolvable into descriptions of techniques and skills for realizing them, it remains uninterested in setting them up in terms that permit us to reflect upon new possibilities. There can be no question that therapy can help to rebuild damaged existential capacities to enable us to move forward with fashioning rationally autonomous and authentically meaningful lives. However, we also need to be mindful that the therapeutic framework serves to diminish the creative potentials of the value ideals that it appropriates.

Therapy culture has appropriated the ideals of rational autonomy and authentic individuality to descriptions of certain types of psychological techniques and competencies. We have seen that this re-construction misses out on the ways in which the pursuit of these freedoms can set the individual on the path to creative explorations of the significance of his/her contexts. So, while the therapeutic might set itself up as a challenge to a liberal construction of rigid private/public boundaries, actually its interpretation of how private freedoms might be produced appears to confirm these impervious borders. At the same time, the lack of a dialectical understanding of the self and its context that reappears within therapeutic appropriations constructs artificial boundaries between the ideals of a self-determining autonomy and authentic subjectivity and this diminishes the cultural power of both.

References

Adorno, T. W. (1972), *The Jargon of Authenticity* (Evanston: Northwestern University Press).

Coetzee, J. M. (1999), *Disgrace* (London: Seeker and Warburg).

Cooke, M. (1997), "Authenticity and Autonomy: Taylor, Habermas, and the Politics of Recognition," *Political Theory*, vol. 25, no. 2, 258–89.

Ehrenreich, B. (2009), *Smile or Die: How Positive Thinking Fooled America and the World* (London: Granta).

Foucault, M. (2006), *Psychiatric Power: Lectures at the College de France 1973–1974* (Basingstoke and New York: Palgrave Macmillan).

Foucault, M. (2008), *The Birth of Biopolitics; Lectures at the College de France 1978–1979* (Basingstoke and New York: Palgrave Macmillan).

Furedi, F. (2004), *Therapy Culture: Cultivating Vulnerability in an Uncertain Age* (London & New York: Routledge).

Giddens, A. (1992), *The Transformation of Intimacy: Sexuality, Love and Eroticism in Modern Societies* (Stanford: Stanford University Press).
Heller, A. and F. Feher (1988), "On Being Satisfied in the Dissatisfied Society," in A. Heller and F. Feher, *The Postmodern Political Condition* (Cambridge: Polity), 300–16.
Horkheimer, M. and T. W. Adorno (2002), *Dialectic of Enlightenment: Philosophical Fragments* (Stanford: Stanford University Press).
Illouz, E. (1997), *Consuming the Romantic Utopia: Love and the Cultural Contradictions of Capitalism* (Berkeley: University of California Press).
Illouz, E. (2007), *Cold Intimacies: The Making of Emotional Capitalism* (Cambridge: Polity).
Illouz, E. (2008), *Saving the Modern Soul: Therapy Emotions and the Culture of Self Help* (Berkeley: University of California Press).
Mestrovic, S. G. (1997), *Postemotional Society* (London: Sage).
Moskowitz, E. S. (2001), *In Therapy We Trust: America's Obsession with Self-Fulfillment* (Baltimore and London: The John Hopkins University Press).
Lasch, C. (1977), *Haven in a Heartless World: The Family Besieged* (New York: Basic Books).
Rieff, P. (1996), *The Triumph of the Therapeutic (*New York: Harper and Row).
Rose, N. (1990), *Governing the Modern Soul: The Shaping of the Private Self* (London and New York: Routledge).
Rössler, B. (2005), *The Value of Privacy* (Cambridge: Polity Press).
Sennett, R. (1974), *The Fall of Public Man* (New York: Norton).
Singer, I. (2009), *Philosophy of Love: A Partial Summing Up* (Cambridge: MIT Press).
Taylor, C. (1992), *The Ethics of Authenticity* (Cambridge & London: Harvard University Press).
Trilling, L. (1972), *Sincerity and Authenticity* (London: Oxford University Press).
Wright, K. (2008), "Theorizing Therapeutic Culture: Past Influences, Future Directions," *Journal of Sociology*, vol. 44, no. 4, 321–36.

9

Privacy and Work

Norbert Ebert

The purpose of this chapter is to reflect on the relationship between work and privacy in late modern societies. Work holds an obscure position when it comes to distinguishing between the private and the public spheres. On the one hand, with the rise of modernity, work helps to define how we see ourselves and the way in which we live. Questions of income, qualifications and lifestyle have become indispensable reference points for identity based on work. On the other hand, while the sphere of work readily lends itself to establishing personal markers for identity in the private sphere, it plays an equally important role in the definition and maintenance of the public sphere, economically as well as politically. Baldly put, work is messy and seeps through each and every facet of our lives. Depending on the perspective we choose, work cannot be located within either the public or the private sphere alone. It has no clear boundaries and probably never had, and yet, maybe because of its fluidity, it still allows us insights into certain aspects of privacy today.

Individualization in particular brings the permeability of the demarcations between the private and public aspects of work to the fore. People are troubled about how to keep work and private lives separate, while, at the same time, the way that work engages energies and capacities nursed in the private sphere seemingly goes unnoticed. My argument is that private life, with all its creative subjectivity and affective charge, is becoming a resource for work under late modern conditions. In particular, the popular management literature conflates privacy and work; I will briefly suggest an example of this later in this chapter. The key question, however, is not whether privacy and work should be kept separate. As with most aspects of late modern life, they cannot be strictly separated. Rather the key question is: how do individuals' private capacities and abilities unwittingly become a resource for furthering economic success in the sphere of work, and how does this, in turn, shape individuals themselves?

The emergence of a public and a private sphere in the forms that are familiar to us today is the result of processes of differentiation. And, while a definition of each of these spheres goes beyond the scope of this chapter, it should be said that the distinction is largely only sharply brought into focus as an analytic device. In everyday life these boundaries are never clear-cut. So one of the tasks we have in hand when discussing modern types of privacy is tracing this everyday fluidity.

The term privacy can have many meanings. For this chapter, I suggest the following working definition: among other aspects, what constitutes an individual's privacy is the capacity to be reflective, to think and act autonomously and independently, and to communicate some of the results of these processes to others only if desired. While this is not meant to be an all-encompassing definition of privacy, I contend that these individual capacities and qualities are some of its defining features. From this follows the equally basic assumption that the public sphere starts at the point at which an individual's articulations and reflections enter public discussion.[1]

9.1. Conflating work and privacy

It is hard to say exactly where work now fits in the private and public spheres, though Burkart makes the important point that their development stands in direct relation to the sphere of work: "The beginning of the separation between the private and the public spheres is marked by the separation between household and economy" (this volume, Chapter 2). In pre-modern societies work and home overlapped strongly, and it was their later separation that led to the establishment of a more emotionally constituted private sphere incorporating a stronger sense of self, together with a more rational economic and political public sphere (see Burkhart, this volume, Chapter 2). With industrialization and the rise of modernity, work and home became separated and with that separation the private and the public sphere became increasingly distinct, while, at least in terms of the functions of production and consumption, these spheres were also becoming interdependent.

Analytically, at least, it is possible to draw a neat differentiation between the norms and expectations that govern work, the private, the public and the self. These boundaries only become messy once we acknowledge that according to these differentiations the value of work has switched from being negative or marginal to an omnipresent measure of everything. Moreover, work seeps through all aspects of life whether private, public, individual, economic or political and renders permeable the everyday boundaries between them. The centrality of work across all spheres on the one hand underlines that its meaning and significance has been universalized. On the other, we seem to be in danger of losing that realm of everyday life that was free from work.

While in antiquity people wanted to be free *from* work, nowadays we seek to free ourselves *through* work, as a means for self-realization. What this means is that every aspect of our daily lives is defined by a particular work ethic. The essence of this is the nexus between achievement and time (productivity), a nexus that explains the universality in every context of the term work. We work to make a living; we work on our selves; we work on relationships; we work on our bodies in gyms; we do housework and most leisure activities have to measure up in contrast to work. Today we are to work at everything, constantly weighing up inputs and outputs. Every cultural, emotional or social endeavor has to be able to "pay off" in order to claim any motivational force. It is easy to see how this utilitarian process of quantification and rationalization works in relation to material production processes. Everything is subject to calculability, measurement and control; to rationalization. Work itself becomes the principle through which individuals rationalize their own behavior (work ethic) against the dimensions of time and achievement, or what I refer to as self-rationalization.

Nowadays we have a nexus not only between time and achievement, but also between time, norms and the self. We no longer experience work simply as the expenditure of mechanical abilities as did the laborers in Adam Smith's pin factory, producing as many pins as possible on the basis of an optimized division of labor (1952, p. 3). We are now, more than ever, emotional as well as psychological workers. The private self, too, must be available to rationalization.

I want to distill three main points from this brief discussion of the changing relationship between privacy and work. First, in pre-modern societies, while a private and a public sphere existed, there was also a crucial overlap between domestic life and work. Because of the changing nature and value of work, the boundaries of the public and private have also shifted. The private is defined in economic, the public more in political terms. Second, the modern separation between home and work establishes the private and public spheres in a different way. Both spheres are dependent on economic prosperity but, more importantly, the political public sphere is intertwined with the economy with all the distortive potentials that this can bring (Habermas, 1979). The private sphere is now characterized by a much stronger sense of selfhood and individuality. Third, and most importantly, despite all the differentiations and functional interdependencies between public and private, home and work, the qualities and capacities of the self at the core of privacy, as well as work, are today completely intertwined. It appears as though most aspects of late modern life drift apart and become fragmented and subsequently a matter of private choice (an example being religion), whereas privacy and work seem to work hand in glove with one another and lose whatever boundaries they had. This obscuring of differentiation between various spheres on the one hand, and the reunification of privacy and work on the other, is experienced as a new kind of complexity and confusion which individuals have to sort through for themselves. Is (un)employment, for example, a social or an individual responsibility? With demands from workplaces, government institutions or service providers to find private solutions to complex problems, the capacities and the qualities of the self are increasingly the only resource that individuals can call upon in their efforts to stay afloat. This call upon the resourceful self is particularly evident in the workplace but is encountered everywhere as we endeavor to manage our way through the demands of late modernity. Privacy becomes a resource to cope with the complexity of life and the individual becomes what Beck and Beck-Gernsheim describe as the "basic unit of social reproduction" (2002, p. xxii). Why individuals have become the basic unit of social reproduction and what that means for their privacy is the focal point of the next section.

9.2. Hyper-differentiation

I contend that late modern societies are hyper-differentiated and as a consequence our sense of privacy is narrowed. Individuals are not only left to deal with a hyper-differentiated environment by themselves but they are left with only their private capacities and qualities as their only resources. I approach the topic of hyper-differentiation from two angles and with the aid of Habermas' distinction between, lifeworlds and systems.[2] What drives the processes of differentiation for Habermas, what he calls the "uncoupling of systems and lifeworlds," is communicative action (1987, pp. 153, 137). Although the lifeworld is not exactly the same as the private sphere, it is fair to say that communicative action belongs more to the private sphere and in political terms more to the public sphere than to the economy.[3] The private realm, the abode of our reflective capacities, might be the underpinning for communicative action, that is, the articulation of our thoughts, feelings or ideas. I will deal with this in more detail when I discuss privacy further in the next section.

The lifeworld resembles a "social cookbook," offering recipes for everyday life situations, ranging from how to respectfully greet people to how to dress appropriately for a wedding reception. It operates as a stock or reservoir of taken-for-granted knowledge, which is basically unproblematic, but can always be communicatively problematized and potentially re-negotiated (Habermas, 1987, p. 124). Habermas refers to this normative negotiation process as the rationalization of the lifeworld. The recipes in the "social cookbook" can be refined and certain ingredients may be added or removed. However, we can also overburden our capacity to process normative questions. As a result of successive processes of rationalization, the lifeworld gains a level of complexity that finally results in communicative overload, where language is partly replaced by steering media such as money and power (Habermas, 1987, p. 155).

Of course money and credit cards offer systemic shortcuts and make life manageable, and yet, late modern life is hyper-differentiated. Facilitation by systems paradoxically means that there are too many choices to be made, too many issues to be negotiated and too much complexity to be dealt with in our daily lives. This can range from insurance claims to applications for residential parking permits, to shopping around for an affordable overseas flight, to juggling childcare and full-time employment, to trying to be politically informed, to getting legal advice on a prenuptial agreement, and so on. Managing our lives has become a time-consuming and busy affair.

Complexity is also one of Niklas Luhmann's main concerns: "The function of social systems is to capture and reduce complexity. They help to mediate between the external complexity of the world and the anthropologically very restricted ability of human beings to consciously process experiences" (1974, p. 116, my translation).[4] But why is complexity on the rise for individuals when systems are supposed to reduce it? Why are our lives filled with more and more tasks on a bureaucratic or organizational level? The problem is, as Habermas points out, that reducing complexity through one system increases the complexity for other systems. One of the reasons, for example, why self-help and popular management literature is in high demand, is that managerialism transfers complexity from the economic sphere into the private sphere.[5] Hence, reducing complexity in the one increases it in the other (Schimank, 1996, p. 138). Without going into greater detail, the core notion of hyper-differentiation for both systems and lifeworlds is that differentiation leads to further differentiation, resulting in hyper-differentiation. This is yet another cause of the omnipresence of work. Reducing complexity in a corporation is the role of management. Working hard in order to reduce work as a manager actually generates more work for individual workers, since they have to engage with the complexity being pushed their way. Systemic processes force the individual to react, cope or conform in a particular way. In such an arrangement, the dialectic between individual and society tends to become a one-way-street. The off-loading of systemic complexities on to individuals blocks opportunities and channels for personal autonomy or solitude and reflexivity, hindering us from articulating what we might genuinely like or dislike.

The important implication of this is that as complexities grow, so does the pressure to manage them individually. Hence, modern privacy is, to a large degree, embedded in a hyper-differentiated context. In particular, the overkill of systemic imperatives and demands that descends upon late modern individuals engages the self to such a degree that it narrows and devalues the sense of privacy until it becomes a mere capacity for systemic problem solving rather than providing a genuine sense of self based on solitude or reflection (see Markus, this volume, Chapter 6).

9.3. Individualization

Hyper-differentiation is one of the reasons why the personal capacities of private individuals have become the basic resource for social reproduction. Processes of differentiation, however, seem to go hand in hand with processes of individualization (Honneth, 2004, p. 463–4). Ulrich Beck defines individualization as:

> The compulsion to lead your own life, and the possibility of doing it, [which] emerge when a society is highly differentiated ... Constantly changing between different, partly incompatible logics of action, they [individuals] are forced to take into their hands that which is in danger of breaking into pieces: their own lives.
>
> (2000, p. 165)

Individualization emerges as a compulsion and a requirement to manage hyper-differentiated life privately rather than publicly.

The most significant development for individuals in contemporary society, however, is not that institutional or more collective reference points become eroded, rather that they are replaced with a general expectation of privately rationalizing one's own life in response to given options. Status and lifestyle are less based on ascription and more on the aforementioned nexus between achievement or merit and time. This liberation underpins the shift from freedom *from* work to freedom *through* work. The freedom to achieve an identity through work is an individual freedom and thus offers the chance of working on one's own performances. Here we can refer to Weber who tells us that individualization emerges as a normatively triggered "inner rationalization" (see also Adorno, 1993, p. 75; Brubaker, 1984, p. 24), or self-rationalization "based on constant self-scrutiny and methodical self-control" (Brubaker, 1984, p. 9). Systemic requirements like, for example, flexibility as a criterion for employability, underpins this process. Hence, individualization in late modernity is the result of liberating as well as coercive processes. It can, therefore, be defined as an individual negotiation process between all the spheres, that is, between work and home, public and private, system and lifeworld. But the question is: how do individuals negotiate and how does it involve their privacy? What do we rationalize when we rationalize our selves? And how does privacy become a resource?

9.4. Late modern privacy

My working definition of the term privacy so far has been the ability to reflect, articulate and communicate independently and autonomously. Based on this preliminary understanding of privacy, it is up to individuals to decide what they want to be publicly known or not. These are the abilities that allow the individual to be the basic resource for social reproduction. What are they and how can we define privacy in more detail? I will briefly look at reflexivity, personal autonomy and the ability to articulate one's needs as examples of core aspects of modern privacy.

The first defining aspect of privacy is reflexivity. Mead, for example, has described reflexivity as "the turning-back of the experience of the individual upon himself" (1956, p. 211). For Giddens (1991, p. 145), it is this concept of the self, as an internal reference point, that lies at the heart of the "reflexive project of the self." Hence, reflexivity refers to the capacity to step back and process information reflectively, not only about oneself, but also about the social environment. As reflections are (at least in the first instance) private, reflexivity can be regarded as a defining feature of personal life. We listen to advertisements, news reports, our bosses and colleagues and politicians, we communicate with strangers, friends and partners on a daily basis or read books and newspaper articles. We immediately deal with the information presented to us. We take some things on board, keep thinking about them or even trace them to get further information or keep them as a discussion point. Other pieces of information we might forget straight away, or decide that the information presented to us is hot gossip, corporate gibberish or even, Orwellian newspeak. And while we might hope to think along those lines, the reflective capacities come under duress in hyper-differentiated circumstances where individuals are supposed to handle an abundance of ambivalent information. This may lead them to react *reflexively* rather than reflectively, that is, to think strategically about what it takes to stay in a job, to gain political votes or to maximize profits, and so forth. We might quietly think the opposite but are not given the opportunity to express these thoughts publicly.

The second characteristic of privacy that I would like to call attention to is personal autonomy (see also Glass, this volume, Chapter 4), and I do so with the aid of Habermas' concept of individuation. Individuation is connected to socialization, which for Habermas refers to the learning of culture, of how things are done in society. The crucial point for Habermas is that the self not only internalizes everyday rules but also matures and learns to reflect on them. Personal autonomy, therefore, is closely linked to reflexivity. This process of maturation, during which the self acquires the ability to think independently and to engage reflectively, pervades Habermas' conceptualization of individuation, or individuals' growing personal autonomy and independence (Habermas, 1976, p. 74).

The third defining feature of privacy, also closely linked to reflexivity and personal autonomy, is communicative competence, which refers to the ability to interpret, debate and contest a society's taken-for-granted norms and rules and draws upon private reflections on the learned culture. This communicative capacity is highly dependent on contexts that both permit the expression of private viewpoints and needs and support efforts to find the grounds of shared understandings. Available at least in principle via the institutional norms of liberal democracies, these required contexts for communicative interactions are less evident in the expectations and modus operandi at the micro levels of social organization. Democratic, communicative interactions can get little hold, for example, in corporate contexts that are structured around power imbalances between boss and employee. By no means a given, personal autonomy can only be achieved in dialogic contexts and entails practical opportunities "to give one's own needs their due in these communicative structures" (Habermas, 1976, p. 78). The autonomy to seek recognition for priorities, to articulate needs, together with the power to remain silent, are the heartland ideals of modern privacy.

Individualization, therefore, is not only a reaction to hyper-differentiation, which leaves individuals no capacity for effective choice. It also refers to our, not yet extinguished, reflective, communicative and autonomous qualities and to (everywhere under threat but surviving nonetheless) capacities to negotiate the social order in which we live. In this sense, individualization refers to processes of active self-fashioning registered as we express needs, wishes, desires, criticisms, comments and opinions, but also as we confirm, contest or challenge existing value descriptions (including, the value of work). Private autonomy is about individuals using these capacities as resources; not only to make functional decisions, but also to shape the society they live in. However, under conditions of hyper-differentiation all this potential languishes. Individuals, we have seen, are required to call upon their private qualities as a resource to coordinate and manage the divides between systems and lifeworlds, the public and the private, home and work. While individuals might develop the competencies to freely articulate their needs, wills and opinions, these energies have to be supported by facilitating social contexts if they are to inform practical aspirations for the self-determined life. As Habermas writes: "[A]n autonomous ego and an emancipated society reciprocally require one another" (1976, p. 71). Individuals, therefore, need privacy, a private sphere in which they can autonomously and critically assess the existing normative infrastructure. And they need an emancipated public sphere in which norms and values are open to discursive scrutiny and review. It is this interdependence that sets the value of privacy along the path of reflexivity, personal autonomy and communication. We have no hope of moving down this track and grasping our potentials for autonomy though unless we first face up to realities about the effective recruitment of our aspirations to private autonomy within the contemporary corporate world.

9.5. *The Fish Philosophy*

Given the abundance of self-help books and popular management literature, one would think that "there is no excuse for remaining stuck in the swamp of negativity. A whole industry has grown up to promote positive thinking, and the product of this industry ... is called 'motivation'"

(Ehrenreich, 2009, p. 97). *Fish* (Lundin et al., 2000) is one of those products. On the basis of my above elaborations so far, this section will engage with the so-called *Fish Philosophy*. What I hope to demonstrate is the way that contemporary management ideologies unreflectively promote the conflation of privacy and work.

Fish is one of the most popular management self-help books.[6] The goal of *The Fish Philosophy* is to learn how to boost morale and improve operational results in a corporation or, as the authors put it in their dedication, "Enclosed are the keys to creating an innovative and accountable work environment where a playful, attentive, and engaging attitude leads to more energy, enthusiasm, productivity, and creativity" (p. 7).

The Fish Philosophy operates on the basis of a widespread assumption presented on the cover of the book: "Work made fun gets done." The more sophisticated version of this slogan is formulated in the book as follows: "*Fish!* Is a parable, an invented story about finding the deep source of energy, creativity, and passion that exists inside each of us by learning to love what we do, even if at the moment we may not be doing exactly what we love" (p. 11). *Fish* is not just a popular management book; it is "a fabulous love story." It promises nothing less than to enable us to "catch our limit of happiness, meaning and fulfillment every day" (pp. 9–10). The love story is based on the fact that "we should not settle for anything less than doing what we love" (p. 11), which translates into loving what we do. While the core of the book takes its cues from the selling of fish, *The Fish Philosophy* is meant to be applied to work cultures, relationships and fulfilling basic human needs, but in particular work situations.

There are at least two sides to this love story. First, we meet Mary Jane, the main character, who is a manager going through a difficult phase in her private life. At the end of the book she gets engaged to Lonnie who works on the Pike Fish market in Seattle. The remaining 85 pages of the book deal with a much more complicated relationship, namely our relationship with work. Mary Jane enjoys her work at First Guarantee until she is put in charge of what is referred to as the "third floor" or the "toxic energy dump" (pp. 20, 24). The third floor is full of people who are miserable and undedicated. Desperate to find a way of turning things around there, Mary Jane escapes from work over lunch to the Pike Fish market in order to reflect on the challenge at hand. At the markets she not only meets Lonnie, but encounters a work environment full of positive energy, enthusiastic people and fun. After she shares the story of the "toxic energy dump" with Lonnie, this "Fish Philosopher" introduces Mary Jane to management techniques that can be equally applied to single parenthood, difficulties with bosses or teams, all of which apply to Mary Jane's situation. From this interchange emerges the *Fish Philosophy*, four "ingredients" with the aid of which Mary Jane turns the toxic energy dump into an award winning workplace (p. 106).

Referring to my earlier discussion, we can say that *Fish* starts with what Habermas describes as "subjectively experienced, identity-threatening crises" (1987, p. 305) on two levels. Firstly, Mary Jane is going through a rough patch in her private life; secondly, the third floor and its operations are in a functional crisis. The concurrence of those two crises results in a compulsion to find biographical solutions to systemic problems. Mary Jane usually finds the solutions to her work problems on a Sunday afternoon at home in her "private time" (Lundin et al., 2000, p. 70), that is, in solitude where she has quiet time to reflect. This confirms that "self-reflexion and psychological self-thematization have become crucial even in the context of *work*" (Burkart, this volume, Chapter 2, original emphasis). The boundaries between work and privacy become blurred as reflecting on her own life leads her to reflect on work issues in her private space. Her lifeworld is filled with systemic problems for which she tries to find personal solutions. And yet, the more genuine questions—whether work needs to be fun or not, or why an individual has to take responsibility for systemic malfunctions—remain unaddressed. Her whole life situation, but in particular her workplace, require self-rationalization, that is, self-monitoring and self-scrutiny.

I will now briefly engage with the core of the *The Fish Philosophy* by addressing the four "secrets" it contains. The first secret is called *Choose your attitude* and follows a simple question: "Who do we want to be while we do our work?" The employees in the book even develop "an attitude menu," where each individual has the choice between "angry, disinterested and bitter" on the one hand, and "energetic, caring, vital, supportive, and creative" on the other. What lies at the core of "choose your attitude" are "personal accountability and proactivity" (Lundin et al., 2000, pp. 78, 99, 101).

While the choice is supposed to be up to the individual, the authors leave no doubt about what the correct choice is when they write:

> we hope the attitude you choose is to bring your best self to work and to love the work you do. We may not be able to do exactly what we love at the present time, but any of us can choose to love what we do. We can bring our best qualities to our work—it is our choice.

> If we can accomplish this one thing, our work area will become an oasis of energy, flexibility, and creativity in a tough industry.
>
> (Lundin et al., 2000, p. 99)

It is true that modern individuals have a lot of choices to make, as more traditional forms of ascription or status have declined in importance. And yet, as Johnson writes: "Rather than an exercise in self-determining autonomy, the attempt to fashion ourselves through choices between already determined goods comes to be experienced as an alienating external determination" (this volume, Chapter 8). A more genuine choice here would have to be based on a different kind of question, for example: Why are only things that are fun positive? Or who is actually flexible when management talks about flexibility? It is the individual that is supposed to be energetic, flexible and creative, not only for themselves, but for the company. The choice that individuals are asked to make here is to rationalize their own behavior, attitudes and thoughts and subjugate their private reflections and perhaps their skepticism in the interests of a smooth organizational process. Individual privacy thus becomes the instrumentalized resource for economic success, by "making emotional life central to the workplace" (Illouz, 2007, p. 16). This seems to be the opposite of what could be called a "self-governing individual" (see Johnson, this volume, Chapter 8). In the case of Mary Jane, "being a good manager increasingly meant displaying the attributes of a good psychologist" (Illouz, 2007, p. 15). On this basis, *The Fish Philosophy* is an attempt to tap into individuals' lifeworlds in order to secure managerial achievements.

The second secret, *Play*, aims to generate more fun and thus energy at work. "The fish guys have fun while they work, and fun is energizing" (Lundin et al., 2000, p. 78). More concretely, this refers to making the work environment more pleasant, including the use of colors and plants but also telling jokes and calling the workplace a playground. It is of course more pleasant to work in a relaxed atmosphere. Work and play, however, are not the same, and yet *Fish* merges them. Elements of the private sphere are imported into systemic environments in order to make individuals feel at home at work and thus increase productivity (see Ebert, 2001). The more serious normative question is once more avoided: Why bend over backwards to love something we dislike? Would it not make more sense to change the things we dislike rather than learning to love them? Play engages and encourages individuals to find private and personal solutions to complex systemic challenges.

Make their day (Lundin et al., 2000, p. 78) is the third secret, the point being how to engage customers, colleagues, friends, partners, children or basically anyone we deal with, and to shape this interaction into a lasting experience. The motivation behind this is no secret: "it is good for business" (p. 93). We could also say that genuine social interaction is exploited for business purposes. Once again, the individual becomes the basic resource for a successfully and smoothly operating organization. Relationships and conversations that belong in the private sphere with partners, friends and family members are at risk here of being instrumentalized for systemic reasons.

The final secret is *be present*, which refers to having a complete focus on work. "When you are present you show consideration for the other person." In more practical terms it means to "never again [...] read or answer emails while talking on the phone with a colleague or customer" (pp. 98–9). Every individual is encouraged to be as efficient as possible. This is, of course, highly ambiguous, as "being present" can mean different things. The suggestion here is to be present for whatever systemic requirements there are and to completely conflate privacy and work.

The Fish Philosophy culminates in the following statement:

> As you enter this place of work please choose to make today a great day. Your colleagues, customers, team members, and you yourself will be thankful. Find ways to play. We can be serious about our work without being serious about ourselves. Stay focused in order to be present when your customers and team members most need you. And should you feel your energy lapsing, try this surefire remedy: Find someone who needs a helping hand, a word of support, or a good ear—and make their day.
>
> (Lundin et al., 2000, p. 107)

9.6. Conclusion

At the end of my reflections on the relationship between privacy and work, I would like to underline four main points. Firstly, work and privacy are conflated in late modern work societies. However, this conflation is built on an ambiguity: on the differentiation of the various aspects of society on the one hand, and the unification of privacy and work on the other. Secondly, in a hyper-differentiated social order, individuals are left to fend for themselves and do so calling on their own capacities and qualities. In that sense privacy has come to be understood more narrowly as an individual resource. This narrowed sense of privacy, thirdly, ties in with processes of individualization. Hence, when we describe late modern societies as individualized, we also mean a narrowed sense of privacy. Finally, I have tried to highlight some of the defining aspects of privacy in reference to reflexivity, personal autonomy and communication.

We have to keep in mind that *Fish* is a fictitious story and as such we must not take it too seriously. However, an enthusiastic reception suggests that popular management principles and assumptions resonate with contemporary needs. The popularity of a book like *Fish* may well be based on people feeling overwhelmed by the value we put on work and the hyper-differentiation of the late modern world. Yet it also suggests that the capacity to reflect in solitude as one aspect of privacy has been devalued (see Markus, this volume, Chapter 6). Thus, under conditions of hyper-differentiation and individualization, privacy increasingly becomes a resource for the negotiation of the public and the private sphere, the systems and the lifeworlds and home and work. In order to do so, individuals have to self-rationalize, self-monitor and self-scrutinize their behavior.

To be sure, this discussion of privacy and work is not intended to identify pathologies in individuals' abilities to be ever more individualistic rational actors. The potential pathologies that I have talked about in this chapter are *social* pathologies that have their origins in inadequate opportunities for individuals to express and articulate the results of their thinking and feeling without having to amalgamate privacy and work.

Notes

1. For more detailed accounts of the public sphere in the Habermasian sense, see Habermas (1989); Calhoun (1992); and Johnson (2006).
2. Like individual and society, work and home, or public and private, systems and lifeworlds are distinct but not separate. I am aware that the public and the private cannot be equated exactly with Habermas' systems and lifeworlds, but find it a useful distinction for my discussion.
3. Strictly speaking the political sphere is both systemic and communicative. Parliament and elections are characterized by communicative action, whereas government bureaucracies are characterized by instrumental or systemic action.
4. "Soziale Systeme haben die Funktion der Erfassung und Reduktion von Komplexität. Sie dienen der Vermittlung zwischen der äußeren Komplexität der Welt und der sehr geringen, aus anthropologischen Gründen kaum veränderbaren Fähigkeit des Menschen zu bewusster Erlebnisverarbeitung."
5. Economists refer to this as the externalization of transaction costs. Other examples are computers and digitalization. I am not convinced that computers,

the Internet or digitalization make work or life easier or reduce work. While the access to information through the Internet is certainly better and more widespread, the amount of information to sift through may be overwhelming.

6. *Fish* was originally published as a movie and has by now developed into a multifaceted approach with various tools and resources. For more information see http://www.charthouse.com/content.aspx?name=home2

References

Adorno, T. W. (1993), *Einleitung in die Soziologie* (Frankfurt: Suhrkamp).

Beck, U. (2000), "Living Your Own Life in a Runaway World: Individualisation, Globalisation and Politics," in W. Hutton And A. Giddens (eds), *On the Edge. Living with Global Capitalism* (London: Jonathan Cape), 164–74.

Beck, U. and Beck-Gernsheim, E. (2002), "Authors' Preface: Institutionalized individualism," in U. Beck and E. Beck-Gernsheim (eds), *Individualization: Institutional Individualism and its Social and Political Consequences* (London: Sage), xx–xxv.

Brubaker, R. (1984), *The Limits of Rationality. An Essay on the Social and Moral Thought of Max Weber* (Boston: George Allen & Unwin).

Calhoun C. (1992), *Habermas and the Public Sphere* (Cambridge: MIT Press).

Ebert, N. (2001), "Vom Produktdesign zum sozialen Design. Bürolandschaft und Erfolgsfaktor Mensch," *Frankfurter Arbeitspapierezur gesellschaftsethischen und sozialwissenschaftlichen Forschung*, vol. 27, 76–95.

Ehrenreich, B. (2009), *Smile or Die. How Positive Thinking Fooled America and the World* (London: Granta Publications).

Giddens, A. (1991), *Modernity and Self-Identity: Self and Society in the Late Modern Age* (Oxford: Polity).

Habermas, J. (1976), "Moral Development and Ego Identity," in J. Habermas, *Communication and the Evolution of Society* (Boston: Beacon Press), 69–94.

Habermas, J. (1979), "Legitimation Problems in the Modern State," in *Communication and the Evolution of Society* (Boston: Beacon Press), 178–205.

Habermas, J. (1987), *The Theory of Communicative Action. Vol. 2: Lifeworld and System: A Critique of Functionalist Reason* (Boston: Beacon Press).

Habermas J. (1989), *The Structural Transformation of the Public Sphere* (Cambridge: Polity Press).

Honneth, A. (2004), "Organized Self-Realization. Some Paradoxes of Individualization," *European Journal of Social Theory*, vol. 7, no. 4, 463–78.

Illouz, E. (2007), *Cold Intimacies: The Making of Emotional Capitalism* (Cambridge: Polity Press).

Johnson P. (2006), *Habermas. Rescuing the Public Sphere* (London: Routledge).

Luhmann, N. (1974), "Soziologie als Theorie sozialer Systeme," *Soziologische Aufklärung Vol. 1*, (Opladen: Westdeutscher Verlag), 113–36.

Lundin, C. S., H. Paul, and J. Christensen (2000) *Fish* (London: Hodder & Stoughton).

Mead, G. H. (1956), *The Social Psychology of George Herbert Mead* (Chicago: The University of Chicago Press).

Schimank, U. (1996), *Theorien gesellschaftlicher Differenzierung* (Opladen: Leske & Budrich).

Smith, A. (1952), *An Inquiry Into the Nature and Causes of the Wealth of Nations* (Chicago: William Benton).

10
Narcissism and the Emergence of the Network Society

Eli Zaretsky

10.1. Introduction: The paradox of narcissism

A life lived in public, it has been said, is a superficial one. If so, then the psychoanalytic claim to depth is well founded. Not only was psychoanalysis a theory of the private world—that is of personal life—it also took place in private. Psychoanalysis revolved around secrets, not exploits, confidentiality was its highest professional value, and one could give no higher testimony to the success of psychoanalysis than to say that it had been forgotten. Given all this, no subject better exemplified the privileged status that private interior space occupied in psychoanalysis than its attitude toward narcissism.

The narcissist, according to the Greek myth, fell in love with his own image. Captivated by the shallow, timeless space of the mirror, he eschewed depth. Loving only himself he did not engage with others. Caught up in an image, he lacked language and therefore had no access to sociality. A psychoanalyst might sum it up thus: lacking an inner world, the narcissist was unable to connect with others. True, there are few passages in Freud more lyrical, even rhapsodic, than those in which he describes the innocence, radiance and self-contentment of "His Majesty, the Baby." But the glory of infancy rests on its transience. Thus, for Freud, narcissism is a *stage* that has to be overcome. When it persists, it signals the absence of the relationship that made analysis possible. Overall, then, classical psychoanalysis effectively defined itself *against* narcissism, that is against that inaccessible residue of an archaic imago of plenitude and perfection.

The psychoanalytic association of narcissism with superficiality and publicity was the flip side of its association of depth with interiority. In classical psychoanalysis whatever went on *between* individuals was mediated by a third, inward dimension that unfolded *within* each of them. This depth or unconscious dimension intruded on the interpersonal plane, especially in the form of transference, enriching it, complicating it, suffusing our relations with mystery, warmth and intensity. The narcissist, by contrast, operated only on the superficial, interpersonal plane, without any access to either his own or another's interiority, and therefore without genuine reciprocity or recognition. Whereas psychoanalysis sought to foster interpersonal communication that included a self-reflective moment, the narcissistic emphasis on appearing, rather than communicating, lent itself to instrumental and impersonal relationships of the sort later termed "networking."

Far from being confined to the psychology of interpersonal relations, the psychoanalytic denigration of narcissism applied also to the psychology of groups. A social democrat living in "Red Vienna"—whose government not only befriended analysis, but also prided itself on balancing the interests of many separate ethnic and national interests—Freud was critical of groups based on exclusive identities. In his view, the narcissistic basis of such groups lay in the mechanism of *identification*: the same skin color, the same national or ethnic origin, the same "book," such as Marx's writings, or the same charismatic leader, such as Mussolini or Hitler. As in the case of narcissistic interpersonal relations, groups based on such identifications evacuated the inner or depth dimension. Suturing the tension between the ego, on the one hand, and the superego, on the other, the group's aggression was projected outward while its internal self-esteem rose.

Finally, the analyst's negative attitude toward narcissism was linked to Freud's skepticism concerning the ability of visual images to communicate interiority. Freud's skepticism drew on two related sources. First, although psychoanalysis was born out of nineteenth-century empirical medicine, with its emphasis on close observation, its deeper roots lay in German idealism, with its insistence that the contents of the mind are conceptual and not simply empirical. In addition, the Hebrew Bible influenced Freud through its prohibition on "graven" images. Whereas Freud's teacher, Charcot, drew and photographed his patients, compiling visual atlases of hysterical postures, and limning cartographies of mental illness, Freud insisted that his patients speak to him in order to open their inner worlds. Although its original subject was dreams, Freud founded psychoanalysis on the translation of iconic dream-images into words by *associating* to them, a process that led him downward into the unconscious. Like Moses, his later subject, Freud instituted a *Bilderverbot* aimed at accessing inner depths: "No images allowed here, only verbal associations," ultimately leading to a narrative. Associating images with immediacy, identity and unmediated wish-fulfillment, Freud followed Gustave Le Bon, the police psychologist-author, in believing that masses or crowds thought in "images."

In Freud's later years, and after he died, the Frankfurt School further extended Freud's negative view of narcissism. Mass consumption, Frankfurt School theorists believed, had eliminated the autonomy of the bourgeois family and, in doing so, shrank the space for autonomy. As a result, Herbert Marcuse wrote, the ego seemed "no longer capable of sustaining itself, as a self, in distinction from id and superego" (1970, p. 47). In the United States, the locus of this development, even psychoanalysis had turned into a shallow affirmative form of reassurance. Relying on positive transference, it lost the distinction between itself and mass consumption therapies, namely the focus on resistance. Still later, Frankfurt School influenced cultural critics like Christopher Lasch (1978) described a "culture of narcissism" which, weakening Oedipal authority, released the primitive, sadistic, self-destructive superego—the lurking violence—of early childhood. As the advertising man in Joseph Heller's *Something Happened* who tried to be a "best friend" to his children complained:

> I don't know why my son feels so often that I am going to hit him when I never do; I never have; I don't know why both he and my daughter believe I used to beat them a great deal when they were smaller, when I don't believe I ever struck either one of them at all.
>
> (cited in Lasch, 1978, p. 123)

Instead of genuine introspection, then, mass consumption gave rise to psychologization, perhaps best captured in Woody Allen's self-ironizing parodies.

In all the key respects—superficiality, identity politics, and the substitution of images for dialogue—narcissism signaled the inaccessibility, or perhaps even the absence, of an inner world. But there was also another, muted strand in Freud's original account of narcissism. The supposedly self-sufficient narcissist, incapable of self-reflection, was also the one who potentially opened psychoanalysis to a new depth of relatedness, precisely because of the intensity of the narcissist's dependence. Far from signaling inaccessibility alone, then, narcissism also suggested deeper and more complex levels of interpersonal, group and cultural connectivity than psychoanalysis had known earlier. In the 1960s, this muted strand exploded onto the scene. In one of the great turning points in the history of psychoanalysis, Freud's critical attitudes toward narcissism were rejected and narcissism was redeemed and reinterpreted.

The redemption of narcissism actually began within American ego psychology. As early as 1946 Heinz Hartmann, Ernst Kris, and Rudolph Loewenstein urged analysts to replace the word "ego" in Freud's text on narcissism by the word "self." Narcissism, they argued, was not the libidinal investment of the *ego* as opposed to the id, but of the *self* as opposed to the world (Hartmann, Krism and Loewenstein, 1946, p. 16). Nevertheless, during the 1960s, narcissism had continued to signal the dissolution of social bonds, the inability to make commitments, to engage in long-run projects, to sacrifice the self for larger purposes, that analysts discerned in the culture of the New Left. By the 1970s, however, this view went into disfavor. As analysts saw their caseloads shift from "symptom-neuroses" to issues of self-esteem and deformations of the self's structure, continuity, and ability to differentiate itself from the object world, the analytic approach to narcissism also changed. Some analysts, notably Heinz Kohut, argued that a psychology of narcissism had to replace psychoanalysis. In the classical theory of transference, Kohut explained, "the id, a repressed drive element, is seeking *satisfaction*; [whereas] in the 'borderline' patient, an injured narcissistic [self] is seeking *reassurance*" (1978, p. 8).[1] Taking what he called an "affirmative attitude" toward narcissism, Kohut called narcissism "an integral, self-contained set of psychic functions rather than a regression product" (1978, p. 618). Portraying the ego psychologists' "courageously facing the truth morality," their "health-and maturity-morality," as suppressing patients' legitimate needs for narcissistic sustenance, he insisted that narcissism had replaced sexuality as the defining issue of the age.[2]

Relational analysis, closely linked to feminism and to the familial revolution that began in the 1960s, continued this trend. Relational analysts see narcissism as a great axis of the psyche, establishing the boundary between the self and others. Comprising one half of the human mind—objects comprising the other half—their new understanding of narcissism includes a new attitude toward women and toward homosexuals.[3] In contrast to classical Freudian psychoanalysis, which foregrounded depth, advocates of this view foreground the interpersonal plane. Analytic practice, rather than being conceived of as an assault on the patient's narcissism, presupposes a "therapeutic alliance" between the analyst and the patient, whom it understands as actively seeking self-knowledge.[4] Individual psychology, analysts of this persuasion would now say, is inseparable from such attributes of identity as gender, race and nationality. Even appearances, including the visual world, have come into their own, especially in analytically-influenced cultural studies; no longer seen as a mere "copy," they are viewed as constituting an autonomous sign system akin to language.

In this essay, I situate the redemption of narcissism in a still broader context than psychotherapy, namely the new "network" society that emerged in the 1960s, variously termed postindustrial, post-Fordist, the information age and globalization. In particular, and in order to foreground the role of agency, I will describe the changed attitude toward narcissism as the expression of a new global social class based on intellectual labor, the two-earner family and transnational culture. The redemption of narcissism, I will argue, was one means by which the cutting edge of that class, namely youth, women and gays, first revealed itself. Self-revelation, in turn, was closely related to the changing boundaries between the public and the private. I will furthermore argue that the changed attitude toward narcissism has its roots in the changed place of labor, especially manual labor, in contemporary society, that is the emergence of a postindustrial, even "post-economic" consciousness. My reason for arguing that the changed attitude toward narcissism is best understood when it is connected to the phenomenological self-constitution of a new class has to do with the place that psychoanalysis occupied in the industrial era, namely that of a charismatic movement facilitating the transition to mass consumption society. In order for a new social class to emerge in the 1960s, then, it had to develop a critique not only of Marxism, that is of the theory of the industrial class, but also of Freud, the theorist of its unconscious. I will make this argument in two parts.

In section 2 I will situate Freud's approach to narcissism in the context of the particular form of family life from which it arose. The core of my argument is that psychoanalysis developed in an industrial society, and as a counterpart to planning and large-scale organization. As a result, it described moral development as a private, inward process cut off from any larger social developments. In particular, Freud assigned a key role to instinctual renunciation linked to self-reflection. For Freud, insight into one's inner life was only gained through such renunciation. For example, in understanding dreams Freud taught that one should take the energy normally devoted to self-criticism (an instinctual demand for Freud) and turn it toward self-observation. Renunciation characterized psychoanalysis and was the basis for its central value, namely the *ego*.

In section 3 I argue that post-Fordist capitalism turned the family into a site of consumption, networking and visual imagery, challenging the public/private divide of the industrial epoch, throwing psychoanalysis into crisis, and bringing the question of narcissism to the fore. The New Left and the Women's Movement, seen as complementary forces, spearheaded the critique of the changing character of capitalism. Because of the centrality of psychoanalysis to twentieth century capitalism, and especially to the changing *spirit* of capitalism, these movements necessarily also criticized psychoanalysis. Small and transient though these movements might sometimes seem, their leaders—facilitated by large-scale (demonstrations, teach-ins, riots) as well as small ("consciousness-raising") group processes and operating in the glare of unprecedented media coverage—picked up on unconscious wishes in the surrounding culture and unwittingly gave them validity. In particular, they repudiated the analytic ethic of instinctual renunciation and thus helped precipitate the new spirit of post-Fordist consumerist capitalism.

10.2. The emergence of an ethic of self-reflection

Marx defined the "economic structure" as the "real foundation" of society. The "economic structure," he wrote, is the total ensemble of social relations entered into in the social production of existence (1970, pp. 20–1). That this conception must include the family would have been perfectly clear in any analysis of a pre-capitalist society. Indeed, it was the association of the family with the most primary and impelling material processes that gave it its connotation of backwardness and the association of women with this realm has been one of the most persistent sources of male supremacy. Similarly, it was the separation of the family from capitalist economic relations per se that created the modern sphere of personal life, giving rise to psychoanalysis, the first theory and practice of modern personal life. As a charismatic movement, facilitating the separation from traditional familial and communal morality, and critiquing Puritan asceticism, Freudian analysis resonated with modern mass consumption's orientation toward leisure, pleasure and self-satisfaction. Offering a non-instrumental conception of the self it tended to ignore practical, economic concerns and to sanction pleasure, consumption, and passive satisfaction. Accordingly, it seemed to validate narcissism.

But this appearance was misleading. Unlike competing paradigms such as experimental psychology, psychiatry, neurology or child development, psychoanalysis had a telos. Never intended to be an empirical description of the human mind, it had a critical, which is to say normative, goal that empirical sciences lack. That goal was self-reflection. Freud's critical attitude toward narcissism resulted from his commitment to self-reflection, but that is where the second, muted strand in the theory of narcissism became relevant. Because it lacked a sufficiently robust conception of the self, Freud's critical attitude toward narcissism also impeded the pursuit of self-reflection. We can see the beginnings of this problem in *The Interpretation of Dreams*. There is a gap between that book's description of the practice of self-reflection (that is, dream interpretation) and its picture of the psyche (the theory of the unconscious). To put the matter succinctly, the unconscious lacked both the motive and the means for self-reflection. This problem has played itself out over the entire subsequent history of psychoanalysis, but during Freud's life time his search for a meaningful, deeply rooted, theoretically cogent conception of the *motive* for self-reflection gave the issue of narcissism its edge.

This is apparent if we begin with the conflict between narcissism and self-reflection. Narcissism is investment in oneself, self-reflection requires distancing from oneself. Likewise, while narcissism is based on an archaic imago of unconditional perfection, self-reflection arises out of unhappiness and lack. Then, too, narcissism is specular, while self-reflection is communicative. In order to make these contrasts, one first needs a proper theory of narcissism. Freud developed such a theory in his 1906–1911 debates with Alfred Adler who argued that egoistic strivings were normal and intrinsic to human psychology. Freud agreed, but he added that sexual aims sometimes operated under the guise of non-sexual egoistic strivings. His 1914 theory of narcissism, in which the infant takes the "I" as its own love-object, was his "settling of accounts with Adler." "The word 'narcissism,' Freud explained, is intended to emphasize the fact that egoism 'is a libidinal phenomenon'" (1976, p. 223).

After 1914, Freud thought of narcissism as the first great tool of individuation, but he stressed that it nonetheless remained deeply embedded in the unconscious, primary process identifications of the unconscious id.[5] The upshot, as we have seen, was that he envisioned narcissism as a *stage* that had to be overcome. By the 1920s, accordingly, when Freud formulated his concept of the ego, he identified self-reflection, autonomy and object-love—in other words, the ego itself—with the renunciation of narcissism. The renunciation of narcissism was one major implication of Freud's incantation: where id was, ego shall be. Narcissism, of course, remains a part of the adult psyche, but it is an infantile part, the part that the superego—still representing the parents of childhood—reassures when it tells the ego that the world is just a joke, nothing to worry about.

Freud's emphasis on the renunciation of narcissism had momentous implications. Self-reflection is, at its core, the ability to look at oneself objectively; it therefore involves a decentering from the narcissism of the child. In human, interpersonal terms, the renunciation of narcissism involves the ability to take up the standpoint of the other. Situated in its historical context—the age of mass production, the age of the industrial working class, the age of the great struggles against fascism—the renunciation of narcissism in the interest of self-knowledge was socially significant. It encouraged a capacious allegiance to the human species as a whole, rather than to particular identities, and the repudiation of racism and nationalism.[6] Overall, the critique of narcissism in favor of self-reflection was an epochal advance.

In a way psychoanalysis arose out of the limits of the nineteenth century doctrines of rationality, utilitarianism and materialist socialism. In contrast to such doctrines, Freud encouraged an ethic of moral growth through self-reflection. This ethic was linked to a historically specific family form, one that culminated in post-World War Two mass consumption society. The ethic was captured through a term used at the time: the "maturity ethic," meaning the renunciation of narcissism. In the 1956 film *Man with the Grey Flannel Suit*, for example, the heroine overcomes the wound to her narcissism inflicted by her husband's wartime infidelity. She accepts his war baby, a triumph over narcissism that also symbolizes America's postwar responsibility for rebuilding Europe. Ego psychology, the dominant form of psychoanalysis in the 1950s, thus stood for a new ethic of "responsibility," and "adulthood," supposedly linked to a new maturity in America's global role, but also geared to the family based, mass consumption societies then being created in England, France and Germany. In the words of Erik Erikson, a person with a mature ego was "tolerant of differences, cautious and methodical in evaluation, just in judgment, circumspect in action, and capable of faith and indignation" (cited in Lasch, 1977, p. 108).[7] The maturity ethic, in turn, was the target of the new social class that emerged in the 1960s.

10.3. The new left and the legitimation of narcissism

In 1956 *The Lonely Crowd* (Riesman et al.) argued that an earlier ideal of autonomy or independence had given way to a new need for mirroring and recognition, that of the "other-directed" personality. In Riesman's metaphor, a gyroscope, an internal steering device (the ego) that keeps one on course regardless of external influences, had become a radar beam (narcissism), continuously scanning the environment for signs of approval or disapproval. Riesman's argument rested on the view that the western world was changing from an industrial society, based on manual labor and goods production, to a postindustrial society, based on services, consumerism and information technology. Whereas ego psychology was a defense of individual autonomy in the age of the industrial corporation, Riesman heralded a personality shift revolving around other-directedness, mirroring and the network society.

In the same year Erik Erikson responded to the increasing disquiet of middle class youth by introducing the concepts "identity" and "identity crises." According to Erikson, adolescence was a historically new stage of life precipitated by the end of the family's role in production, and the accompanying break in the ties between the generations. Although Erikson did not explicitly develop the themes of narcissism and mirroring, he explained identity as the outcome of childhood *identifications* that were selectively repudiated, assimilated, and reconfigured in relation to others, not just the parents, but the community, religion, economic institutions and the state. The goal of these interactions was inner consistency and continuity, which was what Erikson meant by identity (1956, pp. 56–121).[8] The concept of identity presupposed that narcissism could mature and consolidate; it was a departure, then, from classical ego psychology, even as it shared the latter's stress on self-knowledge through instinctual renunciation. In addition, Erikson described the *identity crisis* of adolescence as regression in the service of the ego, that is, a quasi-voluntary surrender of controls, an opening to the id, in the interest of a deeper maturity. In this way he provided a key concept through which the youth movements of the 1960s might be understood.

Riesman and Erikson's insights into the changing character of the self were accompanied by changes in the understanding of social justice, changes that foretold the alienation critique of the 1960s. Whereas mass production capitalism had generated the "distributive paradigm," that is, the idea that justice was a matter of economic redistribution and formal equality, the struggle against imperialism and fascism brought racial discrimination and decolonization to the fore. In 1954 the U.S. Supreme Court decided the issue of segregated schools on the basis of their injury to black students' self-esteem (that is, narcissism), not by appealing to their interests or rights. Early New Leftists criticized communists for not realizing, as Octave Mannoni (1956, p. 8) wrote, that objective inequalities were "embodied in struggles for prestige, in alienation, in bargaining positions and debts of gratitude, and in the invention of new myths and the creation of new personality types." Poets attacked colonialism for injecting millions "with fear, inferiority complexes, trepidation, servility, despair, abasement" (Fanon cited in Césaire, 1955, p. 22). Consequently, the focus shifted from providing material resources for formally equal and putatively autonomous individuals to what later came to be called "misrecognition," understood as an assault on the self-image, that is, on narcissism or, in its later political forms: identity.

When the 1960s dawned, the artistic critique (a cultural revolution and a sexual revolution) emerged first. Mounted by the early New Left, the artistic critique of Fordist capitalism presupposed the material security supposedly provided by mass production society. Beyond immediate needs, the artistic critique was based on intimations of "the affluent society," "cybernation," and "the conquest of space." The long post-World War II period of uninterrupted economic growth, the green revolution, the spread of electronics and mass communications, birth control: all of this made the family centered mass consumption of the 1950s appear dowdy and the ethic of maturity repressive. In place of what began to appear as the gray, regimented order of the Fordist epoch, post-Fordism opened the way for an id-saturated world pulsating with color, vibrancy, and primal rhythms in such areas as rock music, poster design, TV, film, and fashion. An explosive new utopianism and a new sense of limitlessness linked to narcissistic display lay on the horizon. Sublimation—the great moral achievement of the ego—would be renounced in favor of authenticity, expressive freedom and *jouissance*.

The artistic critique was rooted in the shift to a postindustrial service and consumerist society. In that shift ideals of "independence," "integrity," "character," and "achievement" linked to the managerial ethic of goods production gave way to an emphasis on interpersonal relations, networking, "people skills." Narcissism, meaning the ability to impress others with what appeared to be special characteristics of personality, replaced colorless managerial values such as reliability or expertise. At the extreme, self-appointed pundits celebrated "do your own thing" antinomianism. Simultaneously, consumption lost its conformist, "one size-fits-all" character. Capitalism appeared less like a factory and more like an emporium geared to endlessly diverting narcissistic wishes. Driven by such wishes, market forces consolidated a generationally specific youth culture. Intensely commodified, demotic, and antinomian, youth culture overflowed the older family form, encouraging changes in ideals of the self.

The changing place of the family, and therefore of the public/private divide, was at the center of this change. The sexual revolution rejected what was regarded as the suffocating conformity of the family, which privileged genital sexuality (the "missionary position"), and suppressed homosexuality and the so-called perversions, the sexual terrain on which the analytic theory of narcissism originated. Sharp rises in divorce rates, in married women working outside the home, and in the number of people living alone, along with the emergence of explicit homosexual themes in fashion, entertainment and the arts, all reflected and encouraged cultural revolution. In the course of this revolution, the meaning of sexuality, and so of the public/private divide, changed. In the early and mid-twentieth-century imagination, sexuality meant a man and a woman who meet in the middle of an indifferent and unknowing crowd, their love transforming them into a couple with a personal history and meaning. In the 1960s, by contrast, sexuality meant the merger of the couple with the "indifferent and unknowing crowd" as in "wife-swapping," swinging, pornography, explicit sex in magazines and advertising, and the singles scene.

The student movement sought to adapt psychoanalysis to revolutionary ends. This was possible because, as a church, psychoanalysis had a twofold character: it was in but not of the world. The analytic profession, with its renunciation of narcissism, adapted to reality: it accepted the modest goal of self-reflection in the private sphere. But there was also a second Freud for whom the unconscious pervaded society as a whole. The second Freud had inspired earlier heterodox analysts such as Otto Gross and Wilhelm Reich and was represented after World War II by such New Left icons as Paul Goodman, Norman O. Brown and Herbert Marcuse.

The difference between the two Freuds was epitomized in their respective views of the ego. For the ego psychologists, the ego was limited in its powers, having constantly to balance reality, moral demands and internal impulses. Determinedly anti-utopian, ego psychology had meant the acceptance of limits. In Philip Rieff's (1980, p. 8) description, it meant "resign[ing] yourself to living within your moral means, suffer[ing] no gratuitous failures in a futile search for ethical heights."[9] For the second Freud, in contrast, the ego gained access to the id through regression. The second Freud exploded the constraints of the maturity ethic and opened a pathway to the grandiose, narcissistic self of infancy.

Narcissism, Lou Andreas-Salomé (1962, p. 11) once wrote, has a "dual orientation": "on the one hand toward abandonment in the primal boundless state ... conjugation and fusion," and "on the other toward self-assertion." Eventually, both moments came to the fore, but the New Left's first step toward the revaluation of narcissism arose from its embrace of the primal, boundless experience of the loss of self, sometimes associated with mysticism. Rejecting the confining of the self to a private space, the early New Left sought instead to bring *Eros* into work and politics, into the streets and into other arenas of public life. Communes, drug use, attacks on monogamy, rock music, the onstage performance of backstage behaviors, such as nudity, informal dress and self-disclosure, an activist culture, whose only regulative ideal was "participation": these all constituted a social basis for the utopian interpretation of narcissism as merger. The New Left's challenge to the necessity of repression, its insistence that it know the truth about everything, that there be no secrets, arose from the same impulse.

The impulse toward narcissistic merger found its most powerful expression in Herbert Marcuse's *Eros and Civilization*, published in 1955 and one of the most influential books of the 1960s. Like Erikson and Riesman, Marcuse situated his work in the context of the rise of automation, a development that, in Marcuse's terms, made possible a distinction between necessary (biologically given) and surplus (historically contingent, that is, capitalist) repression. Seeking to redeem what he called the suppressed utopian element in psychoanalysis, Marcuse argued that "the autonomous personality [that is, the maturity ethic or the Freudian ego] appears as the *frozen* manifestation of the general repression of mankind" (1955, p. 57, original emphasis). The ego that undertook the rational transformation of the environment, he added, was "an essentially aggressive, offensive subject, whose thoughts and actions were designed for mastering objects. It was a subject against an object" (Marcuse, 1955, p. 109). Thus, the ego was "antagonistic to those faculties and attitudes which are receptive rather than productive, which tend toward gratification rather than transcendence [and] which remain strongly committed to the pleasure principle" (Marcuse, 1955, p. 111). Nature, in particular, the ego's own internal nature, as well as the ecological world, "was 'given' to the ego as something that had to be fought, conquered, and even violated" (Marcuse, 1955, p. 111).[10]

In place of ego autonomy, which Marcuse viewed as intrinsic to the warfare-welfare state, Marcuse went back to Freud's theory of a *primary* narcissism supposedly characteristic of the earliest infant/mother relationship. That is to say, Marcuse went back to the id. There, primary narcissism existed which predated the emergence of the "I," and which reflected the ego's original, "inseparable connection of the ego with the external world" (Marcuse, 1955, p. 168). The id's primary well of narcissism pointed the way, Marcuse (1955, p. 201) reasoned, "from sexuality constrained under genital supremacy" to eroticization of the entire body, and from instrumental rationality to art, play and narcissistic display. Allowed free scope, it might generate "a comprehensive existential order" (Marcuse, 1955, p. 169). In place of Prometheus, Marx's hero from the ancient world who stole the secret of fire and thus served as a symbol of industrial capitalism, Marcuse enthroned the poet/musician Orpheus, who introduced homosexuality to human society. Like Narcissus, Orpheus rejected "the normal Eros, not for an ascetic ideal, but for a fuller Eros" (Marcuse, 1955, p. 171).

Norman O. Brown's (1959) *Life against Death*, another influential New Left text, also defended the pre-oedipal relations and "polymorphously perverse" stage of primary narcissism against the genitally based "ego of mastery." Like Marcuse, Brown valorized "feminine" motifs. Rejecting pseudo-individuation as "based on hostile trends directed against the mother" (Róheim cited in Brown, 1959, p. 129), Brown sought to rescue what he saw as the critical aspect of Bachofen's discovery of the primal mother from "the Jungian *Schwärmerei*."[11] Giving voice to the lived experience of the communes, Marcuse and Brown provided an analytic underpinning to the New Left's critique of instrumental reason, its desire for a new connectedness with nature, and its attempt to liberate sexuality from its genital, heterosexual limits. Neither could know, of course, that the utopian energies of primary narcissism were also preparing the way for post-Fordist capitalism.

So long as the New Left had been preoccupied with issues of peace or social justice, cultural change expressed itself through alternative life styles, drugs, music, sexuality, and "communes." Beginning around 1969, however, the revaluation of narcissism shifted from "abandonment in the primal boundless state ... conjugation and fusion" "toward self-assertion," to invoke Andreas-Salomé once more. The sexual and cultural revolutions associated with the artistic critique gave way to the justice critique in such forms as feminism, multiculturalism and equal rights for homosexuals. By the mid-1970s, the actors involved in the politics of the family were no longer individuals but *groups* organized around axes of subordination such as gender, sexuality and race. A few years later, a term drawn from psychoanalysis would describe these groups: *identities*.

Feminism, even more than the original New Left, was linked to the emergence and consolidation of post-Fordist capitalism. A charismatic force in its own right, feminism reflected and was based upon the destruction of the family wage and the earlier, maternally centered welfare state, and the emergence of the two-earner family. Like earlier movements connected to large-scale transformations of capitalism, feminism espoused respectability, meritocracy, and hard work. Accordingly, feminists adapted the revalued ideal of narcissism to identity, thus pioneering a justice critique based on identity, one that conformed to the American emphasis on individual rights in particular. Nevertheless, the cost of this critique was the repudiation of individual self-reflection. "Individual explanations" were officially discouraged in "consciousness-raising" groups, while what had been forbidden or suspended within psychoanalysis—"acting out"—became privileged. The Oedipus complex was reinterpreted as a "power psychology." Penis envy was actually "power envy." Dora became a feminist icon because she *left* analysis.[12]

A parallel transformation occurred among homosexuals. For classical psychoanalysis, one could understand a homosexual object choice psychologically, but there was no such entity as "a homosexual." In the course of the 1970s, however, efforts to understand the psychology of homosexuality began to seem bigoted, like efforts to understand the psychology of races. In that context, moreover, the last thing homosexuals needed was psychoanalysis: they needed services, community institutions and political organizations. Finally, homosexuals began to understand themselves as persons with a distinct way of life, persons who belonged to a historically specific community. Homosexuality, then, was an identity, something that is based on membership in a community. Lesbians, explained one theorist, are "women who love women, who choose women to nurture and to create a living environment in which to work creatively and independently. ... Lesbians cannot be defined simply as women who practice certain physical rites together" (Phelan, 1989, pp. 73–4).

The final step in the redemption of narcissism came with Jacques Lacan. Lacan rejected Freud's theory of the ego but rather than using that rejection to valorize narcissism, he used it to reinterpret Freud's critique of narcissism, a reinterpretation that placed the problem of the image at its center. Beginning with his famous "mirror-stage" lecture, delivered to the Marienbad Psychoanalytic Congress in 1936, Lacan argued that psychical development began not with agency (as for Freud) but with lack, terror, or the emptiness of non-existence. Narcissism, or what

Lacan called "the ego of narcissism" developed, he wrote, as a defensive response to the traumatic discovery of this emptiness, an imaginary construction, a "crystallization of images" (Fink, 1995, p. 84). Having no basis in the organism's instinctual drives, "the ego of narcissism" was better thought of as an object than an agent.

Deriving his basic orientation from surrealism, which characterized the unconscious in imagistic rather than instinctual terms, Lacan described the psyche as mediating not between id, superego and reality as Freud thought, but between the imaginary, symbolic and real. The imaginary was the aforementioned "crystallization of images" and its basic character was that it was *visual*. Thus the "ego of narcissism," the primal gestalt of the imaginary register, arose from the infant's *specular* and *visual* misrecognition of him or herself as a unity. Misrecognition, rooted in a visual gestalt, situated narcissism in a fictional direction.

Expelled from the International Psychoanalytical Association (IPA) in 1953, Lacan moved at the invitation of the Marxist philosopher Louis Althusser to the *École normale supérieure* in Paris where he identified psychoanalysis with *le champ freudien*. Associated with the slogan "the death of the subject," *le champ freudien* resonated with the broader shift in the self-consciousness of the new class from production and the economy to ideology, culture and the media, and articulated the growing sense that it was through media images, rather than the workplace, and through its effect on the individual personality, and not on the collectivity, that social domination was secured. Lacan's critical approach to narcissism made it possible to understand the ideological effect of a particular text not simply in terms of its content (for example, capitalism, racism, sexism) but rather through the way it sustained an imaginary sense of individual wholeness and unity. In spite of the apparent radicalism of this stance, Lacan spoke for the detached, ironic, privatized and apolitical culture which largely characterized the new class by the end of the decade. Addressing demonstrating students in 1968 he told them: "what you as a revolutionary aspire to is a master. You will have one" (Foucault, 1988, p. 20).

Psychoanalysis, even though it was ostensibly anti-visual, had ridden to power on consumer society's tsunami of images, typified by advertising, photography and film. Nonetheless, even though many of Freud's texts, such as those on hysteria and on group psychology, literally cry out for a discussion of visuality, Freud suppressed not only the image, but even any discussion of images *qua* images.[13] Lacan supplied this theory, at least in its rudiments, with his distinction between the imaginary and symbolic registers. Thus, if, on the one hand, the popularity of Lacan comes from the prominence that visuality (the imaginary register) plays in his work, on the other hand, he remained true to the critical moment in Freud's account of the transition from narcissism to the ego, and thus to Freud's most important point, namely that no overall moral development was possible unless it was based on self-reflection and instinctual renunciation.

Thus, the enormous eruptions of the 1960s ushered in a new society, whose cutting edge was a new social class. Within that society psychoanalysis lost its earlier centrality. Nonetheless, analysis has remained important to post-Fordist society as a result of its relationship to personal life. Representing the product of surplus labor—labor beyond what was necessary to reproduce the society—personal life pointed toward the utopian but increasingly realistic possibility of a society that subordinated economic considerations to human wishes—a post-economic society. This telos remains in place today.

Notes

Some formulations in this article are adapted from Zaretsky, E. (2007), "Psychoanalysis, the Family and Personal Life: Narcissism and the 'Relational Revolution' of the 1960s," *Estudios Interdisciplinarios de América Latina y el Caribe*, vol. 18, no. 1, 1–31, and Zaretsky, E. (2004), *Secrets of the Soul* (New York: Knopf).

1. There may be strong, especially oral, drive elements, but just "as ego functions can become libidinized ... so also can drives be used for predominantly narcissistic purposes" (Kohut, 1978, 8).
2. Freud did not take the term "narcissism" from the Greek myth but rather from the literature on homosexuality, and this also gave the term a negative connotation. Not that Freud assumed that every homosexual was a narcissist; he did not. Rather, he thought of the narcissist as someone who has not gone through the struggle over sexual difference that, Freud believed, was crucial to the ability to recognize otherness in general.
3. Of course, the meaning of this term is contested. For another point of view see Greenberg and Mitchell (1983).
4. The ego originated in the id, but developed out of it, freeing itself from primary, merged, identifications by saying, in effect, to the id: "Look you can love me too, I am so like the object."
5. For this reason, psychoanalysis was intrinsic to the popular front of the 1930s and 40s, which preached universal values against the narrow obligations of the nation state.
6. Lasch's brilliant work, as well as the antagonism it stirred in the post-1960s left, rests in good part on his continued loyalty to the "maturity ethic" of the 1950s. In *The True and Only Heaven* he wrote: "My generation invested personal relations with an intensity they could hardly support, as it turned out; but our passionate interest in each other's lives cannot very well be described as a form of emotional retreat. We tried to re-create in the circle of

our friends the intensity of a common purpose, which could no longer be found in politics or the workplace" (1991, 32).

7. Erikson also argued that identity was a special problem in the United States due to its disparate cultural composition, and he wrote of the difficulty in sustaining ego ideals in a land "characterized by expanding identifications and by great fears of losing hard-won identities" (1964, 647).
8. For the idea that the 1970s constitute a fin-de-siècle see Natasha Zaretsky (2007).
9. Against Kant, Marcuse extolled the philosopher Friedrich Schiller who sought to show that reason was reconciled with sensuality in art and play.
10. Also see Herbert Marcuse (1967).
11. The farewell of Erica Jong's heroine to her analyst in her 1973 *Fear of Flying* was emblematic: "Don't you see that men have *always* defined femininity as a means of keeping women in line? Why should I listen to *you* about what it means to be a woman? Are you a woman? Why shouldn't I listen to myself for once? And to other women ... As in a dream ... I got up from the couch ... and walked ... out. ... I was free!" (1973, 20, 22).
12. This contradiction was apparent when the film, *Secrets of the Soul*, was made in 1926, purporting to explain Freud's theories.
13. This suppression is especially striking in light of contemporary MRI and PET research that suggests that more than half of the brain is devoted to creating, processing and storing specifically *visual* images.

References

Andreas-Salomé, L. (1962), "The Dual Orientation of Narcissism," *Psychoanalytic Quarterly*, vol. 31, 1–30.

Brown, N. O. (1959), *Life against Death* (Middletown: Wesleyan University Press).

Césaire, A. (1955), *Discours sur le Colonialisme* (Paris : Présence Africaine).

Erikson, E. H. (1956), "The Problem of Ego Identity," *Journal of the American Psychoanalytic Association*, vol. 4, no. 1, 56–121.

Erikson, E. H. (1964), "A Memorandum on Identity and Negro Youth," in E. H. Erikson and S. Schlein (ed.), *A Way of Looking at Things: Selected Papers 1930–1980* (New York: Routledge), 644–59.

Fink, B. (1995), *The Lacanian Subject: Between Language and Jouissance* (Princeton: Princeton University Press).

Foucault, M. (1988), *Politics, Philosophy, Culture: Interviews and Other Writings, 1977–1984*, L. D. Kritzman (ed.) (London: Routledge).

Freud, S. (1976), *The Standard Edition of the Complete Psychological Works of Sigmund Freud*, vol. 9, J. Strachey (ed.), (New York: Norton).

Greenberg J. and S. Mitchell (1983), *Object Relations Theory in Psychoanalytic Theory* (Cambridge: Harvard University Press).

Hartmann, H., E. Kris, and R. Loewenstein (1946), "Comments on the Formation of Psychic Structure," *The Psychoanalytic Study of the Child*, vol. 2, 11–38.

Jong, E. (1973), *Fear of Flying* (New York: Holt, Rinehart and Winston).

Kohut, H. (1978), *The Search for the Self* (New York: International Universities Press).

Lasch, C. (1977), *Haven in a Heartless World* (New York: Basic Books).

Lasch, C. (1978), *The Culture of Narcissism* (New York: Basic Books).

Lasch, C. (1991), *The True and Only Heaven: Progress and Its Critics* (New York: Norton).

Mannoni, O. (1956), *Prospero and Caliban: The Psychology of Colonization* (London: Methuen).

Marcuse, H. (1955), *Eros and Civilization: A Philosophical Inquiry into Freud* (London: Routledge and Kegan Paul).

Marcuse, H. (1967), "Love Mystified: A Critique of Norman O. Brown," *Commentary*, vol. 43, no. 2, 71–5.

Marcuse, H. (1970), *Five lectures: Psychoanalysis, Politics, and Utopia*, J. J. Shapiro and S. M. Weber (trans) (Boston: Beacon Press).

Marx, K. (1970), *A Contribution to the Critique of Political Economy*, M. Dobb (ed.), W. Ryazanskaya (trans.) (Moscow: Progress Publishers).

Phelan, S. (1989), *Identity Politics: Lesbian Feminism and the Limits of Community*, (Philadelphia: University Press).

Rieff, P. (1980), *The Feeling Intellect* (Chicago: University of Chicago Press).

Riesman, D., N. Glazer, and R. Denney (1956), *The Lonely Crowd: A Study of the Changing American Character* (Yale: Yale University Press).

Zaretsky, N. (2007), *No Direction Home: The American Family and the Fear of National Decline 1968–1980* (Chapel Hill: University of North Carolina Press).

Conclusion: Futures of Modern Privacy

Harry Blatterer, Pauline Johnson, Maria R. Markus

When Alice in Wonderland asked the Cheshire Cat "Which way should she go?," the answer was simple: "It depends a good deal on where you want to go." This is an important answer for our deliberations on this volume. After presenting a series of analyses of the development and transformations of the modern private sphere we conclude with some reflections about future trends. In the critical theory tradition, we attempt to detect in contemporary experience some of those tendencies that point to the possibility of transcending some of the present problems and unveil alternative grounds and ways of people connecting with each other. Any discussion about the futures of modern privacy cannot just be about trends and their inner dynamics, however. Some conscious transformations are not just possible but also necessary. Some can be initiated by individuals, others need the concerted actions of groups through the existing and emerging channels of civil society. Bauman is right in saying that "[o]nly such future is 'given to us' here and now, as resides in the realm of human imagination" (Bauman, 2002, p.17). So, imagine we must in order to keep open the possibilities for constant revision and adjustment of already existing structures to better suit our needs (where we want to go) and address our fears on an individual and societal level alike.[1] On the theoretical level, and even more so in novels and similar literary works, these fears are expressed in a number of frightening dystopias.[2] On the individual level, as has become clear from many of the preceding papers, the fear of anonymity seems to be pronounced indeed today. Such anonymity—being unnoticed, looked through—is often perceived as humiliation, as the denial of dignity and respect.

To begin sorting through the possibilities of the present we need to have some anchorage about where we are. Let's allow the wisdom of author David Malouf to give us some orientation. For all the changes, he tells us,

> something of an older way of experiencing things persists. Families remain pretty much what they have always been: little word of mouth societies, repositories of facts, skills, stories, teasing secrets (and sometimes insoluble mysteries) ... Children continue, even in an age of technology, to acquire what they will one day think of as their first experience in the most old-fashioned ways. Through codes, habits, rituals that provide us with our first apprehension of how things fit together to make a style of local culture; how power works and who has it and how it can be negotiated—how it can be manipulated, too, and misused; who among those who come and go in a household, belong and to what degree, and who does not and why; all the ins and outs of family lore and gossip that no one sets out precisely to inform us of but which we take in and carry with us for the rest of our days. [...]
>
> This, in the making of young lives, is much and not to be underestimated. What is being shaped here, as the questions arise and are provisionally answered, is a take on the world that will be conditional, as all experience is, on the disposition of the watcher and listener, and in that way tempered to the purely personal view; "We cannot say too little," Emerson warns, "of our constitutional necessity of seeing things under private aspects, or saturated with our humors." And more will come as a life gathers the elements that will in the end define it: love, loss, a vocation discovered and professional skills acquired, partnership, parenthood, perhaps a time at war—the thousand oddities of experience undergone and accidents survived. But what these amplify and build on is what has already been laid down in those first months and years, and was acquired in the most traditional way.
>
> (Malouf, 2008, pp. 36–8)

Personal life, subjectivity and living one's own story mercifully persist. The "constitutional necessity" remains and we need to build on this. Yet we should not be too sanguine either. Beth Elshtain's (1981, p. 353) insistence that we not permit "through our silence things to pass away as in a dream" needs to be heeded too. So what can we say about what's happening to modern privacy? Why does it matter? And what do we need to do to support this little world of particularity?

The news, Bauman and others tell us, is bad. Bauman goes so far as to suggest that we are witnessing the end of utopia; or rather its transformation into something very awful; into the "utopia of the hunters" (this volume, Chapter 1). This would be a society of self-asserting egos lusting only after celebrity and the markers of private success. Hobbes's vision of the "solitary, poor, nasty, brutish and short" life seems a still relevant nightmare. However, Bauman's utopia of the hunters is perhaps most useful as a hypothetical orientation to our questions about the fate of modern privacy. *What if* we don't learn to value and defend the dependencies of autonomous and authentic subjectivity on intersubjectivity and recognition? And *what if* we reduce the public sphere from the ground of recognition between private individuals to a forum where private interests claim power and influence?

All around us collapsing boundaries between the public and the private seem to presage the triumph of the utopia of the hunters. Titled *Smile or Die: How Positive Thinking Fooled America and the World* (2009), Barbara Ehrenreich's recent book has interesting things to say about this. It seems that a regime of "positive thinking" that threatens our capacity to experience either life or death for ourselves is taking over. This is a world that has no place for rationally autonomous selves who are engaged in weighing things up, talking things over and setting their own course. Positive thinking is repelled by a skeptical reason and independence of mind; symptoms of a loathed negativity. There is no easy way out. The medical establishments that treat us, the corporate world that employs us, the media that informs and entertains us, and the religious institutions supposed to guide us are all infected by the spirit of positivity. We have to "feel good" about where we are at, and trust in (not plan!) a future full of riches and success. All this robust confidence has to be enacted in public and the uniqueness of the life story is to be replaced by the repeated code of struggle and triumph.

The "bust through" attitude of positive thinking moves into a space cleared by a therapeutic culture that has invaded the postwar world. Unsupported by enabling social conditions, the demand to be a self-responsible individual has been too hard and the client/individual constructed by therapy culture seems to offer welcome respite for failing private selves. Positive thinking promises to restore a powerful individuality. An energetic assertion of the will is all that is required and our doubting, anxious, individuating ways of making sense of our worlds is all we have to give up. The proposition that reasoning individuals might respond to the impossibility of private self-sufficiency by getting together to plan futures and discuss the sharing of resources (including the resources of toleration and recognition) needed to support private autonomies is, it seems, too negative and slow to contemplate.

A culture that turns dissent from a mandatory self-assertion into a "symptom" is only one of the problems faced by modern privacy. We must also contend with technologies that have little respect for boundaries. Wendy Brown (2004, p. 135) is convinced that the ubiquitous cell phone has done much more than change modern manners. It marks "certain transformations of the public, the private, the intimate"; protection "for the vulnerability of emotional or physical nakedness" which is "one of intimacy's most basic propositions" takes a big loss. The worry is partly that private life—attacked by the rage for endless, featureless disclosure fostered by social networking sites, reality TV and the like—will lose its distinctive qualities of closeness, exclusivity and mutuality. Even more alarming, perhaps, is that nobody seems to mind much that the boundaries have been overwhelmed. What is the meaning of a seeming enthusiasm for technologies that allow us to parade our "emotional and physical nakedness" for the world to see?

Brown (2004, p. 140–1) believes that what is happening here confirms Giorgio Agamben's apprehensions of profound changes in a contemporary cultural landscape. Agamben fears that modern living has drained nothing less than the capacity for experience from us. Nothing, it seems, in the "humdrum daily life in any city" gets taken up and woven into a distinctive personal story (Agamben, 2007, p. 15). Everything is just lived through. "Modern man makes his way home in the evening wearied by a jumble of events, but however entertaining or tedious, unusual or commonplace, harrowing or pleasurable they are, none of them will become experience" (Agamben, 2007, p. 16). This "disturbing incapacity for experience" might be the reason, Brown tells us, that we have become complicit "in an order increasingly indifferent to distinctions between public and private space, and hence private and public experience" (2004, p.140). It seems that there is nothing left to lose.

However, the thesis that the new media have defeated a private life that has lost its value for us appears to be strung between two exaggerated normative poles. The argument is that technologies that wire us into an effortless, compulsive connectivity have overwhelmed private life, whose promise to be a haven to retiring selves (who loved its invisibility) has ceased to matter to us. The picture seems to be too simple on both counts. Certainly new technologies have overseen big changes in the way in which we interact with friends and strangers alike. However, they are not the bearers of radically new needs (for visibility and recognition) nor are they the altar upon which old needs (for privacy and solitude) are sacrificed. As Blatterer and Markus point out in this volume (Chapters 5 and 6, respectively), it is more useful if we look at the way in which new technologies intervene in the "trade off" between these values which, after all, have always been a part of a richly complex private life. A compulsive connectivity is not embedded in the technologies themselves. And, as Robert Putnam urges, we need to begin to reflect not just upon "what the Internet will do to us, but what we will do with it" (2000, p. 180). In this regard, it seems that we have not yet taken the opportunity to think properly about "where we want to go." There is nothing new in the fact that we can't simply go into automatic mode. Choices, now as always, need to be made about checking certain trends that might endanger things we also value in modern privacy. There is not much to be gained either from going into a defensive funk about private life. This is no realm of solemn self-importance; after all this is where the delights of *Twitter* were born.

The "destruction of experience" thesis, which finds that the new technologies have finished off an already hollowed out private life, posts a useful warning, but only that. It tells us that Emerson's very "constitutional necessity of seeing things under private aspects" that Malouf talks about, is under attack. With them, we remain convinced that, despite all the changes and misapprehensions, a private sphere that is knitted together in the "traditional" way from an accumulation of experiences, expressing a mix of needs and values, continues to give our lives substance and worth. Cormac McCarthy's *The Road* (2006) hopes that this little intractable cell of subjective and intimate life might be able to hold out amidst the destruction of all else. It is up to us, however, to reflect on how existing representations of private life have rendered it so seemingly defenseless in the face of threatening trends. We also need to have something to say about how we might rethink the private/public boundaries so as to strengthen each.

The little world of particularity has not been well served by the defensiveness that has colored our representations of its value. Certainly, as Beate Rössler (2005) has forcefully argued, and as some of the chapters collected here have also reiterated, we prize modern privacy because we value our autonomy. However, if autonomy is confused with self-sufficiency and self-responsibility, modern private life becomes mired in enfeebling self-misunderstandings. We cannot, as a triumphant therapeutic culture well knows, "go it alone." As many of our papers have underlined, along with freedom, agency and security, recognition is a need "essential to our being" (Smith, 2006, p. 32); its systemic frustration opens up to a life of humiliation. So, the complex interdependencies between autonomy and recognition need to be grasped when we are talking about what private life means to us. Even our solitude is a quality gifted to our aloneness by the recognition by others (see Markus, this volume, Chapter 6). The point also needs to be made that as long as autonomy is experienced as the requirement that we each shift for ourselves in a society of "hunters," the private individual will inevitably encounter a world that has been completely externally described and defined. The quest for autonomy needs to be underpinned by resources that we have all had a chance to define and given a say in distributing. And it is with this in mind that we can now address more directly the question posed at the outset: "in what society do we wish to live and what problems have to be addressed in order to approach this goal?"

The first necessary step to take toward an answer is arguably also a step that—in societies whose institutions favor "evidence based" outcomes and solutions—is more often than not considered a backward move at best. And indeed, it is perhaps best imagined as a step back, but also as a step "up": "back" from what are perceived immediate problems, and "up" to another level of abstraction from where we may begin to fathom the conditions that frame, foster and reproduce the issues at hand, including the issues raised in this collection. From that vantage point we suggest that only a society that combines decency and civility is a society in which autonomous subjectivity can be understood and then experienced in terms that take seriously the mutual accordance of respect as a necessary condition for flourishing private and public lives. What do we mean by "decency" and "civility"?

Civility in human interactions and relationships is a form of regard for the wellbeing of others. "It is the form that offers the maximum protection for the other's sensitivity, that manifests the respect that is due the other by virtue of being an equal, free and rational member of the same civic community," says Heller (1994, p. 304). As such, civility does not demand an agreement with the other, it demands respect for the other's views, way of life and convictions. As Markus has put it elsewhere,

> Civility, as it has emerged in modernity, concerns in a "society of strangers" the recognition of the other as a bearer of basic and inalienable rights, it demands forms of conduct, which actually respect these rights—be they legally fixed or not—and allow the other to exercise them. It involves toleration toward views, different from one's own, a respect for the right of others to arrange their lives—within the limits of legality—according to their own convictions and values, and a readiness to find a modus vivendi in which these various convictions and plans of life can co-exist.
>
> (2001, p. 1021)

While non-humiliating social arrangements are central also to the concept of decency, here they imply

> something more or at least something different: a respect for the "dignity" of each person and some interest in, and commitment to, promoting the ability of all members of society to lead a dignified, humanly meaningful life. It involves not only the toleration of other views and convictions, but also an interest in, and openness towards what they say and an attempt to understand the reason why it can be meaningful to hold such a view.
>
> (Markus 2001, pp. 1021–2)[3]

Although at this stage the utopian horizon of "civility" in human relationships seems more approachable, we should not give up the idea of decency. If we think about utopia as a yardstick that is as an orientative principle on the individual as well as on the societal level, we may succeed to create a hope for future generations to live under conditions that better reflect their needs and strivings. Under conditions of civility and decency the reality of the link between privacy and autonomy is likely to be self-evident. But more than that, the content and meaning of "autonomy" are then expected to be subject to public deliberation to whatever sphere of life it may pertain. Achieving such goals is no easy task. "At least," as Habermas tells us, "we have to try" (1994, p. 97).

Notes

1. Says novelist Haruki Murakami in *Kafka on the Shore* (2005, 141): "It's just as Yeats said: in dreams begins responsibility. Turn it on its head and you could say that where there is no power to imagine, no responsibility can arise."
2. In the most interesting works we see the imagination working not just as a source of fears but also of persistent hopes that life can be rebuilt from a precious intimacy as illustrated in Cormack McCarthy's *The Road* (2006).
3. Avishai Margalit proposes a somewhat different understanding of the two concepts. According to him, "[a] civilized society is one whose members do not humiliate one another, while a decent society is one in which institutions do not humiliate people" (1996, 1). While he believes that there might be quite a considerable discrepancy between the two, he also notes that while decency as applied to institutions refers mainly to rules and laws, it also includes their actual behavior. Therefore, on this level, the distinction between a decent society and a civilized one is blurred.

References

Agamben, G. (2007), *Infancy and its History: On the Destruction of Experience (*London and New York: Verso).

Bauman, Z. (2002), "The 20th Century: The End or a Beginning," *Thesis Eleven*, vol. 70, no. 1, 15–25.

Brown, W. (2004), "'The Subject of Privacy': A Comment on Moira Gatens," in B. Rössler (ed.), *Privacies: Philosophical Evaluations* (Stanford California: Stanford University Press), 133–41.

Ehrenreich, B. (2009), *Smile or Die: How Positive Thinking Fooled America and the World* (London: Granta).

Elshtain, J. B. (1981), *Public Man, Private Woman: Women in Social and Political Thought* (Oxford: Martin Robertson).

Habermas, J. (1994), "Europe's Second Chance," in *Jürgen Habermas: The Past as Future* (Lincoln and London: The University of Nebraska Press), 73–98.

Heller, A. (1994), "A Reply to my Critics," in J. Burnheim (ed.), *The Social Philosophy of Agnes* Heller (Amsterdam: Rodopi), 281–312.

Malouf, D. (2008), *On Experience* (Melbourne: Melbourne University Press).

Margalit, A. (1996), *The Decent Society* (Cambridge, Massachusetts: Harvard University Press).

Markus, M. R. (2001), 'Decent Society and/or Civil Society', *Social Research*, vol. 68, no. 4, 1011–30.

McCarthy, C. (2006), *The Road* (New York: Alfred A. Knopf).

Murakami, H. (2005), *Kafka on the Shore* (London: Vintage).

Putnam, R. D. (2000), *Bowling Alone: The Collapse and Revival of American Community* (New York: Simon and Schuster).

Rössler, B. (2005), *The Value of Privacy* (Cambridge: Polity).

Smith, D. (2006), *Globalization: The Hidden Agenda* (Cambridge: Polity Press).

Index